The Caravaggio Conspiracy

How five art dealers,
four policemen,
three picture restorers,
two auction houses
and a journalist
plotted to recover some
of the world's most beautiful
stolen paintings

The
Caravaggio
Conspiracy

PETER WATSON

DOUBLEDAY & COMPANY, INC.
GARDEN CITY, NEW YORK
1984

Library of Congress Catalog Card Number 83-45033
ISBN: 0-385-17069-6
First Edition
Copyright © 1984 by Peter Watson
Printed in the United States of America

Library of Congress Cataloging in Publication Data

Watson, Peter.
  The Caravaggio conspiracy.

  Includes index.
  1. Art thefts. 2. Smuggling. I. Title.
N8795.W38 1983   363.2′32

For Lesley

Contents

Author's Note

This is a true story about an attempt to recover stolen old master paintings. For legal reasons, and because of the threat of reprisals, two names have been changed. They are indicated by asterisks at appropriate points in the story.

Part I

The Caravaggio Conspiracy

1

The Man
with the Black Cane

THE DAY DAWNED as clear as a Canaletto. It was Wednesday, 30 May 1979 in New York City. At four minutes before ten that morning, as the sun began to bake the pavements, a tall Englishman with an ebony walking cane limped into the galleries of Sotheby Parke Bernet at 980 Madison Avenue. Like most art dealers, "A. John Blake," as he was shown on his engraved business card, was expensively dressed. He wore a charcoal, double-breasted Savile Row suit, heavy-rimmed, tortoise-shell eyeglasses and a bright, blue-spotted silk bow tie. Like other dealers, he carried under his arm a shiny pink and pale-green sales catalog: it was the day of Sotheby's summer auction of old masters. With the others he took the elevator to the main gallery, on the second floor.

The world's best-known auction houses each hold two "Important Old Master" sales every year, between the end of May and July and again in November. These are the "seasons" in the art world and it is then that the ultrasmooth dealers—the Agnews, the Legatts, the Thaws and the Wildensteins—can be seen jetting back and forth across the north Atlantic, first-class. Sotheby's, Christie's, Bonham's and Phillips always try to dovetail the dates of their sales so that their best customers don't have to spend more than a week or ten days in the Carlyle Hotel or the Hyde Park, the Ritz or the New Berkely; and it is then that the watering holes of the international art world, the Pleiad in New York, Wilton's or the Lafayette in London, echo with the names of Brueghel and Bronzino, Rembrandt and Rubens, Del Sarto and Van Dyck.

Blake arrived early for the sale that day. He wanted a particular seat, halfway down the right aisle, where he could be clearly seen, both by the auctioneer and the other dealers.

Sotheby's in New York has since moved to new offices on York Avenue. But at that time its Madison Avenue gallery was the least intimate of the top auction houses. The building was a carved concrete block, rather like a Texan imitation of a Pharaoh's temple. The auction area itself was shaped like a diamond lozenge with a revolving stage at one angle to aid the orderly presentation of lots; it was a large hall rather than a room, with high green-painted walls, and an overflow gallery upstairs where some of the more secretive dealers preferred to sit.

That Wednesday morning the hall filled slowly. Halfway back were a number of padded chaise longues and sofas, in an eighteenth-century style; here a few of the younger English dealers, in vivid shirts, sprawled elegantly, talking loudly to one another like Members of Parliament in the House of Commons awaiting the arrival of the front bench. They exchanged wary greetings with their American counterparts who, in general, seemed quieter beings, more somberly dressed and, to Blake, apparently more worried by the prospect of that morning's sale. John Blake, too, had begun to sweat.

By the time John Marion, president of Sotheby's in New York and the auctioneer that day, appeared at precisely 10:15, the room had filled and was buzzing with anticipation. The main attraction of the sale, printed in the catalog in full color, was a *St. Sebastian Tended by Irene,* by Georges de Latour, the seventeenth-century painter from Lorraine. Latour's small output—about forty pictures—meant that this one was expected to sell for beween $200,000 and $300,000. It was a rather grisly, realistic painting showing the saint by the light of a lantern with an arrow through his left leg.

All seemed perfectly normal; only the superobservant would have noticed the small exchange of smiles between Marion and Blake as the auctioneer registered where this particular customer was sitting. In no time at all Marion had announced that five lots had been withdrawn (luckily, none that Blake was interested in), that all paintings were offered "subject to the conditions of sale as printed in the catalog" and that lot one, a pair of summer landscapes by Gerard Wieringa and dated 1812, were worth . . . what? The bidding started at $2,000 and the sale was on.

John Blake may have looked for all the world like one of the art market's smoother international dealers. But when he raised his silver Tiffany pen to bid for the Wieringas that morning, it was not only the first time he had bid at auction—it was the first auction he had ever attended. John Blake was, in fact, me in disguise. Earlier that day over breakfast, I had been given a number of bids to make on behalf of three genuine art dealers, beginning with an $11,000 offering for lot number one from Richard Feigen, whose New York gallery is on East Seventy-ninth Street. It was the first public move in our conspiracy to recover some of the world's most beautiful stolen old masters.

As a newspaper reporter, attached to the London *Sunday Times,* I had managed to persuade a few art dealers, policemen and the two main auction houses to join me in what might prove to be a spectacular recovery—or might not. That Wednesday I was extremely nervous—too nervous to admit to Feigen that he was asking me to bid on the first lot in my very first sale.

In fact, I needn't have worried. "Blake" managed to catch Marion's eye when the bidding was at $7,000, stayed in until his limit of $11,000 and then dropped out. The pictures in the end brought considerably more ($23,000), and were knocked down to a woman who, in Max Beerbohm's apt words, was not as young as she was painted.

I relaxed after that and the rest of the day went quite well. Three hundred and five "Important Old Master" paintings and drawings changed hands by 4:15 P.M. and A. John Blake had "bought" twenty-three of them, at a total value of $84,000. He had begun to make his mark on the international art world, which was the whole idea. The plot was off to a good start.

JOHN BLAKE had in fact been born only six weeks before and was chiefly the creation of three people: Rodolfo Siviero, an Italian diplomat who heads a small section of the Italian Foreign Office exclusively concerned with the recovery of stolen art; Don Langton, a bluff ex-policeman, a former head of Scotland Yard's fine art squad and, at the time, running his own private detective agency in England; and Andrew Purches, an imaginative London dealer. Purches was the most deceptive of all. Slight, slow-moving, soft-spoken, he has the habit of puffing away at his pipe for minutes on end without speaking. Hardly the adventurous type, you would think. But for years Purches was used as the front man by the art squad at Scotland Yard.

It was Siviero who had originally helped conceive the idea of a plot to recover stolen paintings. He works in Rome though he spends his weekends in a beautiful house in Florence, on the Lungarno Serristori, overlooking the Arno. This is where the whole conspiracy began.

I had gone to meet him there one cold night in February 1979 as part of preliminary research for a straightforward, factual book which would examine the recent increase in international art theft. The newspaper I worked for, the London *Sunday Times*, was not published just then, owing to chronic labor troubles, and most of the journalists were looking for things to do. Siviero was the world's number one art detective and he seemed a sensible place to start.

The evening light was beginning to fade as I arrived at the house and was shown into a long, narrow sitting room with a huge log fire at one end. Siviero produced a fine malt whiskey and some delicious Italian sugared nuts, then began to talk. Tana de Zulueta, the *Sunday Times* correspondent in Rome, acted as interpreter.

Perhaps it was the whiskey, perhaps it was the log fire adding to the mellowness of the evening, perhaps it was both. But Siviero talked nonstop for three hours that night and it was only toward the end of his monologue that the same thought occurred to us both.

Physically, especially by dim firelight, Siviero is not unlike Pablo Picasso, but in other ways he is more an amalgam of Anthony Blunt and Sherlock Holmes. Think of that familiar, round, powerful Picasso figure with those large globular eyes. Add to the

baldness a few wisps of fine gray hair; replace the Spanish lisp
with an Italian lilt and then clothe him, not in white shorts and
sandals, but in an impeccable suit of English tweed: the trans-
formation is complete.

Unlike Blunt, Siviero is no traitor. But, like the discredited
Englishman, he comes of a patrician background and during the
Second World War flamboyantly combined a practical interest in
art with espionage. Though born in Florence, he comes from an
old Venetian family which has always prided itself on its intellectual independence. Siviero began his monologue by recalling
the Renaissance ancestor who sat as a judge on the Supreme
Court of the Venetian Republic. Having received the acts of trial
against a witch, rather than underwrite the guilty sentence, the
ancestor simply wrote, "If there are witches there is no God, and
if there is God there are no witches. Acquitted. Siviero." It was
worthy of Machiavelli himself.

With that background Siviero's family was not one to have
much patience with Mussolini's inflammatory rhetoric and the
vulgar attempts to compare his regime with the glories of ancient
Rome. As a student in Florence, however, Siviero had at least to
accept the externals of il Duce's regime. Like all students in
Mussolini's day, he was expected to turn out regularly for parade
in full fascist uniform. The very idea repelled him; he haughtily
defined fascism as "an offense to the intelligence." His mother
had bought the cloth which was to be made up into a fascist uniform, but with one excuse and another, Siviero kept putting off
the journey to the tailor.

Eventually, he could stand it no more and made up his mind to
join the Allies. He smuggled himself on board a fishing boat and
made his way to Algiers, where he contacted Allied Command.
From then on he spent the war as an undercover agent in Ger-
man-occupied Italy, crossing the lines several times.

To begin with, many of his operations were purely military. By
1943, however, Siviero was head of the Italian Secret Service attached to Allied Command. This service, which operated only in
German-held territory, was divided into two sections. The job of
the first was to inform Allied Command of the plans and actions
of the German Army in Italy. The job of the second section was
to warn partisan formations of imminent German roundups. It
also oversaw the protection of minorities, Jews and works of art.

The duty was hazardous and its value may be judged from the fact that on the one occasion when Siviero was captured, and sentenced to death by the SS, a partisan commando unit was detailed to rescue him. They made it just in time—but Siviero was so weak his rescuers had to carry him to safety.

It was in his role as protector of Jews in Italy that Siviero had his first success in saving Italian art. His unit came to learn that the famous painter Giorgio de Chirico had fled his house in Florence because the SS were about to arrest his Jewish wife. All De Chirico's paintings had been left behind at the mercy of the maid, whose boy friend was an SS sergeant.

Together with two *carabinieri* officers who were also part of his secret service unit, Siviero turned up at De Chirico's house in a borrowed truck. They briskly identified themselves as police officers come to search the house for anti-fascist Jews. While one of the *carabinieri* kept the maid occupied, the others loaded the truck with the master's paintings and some of his more precious possessions. Before leaving, Siviero took the maid to one side on the pretext of questioning her about her employers; while this was going on another of his colleagues removed a piece from the telephone receiver so the maid couldn't call the SS to check them out. They gained enough time to make a getaway and later hid the paintings by walling them up in the stables of the Pitti Palace —fittingly, since the palace is nowadays once more one of Florence's most splendid galleries.

As the war began to go against the Germans, and they took to stealing paintings and other works of art from Italy under the guise of "protecting" them from the Allies, there was little Siviero could do to prevent it. Instead he tried to keep tabs on who took what from where. It paid off eventually. After the war, and after he had received a letter from Winston Churchill thanking him for his work and expressing "regret" that he wasn't an Englishman, Siviero became the first Italian ambassador to Germany, where he proved a most awkward guest. He used his wartime records to show that he knew exactly where to look for at least some of the countless missing objects.

Among the paintings looted by the Nazis from the Uffizi and which Siviero has helped recover are: Bronzino's *Deposition of Christ;* Antonio Pollaiuolo's *Labors of Hercules;* Domenico Feti's *Parable of the Vine;* a self-portrait by Lorenzo di Credi; a *Nativ-*

ity by a pupil of Correggio; Botticelli's *Primavera* and Paolo Uccello's *The Battle of San Remo*. It was only natural that, on his return from Germany, Siviero should become a minister without portfolio in the foreign office in Rome and be put in charge of the Delegation for the Recovery of Missing Works of Art.

It is here that the parallels with Sherlock Holmes become apparent. Siviero has never married and works by himself, using a network of police officers and art dealers throughout Europe and North America who help out of personal loyalty to him. He lives as well as works during the week in fastidious splendor in a set of vaulted rooms at the back of the Palazzo Venezia, which il Duce himself occupied during the war. Siviero's spartan bedroom is next to his office and through the grilled window you can glimpse the trees and flowers of the palazzo's cloistered garden. His secretary is an elderly Watson-like figure, and is the only one who knows where all the files are located: it is with him that Siviero tries out every move in advance.

Again, like Holmes, Siviero has a phenomenal memory, especially for detail, and, like the Baker Street sleuth, he never gives up. In 1979, for instance, a Canaletto came up for auction at Moretti's in Milan. It was a fairly conventional view of the Grand Canal in Venice, seen from the Rialto Bridge. But to Siviero there was something familiar about it. He searched his memory, then his files. It took a few hours but eventually he found what he was looking for: a Canaletto very like the one on offer at Moretti's. It had been stolen by the Nazis in 1944 from the famous Borbone-Parma collection in northern Italy.

But . . . but . . . There *were* a few differences between the pictures. The view was the same—that was nothing new for Canaletto—but the Moretti picture had more chimneys on the buildings and more clouds in the sky than the one that had been stolen. It also had fewer windows in the walls of a large building seen on the right. Suddenly, Siviero sat up. The picture stolen from the Borbone-Parma collection had two windows, each with its shutters open. These open shutters cast long shadows to the left. The picture on sale at Moretti's had only one window but that was in exactly the same position as one of the windows in the Borbone-Parma painting. However, what caught Siviero's eye was that the shutters to this window were closed but still cast a shadow across the wall to the left. This was against the laws of physics even in Canaletto's day and it was obvious to Siviero that an unknown hand had tried to disguise this painting but had clumsily forgotten to wipe out the shadow after the shutter had been closed. The painting was confiscated before it could be sold.

He doesn't always win, of course. There are many dealers in Europe and North America for whom the mere mention of Rodolfo Siviero is enough to bring an exasperated groan to their lips. Many of them feel his interpretation of the law is too literal, making them out to be criminals when they have bought an object (albeit stolen) in good faith. Siviero certainly is cunning in enticing stolen works back to Italy; no deception is too grand or too elaborate if, in his view, it stands a chance of working. You can quite see why some dealers might feel bruised by him.

The story of the Visso cross is a good example of his buccaneering nature. This beautiful object is six feet tall and wrought of solid gold and silver. At its base there is a carved figure of the fifteenth-century Pope, Gregory XII, and the whole is mounted on a marble stand. "It is a masterpiece of medieval craftsmanship," says Siviero. Others obviously agreed, for on the night of 27 June 1973 it was stolen from a church in the central Italian town of Visso. The Italian police could find no trace of it: the cross had literally vanished.

In the light of past experience, Siviero assumed that it had been smuggled out of Italy. The only thing to do was wait. Sure enough, two years later, he learned that the cross had been sold for 300 million lire ($300,000) by a dealer in Germany. The news came through Siviero's own grapevine and he traveled to Germany to question the seller. The man was reluctant to cooperate, would certainly not say from whom he had bought the cross and in fact seemed quite unmoved by the news that it was stolen. Only under the threat of police action, and much adverse publicity, did he tell Siviero to whom he had sold the cross.

Herr Renato Remschmidt* is a wealthy industrialist in Cologne. He received Siviero, Italian diplomat and minister, with great courtesy. Moreover, he expressed consternation to hear that the beautiful cross he had recently bought was in fact stolen from an Italian church. Now in such cases, rather than open complex international proceedings (the outcome of which is too often unsatisfactory) Siviero prefers the gentlemanly approach. "You say you bought this object in good faith; but now you know it is stolen; hand it over and we part as friends." In this way the buyer's reputation remains intact. Siviero hoped such an approach might prove sufficient this time and moved into a hotel while the industrialist said he would try to persuade his wife to part with the cross. It was, he said, a wedding anniversary present.

Siviero waited at the hotel for three days but heard nothing. He became worried so he telephoned the man. This time the industrialist was decidedly less cordial and, giving his wife as an excuse, let Siviero know that he would not part with the cross.

Disappointed, but not entirely surprised, Siviero was not finished yet. Instead of going back to Rome, he flew on to London and called on a dealer friend in Jermyn Street. He told him the story, and over dinner at Frank's they agreed on a plan which they had used successfully before.

They let a couple of weeks elapse so as to give the industrialist no grounds for suspicion. Then the London dealer asked a German colleague to approach Herr Remschmidt to see if he was willing to sell the Visso cross. Remschmidt, of course, was by now only too anxious to rid himself of the thing, provided he could get his money back: it was an embarrassing object. The ultimate buyer, he was told, was in Switzerland and the deal would be handled by a well-known London art gallery.

Nothing was hurried; all the people who dealt with Herr Remschmidt were bona fide dealers. Unsuspecting, Remschmidt let the cross be moved to London, then to Switzerland, all the while with the dealer's word as guarantee. In May 1975 the cross finally arrived at the Lugano gallery of yet another member of Siviero's network. The gallery owner telephoned Rome to tell Siviero that the cross had been delivered and he was on the plane to Switzerland that night and collected the cross the next morning. Remschmidt was notified by letter of the tremendous hoax which had been played on him.

Imaginative—and effective. Yet there are plenty of people who feel that, in this case as in others, Siviero has essentially taken the law into his own hands. And, in so doing, has punished the innocent members of a chain and let the more culpable dealers and thieves go free. Siviero would not entirely disagree. But as he sees it, anyone who buys a work of art should satisfy himself as to the work's provenance before he parts with his money. Anyone

who does not do so, he would argue, has only himself to blame
for the consequences.

Also, he is charged primarily, not with catching thieves, but
with recovering stolen works. And he must be counted a success.
To date, almost single-handedly, he has recovered 2,500 art
works stolen by the Germans, far more than his traditional rivals,
the *Servizio per le ricerche delle opere d'arte rubate*, run by the
commander general of the *carabinieri*. More recently Siviero has
recovered stolen paintings by such famous artists as Memling and
Masaccio and a sculpture by Michelangelo. It was Siviero who, in
1970, accused the Museum of Fine Arts in Boston of smuggling a
Raphael, *Portrait of a Young Girl*, out of Italy. The museum had
announced that it had bought the "lost Raphael" for $600,000
from "an old European collection." Siviero traced the man who
had carved the portrait's new frame, who gave him the name of
the dealer near Genoa who had commissioned the carving. This
man had a criminal record and, under pressure, confessed he had
bought the painting, for $1,000, from a family that didn't realize
what it had. A search of local hotel registers showed that the director and curator of the Boston museum had stayed in Genoa
hotels for a few days prior to the announcement of the acquisition. It is illegal to export a work of art from Italy without government permission. The scandal resulted in the museum director's resignation. Siviero collected the Raphael in Boston and took
it back to Italy.

IT WAS PAST MIDNIGHT on the Lungarno Serristori. Outside, the
dark green waters of the Arno slid past, murmuring soft protests
as they were forced under the dim brown and red shapes of the
Ponte Vecchio a couple of hundred yards downstream, half lost
in gloom. One by one, the creamy mellow stones of Florence's
older buildings—the Palazzo Vecchio, the Uffizi, the Santa Croce
—could be picked out across the river, colors and shadows worthy
of the greatest of the early Florentine masters, "Hulking Tom"
Masaccio himself. No wonder the Lungarno is regarded as one of
the best addresses in Italy.

Inside, the room had grown quite dark. A suit of armor stood
at attention near the fireplace, blocking much of the light from
the fire; a crystal chandelier flickered above; around the room

were dotted Siviero's marvelous collection of thirteenth- and fourteenth-century metal chalices; pride of place went to a terracotta *Madonna col Bambino* by Sansovino and a bust by Nanni di Banco, the teacher of Donatello. Small modern paintings— including two deep green and red De Chirico portraits—were hung tastefully among their older rivals. Siviero got to his feet and pressed a button set into the wall; the servant appeared and placed another log on the fire. Our glasses were refilled; the evening wasn't over yet.

"I have a suggestion," Siviero said, sliding a sugared almond into his mouth. "Why not try to recover some stolen art yourself? Much more useful than writing a general book—and if you are successful it will make better reading anyway. Find yourself a dealer who will collaborate, who will agree to appear a shade dishonest; put the word around and who knows what you might find? I can help you get started, if you are interested."

There was, he now confided, one particular painting he had tried and tried to recover—but he had always failed. The painting was Caravaggio's *Adoration with St. Francis and St. Lawrence*, usually known simply as the *Nativity*. Stolen in 1969 from the oratory of San Lorenzo in Palermo, it had been missing longer than anything else. Artistically and historically it was of the first importance, but it was also of immense personal interest to him, said Siviero. He believed it had been stolen by the Sicilian Mafia in revenge for something else he had recovered from them with yet another piece of trickery: in a curious way he felt responsible for the loss.

Born in 1571, Caravaggio was a wonderful artist who had revolutionized painting by rendering miraculous events from the Bible as if they were happening to the ordinary, often downright shabby people of his day. Caravaggio himself was not a particularly endearing soul; he argued, he brawled and was given to writing satirical and obscene verses about his painter rivals. He even killed a man and died young while on the run. But, said Siviero, the *Nativity* was one of the last pictures he had painted and stylistically it seemed to indicate a change in Caravaggio. It was a perfect example of a new vision in the mind of a genius. It was vital to recover the picture.

But he had come to the conclusion, he said, that only an approach from outside Italy, from someone who had not the faintest connection with the police or any government agency, stood a chance of getting to the thieves. The authorities were too corrupt to be effective. He was getting old now, he whispered. There wasn't much time left and he had to try more unconventional ways to recover the Caravaggio. If I liked his suggestion, he would help by showing me his secret file. In it were all his suspicions about who was involved in the shadowy world of international art theft.

2

The Plot and the Disguise

THE FILE, marked "Segreto," was in Rome, so another meeting had to be arranged after I had done some elementary background reading about Caravaggio. There was never any real doubt that I would accept Siviero's invitation to take part in the scheme—in fact, something similar to what he had in mind had occurred to me moments before he said it. There was, of course, the problem that we might end up having to deal with the Sicilian Mafia, but . . . well, I didn't dwell on that too much to begin with. Siviero himself had taken them on more than once, and he was still around.

I wouldn't put all my eggs in one basket, of course. If I was lucky enough to recover *any* painting by a well-known artist, that would do as well as the Caravaggio, provided it gave some indication as to how the international traffic in stolen art operated. But concentrating on one painting, at least in the beginning, was an attractive idea because it gave me something specific to aim for. I would even be given the names of suspects, which was the

most alluring starting point of all. If I had any success in penetrating the dishonest elements of the art world, then any number
of stolen works might come my way.

There were possibilities. At that time recent thefts included
Rembrandt's *Portrait of a Rabbi*, El Greco's *Mary Magdalen Be-
fore Christ on the Cross*, Renoir's *Portrait of "Coco"* and Picasso's
famous *Woman with a Sheep's Skull*. Also missing were Pieter
Brueghel's *Harvest*, Van Gogh's *Portrait du Docteur Gachet* and
four Cézannes. From Italy, besides recent thefts of a Botticelli, a
Bassano and a Tiepolo, there were 255 works of art still missing
which had been taken as loot by the Nazis in the Second World
War. These included a Van Dyck, a Rubens, a Poussin, an El
Greco copy of a Correggio, plus works by Tintoretto, Veronese,
Bronzino, two red-chalk drawings by Michelangelo, Titian's *Por-
trait of Ludovico Ariosto* and a number of violins by Stradivari.
Any of those would do just as well.

However, before the project proper could get off the ground
there was the small matter of finance to be settled. My publishers
provided a generous advance. As things turned out, however,
what with the specialist help I had to buy in, the forged documents I had to get, the fancy clothes I needed and the scores of
airline tickets and hotel rooms I had to pay for, that sum went
long before we reached the end of the project. Whatever else it
may be, as my bank manager never ceased to point out, investigative journalism is not cheap.

My first expense against the budget was a ticket to Rome.

THE BRIEFING about the *Nativity* took place in Siviero's office near
the Piazza Venezia in March 1979. This office was almost as
handsome as his house in Florence. Through the grilled windows
one could see the sunlight filter into the cloister across the inner
courtyard. On the walls across from his desk were an Annigoni
drawing, a commemorative plaque from the painter's guild of
Italy and a twisted, six-foot rod. In medieval times this was
believed to be a unicorn's horn, but—disappointingly—it turned
out to be a tooth from a narwhal.

The names of three sets of suspects were listed in Siviero's file.
In the first place there was a collection of thugs who had probably helped break into the chapel and slice the painting from its

frame. For them there were names, nicknames, known hangouts in Sicily, Rome and Milan, and telephone numbers. Next came a much smaller number of names based either in Milan, Rome, Linz in Austria, or Frankfurt in West Germany. Again there were telephone numbers. These names had all been found in note-books belonging to the thugs appearing in the first list. Siviero had had his men go through their luggage in the baggage hall at Milan airport on the occasions when the thugs visited the city. It was Siviero's feeling that this second bunch were international couriers who might have moved the picture around. It was also his hunch that the picture had been moved out of Sicily at least once, in an attempt to sell it. This was because of the third list, which consisted of quite well-known art dealers, two in London and one in Paris. Siviero had heard on the grapevine that these dealers had been offered the painting, had refused but *had not alerted the police*. This suggested to Siviero that these men were less than honest and the thieves had known it. He thought the only reason the dealers had refused the picture was because it was too well-known to resell.

The plot was, essentially, to contact someone on these lists in such a way that he would offer the Caravaggio, or some other stolen painting, to me.

OUR FIRST TACTIC was to see if any of the thugs or couriers had contacts in New York (this seemed far more likely than London, say, or Paris) and whether these New York contacts, if they existed, had links with the art world. Second, we had the names of dealers who had been offered the Caravaggio and who might be persuaded to pass on the name of the individual who had ap-proached them with news of it. Alternatively, if a relationship could be established with any of the dealers, and if they were, as Siviero suspected, dishonest, then they might know of other stolen works.

In order to pursue both lines of inquiry, however, we had to have someone, preferably a dealer, who could logically be inter-ested in the Caravaggio or other old masters *and* who could get himself into a position where he would be offered stolen paint-ings or could legitimately inquire about them. But dealers are businessmen, too busy to have time for plots, especially plots where they are asked to stick their necks out for little reward and where, for a time at least, they would have to appear dishonest.

It was risky, but it soon became clear that the only solution was to turn me into a dealer and in double-quick time to produce a "character" who at least *seemed* to be an international art expert, a specialist in old master paintings, wealthy and, perhaps most important, not above the occasional dishonest deal.

Easier said than done. But this is where Don Langton and Andrew Purches showed their flair. I had first met Don Langton at a conference on art theft at the University of Delaware, well before the idea actually of trying to recover stolen paintings had cropped up. The conference had become a sell-out days before it was due to begin, owing to the theft of a marvelous Greek head from the Metropolitan Museum in New York. It couldn't have been better timed if the heist had been arranged by the university PR people.

Langton gave a talk to the conference on the workings of the Yard's fine art squad and it was he who introduced me to Andrew Purches later on. The pair had worked together while Langton was in charge of the squad, when Andrew was used as the "front man."

Langton is a tall, cheerful, ruddy-faced man who is slightly deaf and so speaks with a booming voice. He had used his years in the fine art squad very well: by the time we came across each other he had his own antique business in East Anglia—*and* a private detective agency.

Don's most spectacular coup while he was at the Yard had been the recovery of two important paintings by Mattia Preti, a seventeenth-century follower of Caravaggio. The pictures Don recovered had been stolen from a church in Taverna, near the toe of Italy. The first tip came unintentionally from a twenty-five-year-old Italian girl, Franca Bakaeva, who was living in London and went to see her dentist there. Under anesthetic she mumbled something about stolen paintings. Later the dentist rang the Yard. Langton and his superior officer then followed Bakaeva and her boy friend, a barman. From this and other inquiries they eventually raided the luggage lockers at London's Euston station where they came across a rolled-up carpet. Inside were the two Pretis, worth several hundreds of thousands of pounds, and a picture by Giuseppe de Ribera. That was when Don had first come

across Siviero: the paintings had been returned to the Italian diplomat and the two men had kept in touch ever since.

Andrew is quite different. He has a kind of bumbling, bewil-
dered manner which invites others to underestimate him. He
never wears a tie; his hands are invariably grimy; he is forever
lighting and relighting his pipe. But he is an excellent part-time
policeman.

Once, when Don Langton had been tipped off that some stolen
paintings were being offered at a gallery in London's High Street
Kensington, Andrew had been sent in. (Don's face was too well
known.) Andrew presented himself as a dealer interested in the
kinds of paintings that had been stolen, English watercolors. It
took several visits to the gallery, and Andrew had to show himself knowledgeable about the genre, had to know, for example,
the difference between Cozens and Girtin, Cotman and Turner.
Eventually, however, he was offered "better pictures, but not
here." A rendezvous was arranged, out in the countryside, and
Andrew was told "to come alone." He did, but Don and a colleague were not far behind in an unmarked police car.

Andrew, who was driving his own car, a white Citroën, followed the two men to a deserted farmhouse. He examined two
paintings—clearly the stolen ones Don had been tipped off about.
He said he liked them and agreed a price. Andrew then said he
would get the money from the trunk of his car. This was the sig-
nal to Don, in the distance, to raid the farmhouse. Unfortunately
the crooks had their own signaling system and they saw Don's car
coming along the drive. They shoved Andrew to one side and ran
from the house, taking the paintings with them. When they got
outside, to the farmyard, Andrew's car was blocking theirs. So
they threw the paintings into the white Citroën and escaped in
that. Don, coming up the driveway, didn't understand what was
going on, but thought that Andrew was for some reason making
an early getaway. Too late he realized he had just passed the
thieves—and the stolen pictures.

There followed a Keystone Kops chase through the English
country lanes: the thieves in a strange car, Andrew in a strange
car, and the police. With their souped-up Rover the detectives
had little difficulty in catching up with the thieves in Andrew's
little Citroën. But the lanes were narrow and Don couldn't get
past. Then, suddenly, the thieves turned off the road and on to a

track across a field. Here the Citroën's superior suspension paid off and the thieves began to draw away.

Andrew, by this time, was miles behind—yet perhaps that was just as well. Before long Don spotted a reservoir in the distance with the Citroën drawn up alongside it. The thieves had stepped out and were pushing the car. Mortified, Don watched helplessly as Andrew's Citroën disappeared down the slope and into the water. As the police Rover skidded to a halt by the two thieves, all that could be seen of the Citroën was a number of bubbles breaking the surface of the reservoir. The thieves made no attempt to escape; the stolen paintings—the evidence—had gone to the bottom with Andrew's car, and were lost. Or so they thought.

The pictures were recovered—damaged beyond repair, but identifiable enough to satisfy the insurance company that they were the ones that had been stolen, and to convince a jury that the two thieves deserved a guilty verdict.

Andrew's car was another matter. It too was recovered, and, after much haggling, the Yard did agree to reimburse him for the trouble of having it cleaned, resprayed and the fish taken out of the carburetor. But that didn't appease Andrew's wife: they had been due to go on vacation in it the day after the chase that had led to the reservoir.

When we met, Andrew was just starting as a printer of artists' lithographs in a shabby, near-derelict wharf in Battersea on the south bank of the Thames. The building had been condemned but that didn't worry Andrew; it was dry, airy and for the year or two before it was demolished the rent was almost nothing. The wharf was just across the river from where I lived, in Chelsea, so we took to meeting in the Phene Arms pub, just off London's famous King's Road, convenient for both of us. There, over a couple of lagers and some ham sandwiches, five major obstacles involved in turning Peter Watson into an art dealer were clarified. One by one they were eventually overcome. But it wasn't easy.

First, what kind of character was this person going to be? Was he going to be a collector, a dealer or should he actually work in a gallery? If the latter, which one? Second, his appearance: should we disguise him? What were the chances of Peter Watson bumping into someone he knew in New York or London or Italy when he was in the company of a Mafioso link man or a dishonest dealer and what should be done about it? Should this character have a different name, with a new set of identification documents? Or was that more trouble than it was worth and carrying things too far? Third, there was the problem of money. How could we conjure up a character out of nowhere *and* make him wealthy, rich enough to pay six figures for a picture? Fourth, we had to remember that this person couldn't be too straight—and how did we go about that? How did we inject dishonesty into his personality without making it seem obvious? Last, but by no means least, there was the general problem of publicity. Whatever character we managed to fabricate, he would have little impact unless we could ensure that the art world as a whole learned about him. We had to ensure that the crooked elements in the art world, whoever they were and wherever they were, heard about our character and his activities, preferably before he ever came into contact with them.

It seemed daunting. But Andrew, puffing away at his filthy pipe, worried at the five problems, drank his lager and neglected his business. His solutions showed he had lost none of the flair since his days with Scotland Yard.

THE FIRST PROBLEM was the one of general identity. What sort of figure in the art world was our new character to be? He couldn't be a dealer since he couldn't acquire either the expertise or his own gallery overnight. Don Langton emphasized that his identity should be as vague as possible so that, depending on our investigations, he could alter course without appearing to behave unnaturally. On the other hand, Andrew thought that the best way to achieve publicity in the art world was to be seen bidding at the major auctions. All the dealers, on both sides of the Atlantic, attend these sales, and if our character was to be seen as an active participant, spending lots of money, he would soon draw attention to himself.

Andrew's argument was a good one. The only type of character who appeared to satisfy all the criteria was a buying agent. Andrew said that the art world was full of these mysterious people who suddenly appeared, and just as surprisingly disappeared, bidding usually on behalf of others. So it would appear not at all odd if I suddenly started showing up at the auctions acting as an agent. Such people, Andrew said, knew a bit about art but didn't need to know anywhere near as much as dealers. Further, as an agent, I could easily pretend to be acting under instructions for several clients, so could claim a legitimate lack of expertise in some areas.

The name of this buying agent was the second thing we settled. Siviero had by now become most insistent that nothing be done by half measures. We needed a complete background—a new record, a passport, other documents, a life stretching back at least a few years and so on.

We could have chosen any name since we planned to buy the necessary documents to establish a false identity. In London, in 1979, provided you knew the right people (and most journalists who have covered criminal cases know the right people), the going rate for a British passport was £500, plus the cost of the photograph. A driver's license cost between £150 and £250. In both cases the documents would be stolen. I consulted George Fenyo, a Hungarian living in Earl's Court who made his name among certain people by forging German documents in concentration camps in World War Two. His view was that the then recent British practice of wrapping a shiny, clear plastic strip around the page of the passport which contains the photograph was a brilliant innovation, extremely difficult to change and just as difficult to forge. He also pointed out that, since the passport would have to be stamped with an American visa, it would have to stand up to special scrutiny, not just the cursory glance most immigration officials give to documents. So one of George Fenyo's forgeries would not do and we decided to test out *The Day of the Jackal* method.

In that marvelous thriller, Frederick Forsyth shows how easy it used to be to obtain a British passport in a false name. The "Jackal," the Englishman who has been retained by a group of disaffected French soldiers to assassinate President Charles de Gaulle, visits an old churchyard in the Thames Valley looking for the gravestone of someone born roughly at the same time as himself but who died very young, before he could ever have applied for a passport. Under some pretext, checking the parish records for this person, the Jackal finds who the parents were and their address: this gives him a clue to where the birth was registered. Using another excuse at the registry office, he is able to obtain a copy of the birth and the death certificate—applying for both shifts attention away from his interest simply in one end of this person's life. Discarding the death certificate, he is then free to use the birth document to apply for a passport in the dead person's name, safe in the knowledge that no one has used that particular set of details to apply for a passport before.

However, our experience suggests that, although the technique outlined by Forsyth works eventually, it may be that he never tried it out himself. We found some subtle variations.

We tried several churchyards to the north of Oxford—Chipping Norton, Morton-in-Marsh, Stow-on-the-Wold, Bourton-on-the-Water—traditional Cotswold villages (and all very beautiful). In each, however, the pattern was the same and not at all helpful. To start with, churchyards were not much use. Most did not accommodate corpses after the early nineteenth century—where we could read the gravestones, that is. For the most part, the weather had eaten away at the chiseled details so that names and dates were indistinct. But, even more important, churchyards were invariably full by 1850.

This means that mid-nineteenth-century deaths are almost always accommodated in municipal cemeteries, which rarely adjoin the old churchyards. (The exceptions are where a family has a plot or crypt going back a hundred years or more. In these cases, the old crypts may be opened for later members of the family to join their ancestors.) These municipal cemeteries saved us a lot of work since improved materials (and the shorter life of the gravestones) were easier to read. Added to that, the municipal mind, in contrast with the ancient clerical one, seemed more prone to lay out the graves in rough chronological order. Thus we didn't have to scour the entire graveyard but simply locate the patch encompassing deaths which had occurred at roughly the time of my birth, 1943. In any case, however, not even this was much use. In the cemeteries we examined we found no one who would fit the bill.

Then it struck me that, perhaps in these well-to-do rural areas, child mortality was relatively low and that our purpose would be better served in some larger town, with more poverty, overcrowding and all the other factors that, sadly, are associated with increased child mortality. During the following week I tried the South Yardley cemetery on the southern outskirts of Birmingham. It was May the third, general election day, and within hours Margaret Thatcher would become Britain's first woman Prime Minister. This time I couldn't have chosen better.

Yardley cemetery is enormous—several hundred acres at least. But it is well cared for, busy—in the sense of there being several new additions every day—so my investigations passed unnoticed. Moreover, it is laid out extremely systematically. Every decade appears to have its own patch of land, separated from others by walkways and driveways. It took less than ten minutes to find the patch given over to deaths that occurred in the 1940s.

As you might expect, this patch was larger than most since Birmingham suffered such terrible bombings between 1941 and 1943. It was a sobering experience to study the graves, as I could not help doing, of entire families wiped out. Saddest of all were the families who lost two or more sons in the war; in many cases the parents themselves seemed not to survive past the end of the war, as if the deaths of their children had broken their will to live.

But even though the patch I had to search was larger than any other, there was another practice, evident in Birmingham but not in the Cotswolds or in *The Day of the Jackal*, which made the task easier. This is the custom, particularly among Catholic families (who of course would not be present in a Church of England graveyard), of mounting a small stone angel above the grave of a dead infant. This meant that, instead of examining the wording of each grave, I simply had to look for those bearing the small stone figure. I also appeared to have been right in my amateurish foray into demographics. In South Yardley there seemed to have been plenty of child mortality: within three quarters of an hour I had found eight children whose deaths occurred around 1940.

At the cemetery office I posed as a researcher investigating child mortality for the World Health Organization. In no time I was shown the register of burials by helpful assistants. This listed who owned the graves—in most cases the parents—and the addresses from which the children had been buried. From these addresses I could identify the parishes where the children had been born and, in the parish churches, find the birth register with the exact date of birth and the full name of both parents (which you need to apply for a birth certificate).

Owing to the amount of movement in the early 1940s I was not able to trace all the names back to parish churches—many people presumably had been bombed out of their own homes and, at the time of their deaths, were staying with friends or relatives in different parishes. In fact, the eight names shrank to two in the end. These were Peter Joseph Morrison, who died on 11 June 1947, aged thirteen months, and Ailiffe John Blake, who died on 9 February 1939, aged five weeks.

Peter Morrison had two advantages. The first was his Christian name. There was always the risk that, while I was in disguise or acting my part as a buying agent, I would come across someone who knew me as Peter Watson. If I was using the name Peter Morrison and a friend chanced to call out "Peter," my cover would not be blown. A second advantage, though less important: Morrison had been christened in the same church as I on the outskirts of Birmingham. This meant that I automatically knew little details about Morrison's background that might, at some unforeseen point in the future, give my cover credibility. On the other hand, if Peter Morrison were alive today he would be four years younger than I. Since I look three or four years older than I actually am, this was a considerable disadvantage.

Ailiffe John Blake, were he alive today, would be four years older than I—but we judged that an asset rather than a drawback for the same reason that Peter Morrison's age was a problem. Blake was a Catholic, baptized *e pericoloso de mortuis* [in danger of death]: there was absolutely no chance that there would be a passport in his name. But what clinched it was the information, also in the parish records when I tracked them down, that the infant's mother had died in 1941. This made it less likely that there were any brothers or sisters around now to be upset by our activities in using their dead brother's name. So I opted for A. John Blake (shortening Ailiffe to "A." was another touch of Andrew's), and duly applied for a passport in that name.

Next, the driving license. We needed one because Blake might, in some remote part of Italy, need to be mobile. I could have applied in the ordinary way and taken a driving test under an assumed name, but in London at that time the whole procedure took months and we couldn't wait that long. Using my contacts made as a crime correspondent, I bought one. It took three weeks and cost £250. I obtained that in Birmingham, too.

Other things were simpler. A checkbook and credit card were acquired with the help of William Whelan, a coin and bullion

dealer of Crown Passage, a narrow alleyway just off Pall Mall in
St. James's. Whelan, a tall, cheerful man with a young face and a
prematurely bald head, was another contact of Langton's from
his time at Scotland Yard. He agreed to "employ" Blake for the
purposes of bank references and so on, "paying" a salary of
£12,000.

Blake's identity was finished off in two ways. First we got him
membership cards for the sorts of things an art dealer might be-
long to: the Friends of Covent Garden, the Institute of Contemporary Arts, the National Film Theatre and so on. Second, his
briefcase and pockets were peppered with letters to him from
well-known figures in the art world: dealers, picture restorers and
curators. Through a friend, I arranged to filch some official notepaper from the Metropolitan Museum in New York. A business
diary apparently collated details of Blake's sales and purchases
during the previous months. Several items referred back to deals
made in earlier years. Blake's briefcase was also crammed with
color photos of paintings he was either buying or selling. Whenever he went out, all the trappings went with him.

One final—but important—detail needed to be sorted out. Blake
needed a base, an address to work from, and this was tricky. The
budget wouldn't stretch to a separate flat for any length of time,
especially as it would have to be in the best areas of town—
Mayfair, Belgravia, Chelsea. Nor did we judge this entirely necessary. In the end A. John Blake's business card showed just two
telephone numbers—one in London, the other in New York. The
numbers were real numbers, of real (girl) friends who were taken
into our confidence and agreed to pretend, should the need arise,
to be John Blake's secretaries. If called, they would simply say
that he was out of town and they would pass on messages. Having a number both in London and New York was particularly impressive, we felt. It impressed us, anyway.

The disguise was easier to settle. A close friend worked for the
makeup department of the BBC and was perfectly placed to offer
advice. She suggested two changes: Blake should have straight
hair rather than curls—easy to do since once wetted and combed
straight it would stay that way. Second, a pair of heavy, horn-
rimmed glasses. This was lucky since I'm nearsighted and needed
spectacles anyway. Don Langton suggested that an odd touch of
flamboyance in Blake's clothing would not go amiss since it

would help people in the art world to remember him after only one or two encounters. We settled on a bow tie as sufficiently unusual these days to do the trick, plus a limp and a cane. To ensure that I never forgot to limp I always wore a pair of shoes bought a year earlier in Venice by mistake: they were so small that I couldn't wear them without hobbling. I hoped Blake would never have to run.

Andrew also emphasized that Blake would have to dress as well as behave like a Bond Street dealer. So one Savile Row suit, three Turnbull and Asser shirts, a sterling-silver Tiffany pen, a Dunhill wallet and gold-edged writing pad all went on expenses. And how right Andrew was. Unlikely as it may seem, weeks later that Dunhill writing pad helped avert a disaster.

The final plank in Blake's disguise was his history. Had he always been in art? If not, what? We decided that he had to be a relative newcomer to the business, otherwise he would have to know more than I did (and I was by now of course reading all sorts of books, from a biography of Caravaggio to Vasari's *Lives of the Artists*). A year or so earlier I had written a book about psychological warfare so we agreed that I had been working in this field for the British Army in a secret capacity. In any conversation about psywar, I could keep my end up and it would be a field impossible for most people to check out. This reminded Willie Whelan of Malcolm Henderson, a friend of his who had once been a mercenary and now ran a gallery in Washington. Malcolm agreed to say, if asked, that Blake and he had met in mercenary work and that, after he had left the army, Blake had worked for him for a couple of years, helping to sell prints in the U.S.A. This was useful for it helped explain how Blake got into art, how he might have acquired his clients, where he had been these past few years and why he had never needed to learn any languages other than English. (Many dealers speak Italian.)

All that took four or five weeks to organize, but toward the end of May A. John Blake arrived on New York's Upper East Side in time for the first big sale of the season. He had his black cane, his limp, his bow tie, his expensive clothes, two hundred posh business cards and the rest of his fake identity. There was just one thing more he needed to complete his disguise as an art dealer. Money. Lots and lots of money. This was the most difficult pretense of all.

3

Cheating at the Auctions

A DISGUISE was one thing, but acquiring enough money to bid in the major old master auctions was quite another. Yet Blake had to do this if he was to attract attention from the rest of the art world. Andrew and I had spent several lunches at the Phene Arms discussing how Blake might acquire the necessary funds but had failed to come up with anything. Then, early one morning halfway through May, the telephone rang. It was Andrew. "Do we know how much the Caravaggio is expected to fetch?" he asked without any preamble.

In 1972 the *Nativity* had been called a seven-figure painting (in sterling) so it was probably worth at least half as much again by 1979. "But," I added, "that's on the open market. As a stolen picture Siviero's guess is that it will change hands for anything between £40,000 and £150,000. Stolen art tends to fetch seven to ten percent of its open-market value."

Andrew already had his first pipe of the day on the go and there was a delay before he said, "So Blake doesn't have to be worth millions?"

"No." I was puzzled. "Only hundreds of thousands." I didn't see what difference it made.

Another pause, then: "I'm coming up to town later this morning." Indirect as ever, this was his way of proposing lunch.

"I think we can do it," he said when we had settled down with the beer and sandwiches. "It will mean taking one or two more people into our confidence—but without that we are getting nowhere anyway. As I see it, there are three possible ways and we need to make use of all three, just in case.

"First, we need a legitimate old master dealer here in London, and another in New York, whom we can trust. With luck they will be buying at the auctions and they might let you bid on their behalf. That way you can actually be seen to raise your hand in the auction room and, if you get anything—as you must do if you have enough bids—the auctioneer will call out Blake's name.

"Second, we need the help of the auctioneers, Sotheby's and/or Christie's. In every major sale there are usually a number of 'order bids'—bids sent in in writing by people who either can't make the sale or else want to remain anonymous. If the auction houses get some of these, from people outside the trade, and they are willing to play ball, then any order bids that are successful could be knocked down to John Blake as well. You wouldn't be able to bid openly, to raise your hand or anything like that; but if you looked hard enough at the auctioneer, and he looked hard enough at you, people would think you were bidding in a secret code. It happens all the time. If, after all that staring, he were to call out Blake's name, it would probably attract as much attention as cruder methods of bidding, because people would be intrigued to see what code you were using.

"Third, any lots that are 'bought in' could also be knocked down under Blake's name."

" 'Bought in'?"

"Ah—you don't know what I mean. Well, as you probably know, most paintings sold at auction have a reserve price put on them. That is, if the bidding does not reach the reserve it is 'bought in.' "

"What happens?"

"Assume a painting has a reserve of £50,000 and the bidding stops at £40,000; the auctioneer simply pretends that someone at the back of the room has bid, say, £42,000 and, if no one bids any more, it is knocked down to a fictitious name—and bought in. The auctioneers go into each auction with a long list of these fictitious names, just in case. John Blake could be one of them."

"Why do they do it?"

"It helps maintain the image that the art market is buzzing. If the auctioneer called out 'No sale' every so often it might depress prices all around; you can never be exactly sure something has been bought in and the fictitious names help maintain this ambiguity."

I thought over what Andrew had said. It seemed a good idea but there had to be some drawbacks.

"Yes," he said, "but if people are going to help they can also help minimize the dangers. With the first technique, for instance, it would be useful if the dealer who lets Blake bid for him didn't put any pictures knocked down to Blake on show straightaway after the sale. People might notice that the paintings had been knocked down to one person, but then turned up in somebody else's gallery. Or, if asked why he is showing a painting knocked down to Blake, he would have to be prepared to say that he bought it from you immediately after the sale. That's okay. It happens quite a lot.

"With the second technique we shall have to make sure that any order bids knocked down to you—I mean to Blake—come only from people outside the trade. Some dealers prefer to buy anonymously through the chair and if they attend the sale and see a painting they have bought knocked down to Blake they are going to wonder what is going on. But if the auctioneers agree to help they will probably anticipate this danger and avoid knocking anything down to Blake that could compromise him.

"Buying in is the most dangerous. Dealers often try to buy paintings they think have been bought in immediately after the sale. If they made any inquiries about John Blake, how they could contact him and so forth, to buy such and such a picture off him, the auction house would have to admit that they had used Blake as a buying-in name. You'll have to decide whether to take that risk."

That was the final plank in our elaborate deception. I thought it over for a few days, and discussed it with Don Langton. We could see it presented problems but could not think of a better scheme. And Andrew's idea had plenty of merit anyway, not least the fact that it would guarantee maximum publicity for Blake since almost his entire activity would take place in the main auction rooms. We decided to give it a try.

We wanted to keep moving as quickly as possible for, besides other considerations, major paintings were still disappearing regularly. Two Rembrandt portraits, of Rombartus and of a sleeping woman, were stolen from Amsterdam that month, yet another Renoir, *Sous-bois,* from a collection in Paris, and a Utrillo taken in the same theft; El Greco's *Jesus Salvador* was also stolen in May 1979 from Caceres, in Spain, and so was Eugene Boudin's beautiful rendering of sailing ships at anchor in Brest Harbor, looted in Vancouver, Canada.

Our next move, therefore, was to enlist the aid of a couple of dealers and the auctioneers. It was now 20 May and the first major sale, in New York, was to take place ten days later.

The art world is full of rumor and counter-rumor and neither Andrew nor Don felt that they could trust many of the larger old master galleries to keep our secret. Then Willie Whelan, the coin and bullion dealer in Crown Passage, happened to mention one of the smaller Bond Street dealers, Johnny van Haeften, a specialist—as his name would suggest—in the Dutch school. Willie knew him only vaguely, but by coincidence Don Langton had known Van Haeften quite well several years before, when Johnny had been on the staff of Christie's and Don was at the Yard. We decided to approach him.

The Van Haeften gallery is now in Duke Street, St. James's, but in 1979 it was in small but perfectly situated premises at the junction of Old and New Bond streets over the famous jewelers Boucheron. It was beautifully appointed: a uniformed doorman showed you to the elevator and Johnny's attractive wife (and secretary), Sarah, welcomed you into the gallery. A window made up one entire wall, with a view along Burlington Gardens. The lighting, the salmon-colored carpet, the leather Chesterfield sofa all gave the gallery a luscious elegance.

Right from the start the Van Haeftens were extremely cooperative. Within seconds of my arrival, Johnny had shut up shop and plied me with a stiff gin and tonic. He and Sarah sat rapt as I outlined the plot.

It was a risk we had to take time and again. We felt we could not ask people to jeopardize either their reputations or their money if they didn't know exactly what we were up to.

But we needn't have worried with the Van Haeftens. They would be pleased to help, they said, and asked fondly after Don Langton. They also suggested two people in New York who might cooperate, Clyde Newhouse and Richard Feigen, both well-established old master dealers. The plan was that I should leave for New York the next day to see Newhouse and Feigen and try to persuade the auction houses to help. Then I would return in a few days, see Johnny, who by then would have some bids for me, then almost immediately return to New York as John Blake. (The London sales were not until mid-July.) I left the Van Haeftens much encouraged.

In New York, however, we had our first disappointment. Clyde Newhouse, who has a splendid gallery on Sixty-sixth Street, listened attentively to the plan, agreed to help, but a day later changed his mind. His health was not good and he had been advised by his doctor, he said, not to take on anything new unless it was unavoidable. There was nothing I could do but it meant that there was now at least one individual privy to our plot who was not part of it.

But this setback was offset by progress on other fronts. Richard Feigen, a tough, good-looking Chicagoan, promised full support and was to prove, with Andrew Purches, the project's most imaginative adviser throughout. Both the auction houses also promised full cooperation.

I had been told often enough by members of the art trade that the rivalry between Sotheby's and Christie's was intense and on several occasions I was able to make use of it. More than once during the life of the project I felt that the auction houses were cooperating because I "happened" to mention their rival had already agreed.

Not that those strictures apply to John Marion, head of Sotheby Parke Bernet in New York and the company's chief auctioneer there. He listened attentively as I outlined the plot, asked one or two pertinent questions (like did I have any identification and where the hell was it?) and then agreed to wholehearted cooperation, provided it was in writing. It was a strange document that he had his lawyers draw up, but it did the trick.

Christie's president at Park Avenue, the Honorable David

Bathurst, listened literally open-mouthed as I outlined the plot, but to do him justice, when I had finished a broad grin spread over his face and he immediately took me down to meet his chief sales clerk Peter Villa and instructed him to give us all the help we needed.

Then it was back to London to keep my appointment with the Van Haeftens. I had been in New York less than seventy-two hours and was already beginning to live like a jet-setter. It was the year when the cheap, north Atlantic stand-by air fares came on the market and I was making full use of them.

The minute I walked into the Van Haeftens' gallery the next evening I sensed a change. Johnny wasn't there, and Sarah seemed flustered and embarrassed. She said she knew where Johnny was and would get him on the phone. After my experience with Newhouse, I recognized the signs and, sure enough, when I spoke to Johnny on the phone he said he had talked it over with Sarah and they had decided they couldn't help. The reason for their second thoughts, I suspected, was a general reluctance to get mixed up in "hothead" ventures, but that wasn't the reason Johnny gave.

He said that most of his bids in New York, the following week, would be joint bids with another dealer. Obviously we couldn't take this second dealer into our confidence, but he would be at the sales and so if Blake was doing the bidding he would want to know what on earth was going on. Since it was all so complicated, Johnny thought he had no choice but to back out. He was sorry, but it couldn't be avoided, et cetera, et cetera. . . .

I was tired, still suffering from jet lag, and I acquiesced. I must have looked pretty crestfallen as I put down the phone because Sarah took pity on me and gave me a large gin and tonic. We sat talking for a while and then I had another drink. It hadn't been my intention to stay, but while I was on my third gin, Johnny returned.

He had with him another young dealer, Rafael Valls, slim and sleek, with dark good looks. He, too, had his own gallery in Bury Street, St. James's. This was the man with whom Johnny would be bidding next week.

Johnny was obviously surprised to see me still in his gallery (it was now well after seven), but he took me to one side to explain more fully his feelings. By now I had had time to weigh the situation and I realized that if our approach was to work we needed the help of dealers in both New York and London. If Johnny wasn't going to help then here was yet another person in the know and not part of the plot. So I said quite bluntly that I had no objection to Rafael Valls being told. Johnny was surprised and, for a moment, disconcerted. Instinct, I think, told him to steer clear of the project. But now he had, at the least, to put it to "Raf." He may have thought that Raf, too, would not wish to be involved, but if he did he could not have been more wrong.

Like Johnny, Raf cut his teeth in the art world by working for one of the bigger organizations—in his case, Wildenstein's, a large gallery in Bond Street, opposite Sotheby's. An international firm, Wildenstein's head office is in Paris and this accounts for their expertise in French painting of all types as well as old masters in general. The Wildenstein family has good links with the National Gallery of Art in Washington, D.C., and have helped that museum make some notable acquisitions. The Wildenstein stock of paintings is legendary in the art trade. At one point, for instance, it was revealed that their New York storerooms contained over two thousand pictures, including a Fra Angelico, two Botticellis, eight Rembrandts, eight Rubenses, three Velásquezes, nine El Grecos, ten Goyas, five Tintorettos, four Titians, a dozen Poussins, seven Watteaus, seventy-nine Fragonards and always, "on principle," at least twenty Renoirs, ten Cézannes, ten Van Goghs and ten Gauguins. At another time they held as many as 250 Picassos.

Raf's own gallery had been burgled about a year before and he had lost £100,000 worth of paintings. Some of the paintings had been his own, some had been Wildenstein's; none of them had been recovered. He was still livid, his pocket and his reputation still smarting. When I outlined the plan to him, he was very keen to help.

The situation was transformed. Raf's enthusiasm ensured that Johnny would help too. The pair had still not decided which pictures they wanted to buy the following week but we all arranged to meet in the bar of the Carlyle Hotel on Madison Avenue on the Tuesday evening before the sale. They would tell me then which pictures John Blake would be able to open his account with.

I had one more card to play before I left for New York. We

knew that Siviero had a network of dealers around the world who fed him information and that at least one was in London. It had occurred to us that this dealer might be able to help so we had asked Siviero to explain to him what we were up to and persuade him to get in touch. It took a couple of weeks, but a few days before the New York sale, I got a call from Andrew Ciechanowiecki.

Andrew is a Pole and the guiding light at the Heim Gallery in Jermyn Street, London. Heim's headquarters are in Paris, but it is also one of the very biggest London galleries (specializing particularly in French classical art, Claude, Poussin, etc.). Ciechanowiecki is both a very nice and a very shrewd man. He said he had no bids for the New York sales at that moment, but was expecting a couple. He would telephone me in New York on the day of the sale. He didn't seem to mind handing over the bids to a stranger.

So when John Blake left London, on 29 May, he still didn't know which paintings he would be bidding for the next day. He couldn't even be certain that there would be any.

THE RENDEZVOUS in the bar of the Carlyle took place exactly as scheduled—second thoughts seemed to be a thing of the past—and Johnny and Raf produced six bids for the auction. Richard Feigen also called from his breakfast table at 8:00 A.M. on the day of the sale, as arranged, and offered two more bids, including the (to me) terrifying news that he was interested in lot number one. Ciechanowiecki actually cabled me—as John Blake—halfway through the sale at Sotheby's with a bid.

London still outranks New York in the quality and value of the old masters offered for sale. (New York is better for modern paintings.) But the most spectacular piece of auctioneering, as far as our project was concerned, was the performance by John Marion on that day when John Blake first appeared in the art world.

All auctioneers are smooth, well-dressed characters: it is part of the image. Examine any Christie's or Sotheby's catalog and you will find its staff list cluttered with mini-royalty: lords and honorables, baronets and brigadiers, English double-barreled names, Frenchmen called *de* this and *de* that, and Germans *von* here or *von* there. But Marion was also a consummate actor.

Better than Blake, I suspect. Blake was very nervous that Wednesday. First, because he felt a shade silly with his bow tie, black cane and slicked-down hair. Johnny, Raf, Dick Feigen and Clyde Newhouse were all in the room, watching. He didn't know if he looked natural or was clearly a fake. Mostly, however, he was nervous because he had no idea what the form was at auctions. He had simply forgotten to take the elementary precaution of attending a sale in the previous days to see what happened. Was there a particular way in which one bid? One heard all sorts of stories about the established dealers and collectors who used complicated ways of taking off their spectacles, or scratching their ears, or surreptitiously winking at the auctioneer to let him know they were bidding without their rivals seeing. Blake fingered his silver Tiffany pen and gripped tightly his Dunhill writing pad, hoping against hope that he looked more genuine than he felt. To cap it all, bidding on lot number one, he wouldn't even have a chance to look around to see how other people were behaving. He could get his first actions wrong, and either waste the opportunity of a good buy for Dick Feigen or make such an embarrassing mistake that the whole thing would be blown there and then.

As we have seen, Blake didn't get Lot Number 1. He attracted Marion's eye when the bidding was at $7,000 (he had been told not to raise his hand too early, since it only helped the price rise quickly) and had dropped out at his limit of $11,000. (The picture eventually fetched $23,000.) But before the day was out, Blake had "bought" twenty-three paintings and had been seen to "spend," in total, the useful sum of $84,350. Besides the six bids from Raf, Johnny, Ciechanowiecki and Feigen, Marion had engineered a number of other order bids and a handful of buyings in. The "stars" of the Sotheby's sale that Blake netted included a *Holy Family with Saints Elizabeth and John the Baptist,* from the workshop of Raphael ($15,000), a *Still Life with Flowers* by Gaspar Verbrugghen the Younger ($8,000) and a *Portrait of a Boy in a Black Velvet Cap* by Jacob Van Loo ($6,000). And this was only part of the picture. On four other occasions Blake showed himself "willing to spend" another $57,000 for pictures that, in the end, he didn't get.

These were the order bids that failed. Andrew Purches had said, as usual quite rightly, that for our purposes it was just as important to be seen as the underbidder as to actually buy the painting. This is because other dealers (and the press and the auction houses themselves) take almost as much notice of the bidder who is forced to drop out at the last moment as they do of the successful buyer.

Marion's genius was to draw attention to Blake as much when he was the underbidder as when he was successful in buying a picture. Lot 37, for instance, comprised two very nice river landscapes from the circle of Anton Mirou, delicate blues and greens with a lot of activity. The estimate (a guide to what the paintings are expected to bring and usually printed in the back of the catalog) was $18,000 to $22,000 and bidding started at $8,000.

At about $17,000 Marion looked hard at Blake, who, sensing this, sat up in his chair and stared back at Marion: an order bid was in action. Marion had on the lecturn in front of him a bid from a prospective buyer who either wasn't at the sale or didn't want to be seen bidding. Marion would have a top figure and would, in effect, be bidding himself for this client. He was bound, of course, to secure the painting for this client for the lowest possible figure. From Marion's movements, however, the order bid had a serious rival on the floor. Marion's gaze shifted regularly between the far left-hand side of the room and back to Blake.

"The bid is in the aisle in front of me here." Marion indicated Blake, with a movement of his head. "At $17,000."

He nodded across the room as the rival bid again: "$18,000."

He looked down to Blake; after a pause Marion tossed his head with a smile and looked across the room: "$19,000." We were in.

The rival soon decided to increase his offer to $20,000 and Marion was again looking quizzically at Blake.

Blake didn't move, but this time Marion jerked his head back again to the rival: "$22,000."

Bidding proceeded faster now that it was in $2,000 steps. (Bidding is usually in $500s up to $1,000, $1,000s up to $20,000, $2,000s up to $50,000, $5,000s up to $100,000 and $10,000s after that.)

In no time we were at $30,000. This was the rival's bid and Marion looked hard and long at Blake. "It's against you, Mr. Blake," he said, loud and clear, and smiled. A long pause, he raised his hammer, and then, just as he was about to bang it down he shot his gaze back across the room: "$32,000—against you, sir," he said to the nondescript rival.

But the rival came back again, with a bid of $34,000 and Marion focused on Blake once more.

"Against you again, Mr. Blake." Pause. "Try another, Mr. Blake?" Another pause, this time covered by a smile. "Fair warning, Mr. Blake." He raised his hammer, tilted his head a final time at Blake . . . and knocked the picture down to the rival. The order bid lost but everyone in the room knew who *hadn't* bought the picture, even though there was no clue as to the identity of the successful buyer. A brilliant piece of acting which was repeated three or four times throughout the day.

If anybody had been totting up what Blake had spent, and how much more he was willing to spend, the total would have come to the tidy sum of $141,350. It is extremely unlikely that anyone was watching him that closely, but even so the general impression in Sotheby's that day must have been that here was a new figure who had money to spend and was eager to spend it. It was a good start.

The Christie's auction was the following day, and although the pattern of the sale was somewhat different, for Blake it was just as nerve-racking.

Situated on the corner of Fifty-ninth Street and Park Avenue, Christie's auction rooms in New York are far more intimate than Sotheby's. The main room is longer, narrower and a great many of the pictures for sale are hung around the walls. This means that dealers can get up, stroll around and make last-minute inspections of any works they are thinking of buying.

Once again John Blake arrived early so he could claim a seat halfway down the aisle where he could see and be seen. He was dressed as the day before, with his spectacles and cane, but had changed his blue bow tie to a bright brown and red one, hoping to draw attention to himself.

Blake had only two bids that day—one from Feigen and one from Raf and Johnny—but in the end it didn't matter.

The chief sales clerk at Christie's, Peter Villa, had briefed the auctioneer, Ray Perman, giving him David Bathurst's instructions. Perman, however, was not as experienced an auctioneer as Marion, and he refused to use order bids in the dramatic way Marion had: Perman said it would confuse him. He did agree, however, to use Blake as a buying-in name from time to time.

This was worrying because even after one day at the sales,

Blake could see that buying in, under fictitious names, was not a technique that fooled experienced dealers. Far from it. All sales catalogs include, at the back, a printed list of estimates, the prices which the paintings are expected to fetch. These estimates are fair guides to the reserves which have been put on these paintings. An estimate of £50,000 to £80,000, for example, would probably conceal a reserve of £45,000, which was true of one case to which I was privy. If a painting goes—or appears to go—for much less than the estimate, the chances are that it has been bought in. So we did not want many paintings being knocked down in Blake's name for sums well below their reserve.

As it happened, Ray Perman appeared to forget the existence of Blake until well into the sale. Nothing was knocked down to him in the early stages and by the time his first bid fell due, lot 77, he was beginning to worry. But then occurred one of those curious, unpredictable events which occasionally make auction houses such exciting places.

Contrary to what people think, it is not always the biggest pictures that attract the attention of dealers. Just as intriguing for the professionals are those personal tussles between two people who, for one reason or another, want a painting so badly that they are willing to pay far over the odds for it. Such was my luck with my first bid at Christie's.

Lot 77 was *A Wooded Landscape* by Jacob Grimmer. It was a vivid, predominantly green painting, measuring about ten by fifteen inches (a "good size" according to the experts—meaning it would fit many different-sized rooms and alcoves). It showed "apple pickers and peasants near a cottage, and buildings on a river estuary in the distance." Its estimate was for $18,000 to $20,000, and for some reason Johnny and Raf really wanted it. I had been given a limit of $30,000 "plus one."

The words "plus one" refer to the fact that, because you can never be certain when you will catch the auctioneer's eye, any limit you set yourself may be reached with someone else's bid. For example, if your limit is $30,000, the bidding may fall so that you bid $28,000 and your rival bids $30,000. All dealers therefore, in practice, have two limits: a given amount *plus* the next bid in case the progression is against them. In other words, if my limit is $30,000 plus one and the bidding progresses to a point where a rival bids $30,000, I will go plus one and bid

$32,000. If, on the other hand, my rival bids $28,000 and I bid $30,000, and then *he* bids $32,000, I do *not* go to $34,000.

The psychology of bidding is beyond me. The wiser dealers hand out their bids to agents who have a limit and daren't go over it. On the other hand, many dealers like to bid for themselves and no doubt sometimes pay more for a picture than they intended. Perhaps my rival on this occasion thought that I was using my own money and that by bidding quickly he was conveying the impression that he had virtually unlimited funds and was determined to get the picture whatever the cost.

Other people presumably thought so, too, for the tussle began to attract attention even though the amounts, by salesroom standards, were not large. The general chatter in the room fell away and heads turned to see who was bidding against whom. Dealers strained their eyes to view the small painting on the easel at the front of the room as the price rose agonizingly from $19,000 to $20,000 (my bid) and then jumped quickly to $22,000 (my rival's). I waited an age before going to $24,000, but as soon as I did so, my rival jumped to $26,000. Another long pause, Ray Perman smiling gently as he gazed at me, waiting. Eventually I inclined my head—$28,000, only to see my rival rush in straight away with another bid, at $30,000.

It was my turn to bid and I was slower than ever. Probably, many of the other dealers thought that I was using my own money and was already beyond my limit. Ray Perman lifted his gavel against me.

But I had figured that my rival had a limit, too, whoever he was. I figured that his limit was the same as mine—$30,000 plus one. And the bidding was in my favor—I still had one bid to go. Just as Perman started to bring down his gavel, looking all the while at me, I nodded my head. He held his left hand in midflight and chuckled: "$32,000." My limit.

Perman looked across expectantly at my rival but he was just as prompt and businesslike in shaking his head as he had been in nodding it.

I had been right; his limit had been the same as mine. I had been lucky, and the picture was Raf's and Johnny's. Seconds later, the gavel swung down, loud and final, Ray Perman smiled down at me from his rostrum and called out, "Blake," loud and clear. The murmur around the room showed that I had been noticed. I hoped several dealers registered that Blake was the man who had bought so many paintings the day before.

It was just as well that the second day at the sales started in this way. I didn't get my second bid (although I went up to $24,000) so had to rely on bought-in lots. It was only after the tussle over the Jacob Grimmer that Perman seemed to recall that I was there, but after that he played his part well. There weren't as many bought-in pictures at Christie's as there had been at Sotheby's, but on the other hand what there was was of better value.

Blake "bought" twelve other paintings that day (including a *Street in a Town* by Jacobus Vrel for $28,000). Together, the twelve pictures, when added to the Grimmer, came to a combined total of $80,825. Christie's also made more fuss of the bought-in lots than Sotheby's had done and this was useful in attracting attention to Blake. Peter Villa, who was standing next to Perman, saw to it that, whenever a bought-in painting was knocked down to Blake, a girl would rush over to him with a card. Buyers fill in these cards to confirm the sale. Dealers could not have failed to notice the number of times these girls came over to where Blake was sitting.

It was an exhausting couple of days. Posing as someone else means you can never relax; you must always think ahead if only to make sure you are not about to bump into someone who you knew in your other life. Blake had "spent" $165,200 and been seen "willing to spend" another $81,000—$246,200 in all. Not too bad for a beginner. Relieved, I traveled back (first-class) to London, where the sales were to prove very different.

4

Caught Out

WE HAD MORE TIME to orchestrate our plan of campaign for the London season. The art world was buzzing at the time with the news that two Goyas had disappeared in Madrid. The general feeling was that the work of Spain's principal painter to the King would be too well known to surface in his own country and that a natural resale point for these portraits would be London, New York or Paris. I licked my lips.

Christie's main old master sale was three weeks off, at the end of June, and Sotheby's was ten or eleven days later, well into July. There was no question but that they were better quality auctions than in New York. The Christie sale, for example, was to include a *Madonna and Child* by Fra Bartolommeo, expected to fetch £1 million. There was also a Goya *modello*, a Bellini, a Bronzino, a Canaletto, two Brueghels (one elder, one younger), two Watteaus, two Van Ruysdaels and four Guardis. The Sotheby's sale was not so highly regarded in the trade, but even so was scheduled to include a Tintoretto, a Velásquez, an Andrea del

Sarto, a Canaletto, two Brueghels (again, one elder, one younger), a Murillo, two Van de Veldes and two Guardis. Both were all-ticket sales with the best seats reserved for the auction house's best customers and the entire art market would be there, not to mention the press and the television crews.

But given that we now had more time to play with, our plans for Blake extended beyond his visits to the main auctions. One of the ways in which the London sales differ from those in New York is that the main houses have more than one old master auction. Phillips and Bonham's, the smaller houses, have a single auction, but for the big two the sales are divided into four days. At the top end of the market are the "Important Old Master" sales, which include the Fra Bartolommeos and the Bellinis, the Bronzinos and the Brueghels, the Canalettos and the Del Sartos, and so on. All the pictures are photographed for the catalog and sometimes in these sales the prices are so high that, as with the Fra Bartolommeo, the estimate is not printed in the book and you must call the auction house and prove you are a bona fide buyer before they will tell you.

Second come the "Fine Old Master" sales, which are not all illustrated in the catalog and tend to fetch sums ranging from £600 to £8,000. Plain "Old Masters" start at £200, roughly, and rarely go above £3,000. Finally, there are "Old Master Drawings and Prints," where people tend to think in three figures rather than four.

So, for a period of two to three weeks, at the end of June and beginning of July, there is an old master sale of one kind or another every few days. Besides these, while the world's dealers and collectors are in town, various galleries in London often mount exhibitions of their own. Colnaghis, for instance, had a collection including, as it happened, some Caravaggesque paintings of the Neapolitan school and a beautiful, if small, Rembrandt ink drawing. And, in St. James's, the Brod gallery had a Jan Brueghel exhibition. Jan, called the "Velvet Brueghel," was the younger son of Pieter, the great Dutch painter. I learned that Jan is chiefly remembered for the fact that he collaborated with Rubens and because no fewer than 3,000 paintings have been wrongly attributed to him. The information I picked up at this exhibition was to prove invaluable later on.

Andrew advised that Blake should be seen wandering around

these galleries, looking at pictures with his magnifying glass, asking about prices, taking away color photographs, and generally attracting attention to himself, besides being present at the main sales. We also planned visits to the chief watering holes of the art dealers, Frank's Restaurant in Jermyn Street, Lafayette along the road from Christie's in King Street, and Wilton's fish restaurant in Bury Street.

All this activity meant that, for three or four weeks, John Blake put in an appearance somewhere every day. One day it would be lunch with Dick Feigen in Frank's. I would read up on a particular painter, say Andrea del Sarto, the best Florentine colorist, a man who had made a disastrous marriage to a beautiful widow. Dick and I would spend the meal talking as loudly as we dared, showing off our scholarship. We would become enthusiastic about the way Del Sarto adapted Dürer engravings, and compare opinions on his copy of Raphael's portrait of Pope Leo, which was so close to the original that not even Giulio Romano, Raphael's chief assistant, could tell the difference. (A special mark had to be put on the back to identify the real one.)

Blake would always pay for these meals, of course, and as ostentatiously as possible. The next day he would go viewing the old masters on show at one or another of the auction houses, accompanied either by Raf or Johnny. He would listen quietly to what they had to say. The day after that Blake would visit one of the exhibitions, the Brueghel, say, again having first done his homework on the painter in question. While in the gallery he would question one of the dealers on a particular picture, once more in such a way as to show off his knowledge, and take away a photograph as if he were contemplating a purchase. He would of course have inquired discreetly about the price.

Then on the fourth day Blake would perhaps return to either Christie's or Sotheby's and look again at the paintings he had seen a few days before. He would be accompanied by either Raf or Johnny, whoever had *not* been with him on the previous occasion and this time show off to them the knowledge he had picked up earlier. The bow tie, the limp and the cane became a familiar sight in the London art world that summer, and anyone who overheard Blake speak, which was not difficult to do, was meant to come away with the impression that he knew what he was talking about.

There were, however, many tricks of the trade that Blake had still to learn. . . . Like how to look at a painting. Johnny van Haeften explained this one day at a Christie's viewing. First you just stare at the painting, "taking in the general effect." Next you move in close and study some of the finer workings. For a dealer, size is important, so unless you have a particular house in mind you don't want a picture that is too big or too small. You may therefore hold the picture and turn it around to see how it is framed and to see whether there is any more canvas, copper or panel behind the frame that might change its size. Another reason for turning the picture over is to see whether it has any of the auction houses' earlier marks on it, indicating that it has come up for sale before. If it has, you can check its price, who has owned it and so on. Then you will look for the signature, if there is one. You do this by gently spitting on your finger and rubbing it over part of the painting. You also do this to see how the picture might look cleaned up—it gives you an idea how much detail will show through. If a picture on show appears to have been "licked" in one place rather a lot—beware. This means that several dealers have doubts about it or are worried that the signature, at least, is fake.

Detail is very important for dealers. Besides a satisfying overall composition they look for pictures "with a lot going on." They will look at a small portion of a Brueghel, say, where tiny people are dancing and dogs are snarling and describe this area as "fun." Elsewhere the sky may have few birds and even fewer clouds— that will be called "a bit thin." Too many thin parts in a painting detract from its value.

You will also look at the competence of the draftsmanship—and here you are not influenced by the supposed authorship of the painting. Brueghel, Tintoretto, Canaletto, Goya—all had their off days, all except Del Sarto, who was known as "the painter who never made a mistake." If the draftsmanship is in any way weak, many dealers will shy away. I was impressed, or at one point thought I was impressed, by a Guercino drawing on offer with an estimate of only £400. I'd even thought of buying it for myself. Rafael Valls warned me off in no uncertain fashion. It was a picture of some people crossing a bridge and there were trees to one side. "It seems to me," said Valls baldly, pointing to the bridge, "that Guercino couldn't draw arches."

I thought it an extraordinary thing to say about a famous old master, but Raf was right.

Another trick of the trade that I needed to learn was how to research a painting. Art dealers don't give their secrets away easily, of course, but most *coups*—like when a dealer discovers that an unknown painting is a Titian or a Rubens—appear to be based on the fact that many pictures are, quite simply, not by the painters to whom they are attributed. This is no surprise to the dealer, but it takes a bit of getting used to for the layman.

One of the most fascinating places in London is the Witt Library. The Witt is part of London University, a segment of the Courtauld Institute of Fine Art and is located in a cozy but rather shabby building in Portman Square, just behind Marble Arch. Anyone can use the Witt and it costs nothing to do so. I have never seen it busy and, presumably, art dealers like to keep it that way: this is one of their first ports of call when they are researching a picture. Here every artist you have ever heard of, and thousands you haven't, has a green box file to himself with reproductions of most, if not all, the paintings he produced.

There are yards and yards of these green boxes, divided according to country and century. A painter like Canaletto, Tintoretto or Picasso would have six, ten or fifteen boxes all to himself. I was amused by the very practical way the reproductions are organized. They are not laid out in any chronological or artistic sense, "Picasso's Blue Period" for instance, but much more to help the researcher or dealer who has been offered a painting whose attribution he doubts and who therefore wishes to look up all known pictures of a particular composition to see what else it might be. Tintoretto portraits, for example, are organized under such categories as "Male, identified, facing left, with hands"; Renoir's come under "Female, unidentified, turned to left, without hands but with hats." Sisley's landscapes are divided into those with and without snow. My favorite label was "Delacroix: Battles and Rapes."

One message that comes over loud and clear from the Witt is the uncertainty about the authorship of many paintings. For example, in the Tintoretto box is the reference "See Bassano." In the Bellini file you will be cross-referred to Beccafumi; and in the Titian box there are several cross-references to Giorgione. This is where the scope lies for scholarship and research which may "improve" the authorship of a picture.

Later on in the project I had occasion to use the Witt as a dealer would. I needed to learn about a certain painter called Gaspard Dughet. He is not widely known to the public but most dealers are familiar with him: he was the brother-in-law of the famous French classical painter Nicholas Poussin and so is also known as Gaspard Poussin and as Le Guaspre. As another element in the plot to make John Blake look real, Andrew Ciechanowiecki had given me some photographs of a Dughet painting, a landscape. He had a couple of paintings which he wanted to sell, preferably in New York; so on his visits there Blake could carry photographs of them and appear—genuinely—to be selling as well as buying.

The one problem with the Dughet was that it had no date. This was important because the date of Dughet's work affected his price. I learned from the Witt that, in fact, Dughets are notoriously difficult to date but I found there a photograph of a painting very similar to "mine." Some of the buildings in the background and the landscaping of the trees were identical with my picture: only the figures and the clouds were different. The other picture, according to the details in the Witt, was in the Ashmolean Museum in Oxford and was dated *circa* 1658. This was very useful for it suggested that my picture was painted at about this time—and this was a time, according to articles on Dughet also contained in the Witt, when the painter had achieved his maturity and was producing his best work.

So my picture was a good example of Dughet's work, worth more rather than less. This kind of research helped give John Blake a spurious knowledge about painters which improved his credibility and also helped in a genuine way to assess accurately the worth of this particular painting.

Besides the Witt, most dealers also make use of two other reference works, which they like to call their "bibles." One is the eight-volume Dictionary of Painters and Sculptors by E. Benezit, first published in Paris as long ago as 1806 but updated several times since then. It lists 300,000 artists, acts as a quick guide to their place in history and therefore to the approximate value of a minor painter. It is a matter of casual pride to dealers to discover an artist of merit, however thin, who is not in Benezit. The second bible is the forty-three-volume Thieme Becker, with 150,000 artists described.

Dealers, of course, have their own specialties. Wildenstein, besides old masters, deal in Impressionist paintings and French eighteenth-century works; Agnews like English watercolors and old masters; Brod concentrate on Dutch pictures, Eyre and Hobhouse on Indian works. Among those dealers who were privy to our plot, Raf's specialty was paintings of the Spanish school, Johnny knew about Dutch pictures and Dick Feigen was something of an authority on French works. And it was Dick who at this point involved Blake in a major *coup* that made headlines and did Blake's search for notoriety no harm at all.

As well as the major Christie's sale, Blake also attended a sale of "Fine Old Masters." He had five bids from Raf and Johnny. The auction room wasn't full and, partway through the sale, he noticed Dick Feigen near the opposite wall talking to another man. Blake waved and Dick grinned, looking healthy and handsome alongside the fat, white London dealer. A few minutes later Dick strolled over and said in a whisper that there was a particular lot, a landscape with figures, that he would like Blake to bid on: Dick was being watched by the London dealers who might push the price up if they saw he was buying. He gave me the lot number and a limit of £1,700, plus one. I was delighted of course and casually flipped ahead in the catalog to check out the painting. It wasn't an expensive picture; the estimate was £800 to £1,200 and the artist was Herman van Swanevelt. I had never heard of him.

When the lot came up a few minutes later there was little interest in the picture, only one or two others bothering to bid. In less than a minute the painting was knocked down to Blake for £1,100, well inside what Dick was willing to spend. I hoped he was pleased.

He was—more than I knew. For Dick had spotted this picture and believed that it was in fact a "lost" painting by the French master Claude Lorraine. Within days, when Dick was back in New York, he had contacted the renowned Claude expert Professor Marcel Roethlisberger, who confirmed that the landscape was indeed by Claude and, moreover, "in the best possible condition." The painting went on sale in Dick's gallery—for $300,000—and Dick's *coup* was written up in both the New York and London newspapers. With luck, the gossips in the art trade would have noticed that Blake had been the man bidding for Dick on that occasion and maybe a bit of his clever scholarship would rub off.

CHRISTIE'S "Important Old Masters" auction of the summer was on Friday, 29 June, at 11 A.M. "precisely." (All auctions begin promptly, even in Britain.) The auction house is an imposing building, in King Street, St. James's. A polite commissionaire helps customers out of taxis and thanks them when they leave. Downstairs in the entrance lobby there is always an expectant bustle as young men in pinstripe suits and women in tailored outfits scurry to and fro. The stairway to the main floor, where the three auction rooms are situated, is wide and graceful. When the skylights above flood it with sunshine, it is rather like mounting the steps of a cathedral. Years ago Lord Curzon would climb these steps majestically, a flunky at his side, carrying a reference book on a cushion: his lordship liked to argue a fine point of connoisseurship before making a bid.

At 10:30 that Friday morning there was a milling throng outside the auction room. You couldn't get into the main room without a ticket (John Blake, of course, had one), but in the other rooms people could watch the auction from unreserved seats through closed-circuit television.

The main room in Christie's is a high-ceilinged, octagonal hall, festooned, on an auction day, with the larger works for sale. There was a much greater sense of excitement that morning than there had been in New York. All the foreign dealers—the Italians, the Swiss and the Germans—were there, snatching last-minute inspections of the pictures on the walls. Television was there, the crews trying out the bright lights they would use when the really important pictures came up. And high above everybody was what looked like an electronic scoreboard. Here, in lights above the auctioneer, the current bid for any picture would be translated into, first, dollars, second, Swiss francs, third, lire, fourth, German marks and, fifth, yen. It was the biggest sale of the season and the hubbub was deafening.

One minute before eleven the Honorable Patrick Lindsay strolled casually to the rostrum, nodding here and there to people

he recognized. Lindsay holds a special place in the art world. It is
not just that Christie's seems to have a monopoly on the honorables: Lindsay, Bathurst, Charles Allsopp (Sotheby's has its
knights and earls). It is more that, although Sotheby's is older
than Christie's (1744 as opposed to 1766), Christie's has the "better" image. Sotheby's is regarded as the flashier house whereas
Christie's is more traditional. This is partly due to its undoubted
preeminence in the old master field, and recently this preeminence is generally credited to Lindsay. Many dealers will tell you
enviously that Lindsay is on first-name terms with almost every
owner of a stately home in Britain. It follows that he knows
where almost every picture of importance in the country is
located and that when they are sold they come up for sale at
Christie's. As a child Lindsay was raised in a nursery that contained a Duccio, which belonged to his mother, the Countess of
Crawford and Balcarres. Later it was sold, at Christie's, of course,
for £1 million.

In appearance he is the perfect English gentleman: navy-blue
double-breasted suit, guards tie, ever so slightly drainpiped trousers, spiky eyebrows and a way of pronouncing pounds (as
"pineds") as though it is a currency that exists only in the hundreds of thousands.

I had seen Patrick Lindsay earlier that week, with Andrew
Purches, who was, of course, an old friend. Lindsay had said that
he could not help with order bids for the simple reason that the
sale was so important all the dealers had opted to come themselves and no order bids had been received. But he said he would
use the Blake name as a buying-in name from time to time. "If,"
he added with a twinkle, "anything is bought in."

He settled a ticket for Blake, however, in a splendid way. He
asked for the seating plan of the sale to be sent up and, when it
arrived, there were all the names of the big dealers—Agnew, Colnaghi, Brod, Kroetser, Leger, McGill, Wildenstein—laid out on
the plan. There weren't many seats left, but unhesitatingly Lindsay pointed to one at the end of a row against the wall about
halfway back.

"That's where you want to sit," he said. "I shall be able to see
you easily there, you can be seen by most of the big boys—and
you will be surrounded by some of the loudest gossips in the

business." We couldn't have known then how important this choice of seat would turn out to be.

As Lindsay mounted the rostrum that Friday, he glanced down to his right and, like Marion before him, gave me a flicker of recognition as he registered that I was in my place. The hubbub died down and all eyes turned to Lindsay.

I was grateful that morning that I was posing as a dealer and not as an auctioneer. I knew enough by then to appreciate that auctioneering is far more complicated than it looks. On the rostrum, Lindsay, or Marion, or Perman will have a heavily annotated catalog of the sale. This will contain the reserves on each painting but will be written in code, in case any unauthorized person should sneak a look. The auctioneer must decipher this code as he goes along. Moreover, some reserves are not firm but approximate figures ("£45,000, with discretion" in the jargon). More complicated still, a seller will offer, say, four pictures and leave instructions that he or she wants "£20,000 for the lot." So the auctioneer can let one or more of this group go cheaply if he has already done well enough with the others. However, it is common for these pictures to be spread through the sale so that buyers do not realize what is going on and the auctioneer has to remember which paintings are "related" to which others. As if this is not confusing enough, there may be more than one group like this in any particular sale.

Next, the auctioneer has his list of buying-in names to remember. To make this part of his task easier, they are often chosen according to a theme—opera, for example, is popular at Christie's and names like Seville, Sullivan or Grimes will recur. The auction houses also have traditional names that they use, such as Martens and De Witt at Christie's.

Yet another thing the auctioneer has to remember is that he must enter the bidding for any order bids at the right moment. Say he has a bid of £30,000, he must enter the bidding at either £19,000 (an odd number) or £22,000 (an even number) so that the progression will fall his way and he will not need to go plus one. (The order bidder thus has an unfair advantage over people in the room who cannot always arrange their bidding so neatly and often need to go plus one because they are on the "wrong foot.")

Finally, the man on the rostrum has to remember all the idio-

syncratic ways in which secretive dealers like to bid. One American dealer, for instance, is "in" only when he is holding his walking stick, another uses only his eyebrows (and he wears spectacles!), while a third is bidding only if he is *not* wearing his
spectacles. Simply seeing these foibles is hard enough; remembering which apply to whom is near-miraculous.

The pattern of the sale that Friday morning turned out to be
unusual. There were some exceptionally high prices—for example,
a wooded landscape by Jan Brueghel the Elder, estimated at
£150,000 to £200,000 went for £440,000. The Canaletto, a
view of Greenwich, went for £140,000, £20,000 more than the
estimate; and a very beautiful estuary scene by Jan van de Cappelle went for £510,000, better than the (unpublished) estimate
of £400,000 to £500,000. On the other hand some of the paintings by equally famous old masters appeared to be bought in. A
beautiful *Martyrdom of St. John,* done in gold, pinks and reds by
the splendid Italian fifteenth-century painter Giovanni di Paolo,
was knocked down for £80,000 when it was expected to bring at
least £100,000. The Goya, too, was expected to fetch six figures,
but bidding stopped at £80,000. For me the most surprising failure of the sale was the Fra Bartolommeo; confidently expected to
bring £700,000 and maybe a million, it was knocked down at
£400,000.

With prices apparently fluctuating wildly, the room's attention
was riveted on the auctioneer. It was fascinating to watch Lindsay, but to begin with, Blake did so with no real enthusiasm. The
truth was that for this, probably the most important sale John
Blake would ever attend, he had no real bids. Richard Feigen
was over from New York but, since he was planning to spend so
much money, he wanted to bid for himself. Valls and Van Haeften were interested in lot 9—a *Madonna and Child* by the Studio
of Bronzino—but they had their clients with them, on whose behalf they would be acting. They could not pass this bidding on to
me since their clients might change their minds about their limit
at the last moment. Ciechanowiecki didn't even attend the sale.
(There is a brand of dealer who avoids salesrooms on the perfectly reasonable grounds that anything you buy in this way is
known to the rest of the world and is bound to affect the markup
you can put on a painting.)

All that Blake had that morning was a piece of inside knowledge from Valls. A client of Raf's had a painting in the sale, a *Madonna and Child* by Dieric Bouts, a fifteenth-century Dutch painter especially adept in rendering the effects of light on landscape. It was estimated at £50,000 to £80,000, and Valls happened to know that the reserve was £45,000. This meant that Blake could bid up to, say, £40,000, be seen to raise his finger and still be safe in the knowledge that he wouldn't inadvertently land himself with a picture he couldn't afford. It was a slightly unethical maneuver, but in the event it averted catastrophe.

It happened in this way. Lindsay was doing a splendid job, and, throughout the morning, bought in eight or nine pictures in Blake's name, together worth no less than £35,000, making it theoretically his best day to date. However, although Patrick Lindsay made a nice show of looking hard at John Blake when calling out his name, some of the pictures were bought in at so much below the estimates that it became dangerously obvious what was happening. A mountainous landscape by Joos de Momper, the Younger, for instance, estimated at £10,000 to £15,000, was knocked down to Blake for £8,000. An Elout still life (estimate £12,000 to £15,000) he got for £7,500. And a pair of portraits by Juan Pantoja de la Cruz were his for £4,200 when they should have sold for at least £6,000 to £8,000.

Imagine my horror then when suddenly I heard a gossipy voice behind me say of lot 23, a portrait by Corneille de Lyon, "I think that must have been bought in. It was expected to fetch £4,000 to £6,000, but the bidding stopped at £2,400." Then the voice added, "Blake must be one of the buying-in names used by Christie's."

The television lights went on soon after that, as another very nice Joos de Momper came up for sale, but even without the lights Blake would have been sweating. What could he do?

He could walk out. That way at least he wouldn't have to hear any other worrying things the man behind him might say. But there was no way of telling Patrick Lindsay to stop his part in the plot, and if more things were bought in in Blake's name and the figure behind Blake was able to confirm the deception and started telling other people, Blake would never know. No, he couldn't leave.

Fortunately, nothing else was bought in for quite a while—Johnny and Raf didn't get the Bronzino, it went for £17,000, well above its estimate of £5,000 to £8,000. Then a few other things appeared to have been bought in but Blake's name wasn't used. "Good," he thought, "at least Patrick isn't overdoing things."

But just as I was beginning to stop sweating, up came the De la Cruz portraits. Blake stared at the reserve—£6,000 to £8,000—as bidding started at £2,000 and remained sluggish throughout. Blake was willing the bidding to go up, and would not look at Patrick, fearful that if he did so the pictures would be knocked down in his name. Agonizingly, the bidding rose through the three thousands but there was no way it was going to get anywhere near £6,000. In the end it just topped £4,000 and stopped.

Blake could see it coming. A slight pause. "Any more?" Lindsay asked of the room in general. Another pause, longer this time, and then the hammer came down and with it Patrick's voice, loud and clear: "John Blake."

Behind me the voice was jubilant, pleased with its own cleverness. "There you are; those were bought in too—way below the estimate. Blake *has* to be a buying-in name."

This was serious. Patrick had to be stopped—we couldn't rely on there being no more pictures bought in today. Or, a different possibility, the person behind had to be "fixed." Blake was just mulling this over when the solution was landed in his lap.

The television lights were going on again and a picture he recognized was being lifted onto the easel. It was a *Madonna and Child*, the madonna seated on a wall and wearing a red cloak. Blake's heart missed a beat and he swore to himself, "Oh, no! It's the Bouts, the one I'm supposed to be bidding on." He quickly scanned the catalog to check the figures and sat up straight in his seat, the better to be seen by Lindsay.

Bidding started at £8,000 and Blake let it rise to £14,000 before he raised his arm. But then panic again: Patrick hadn't noticed him and already it was at £16,000. Blake raised his hand again—still no luck. The bid was in the back of the room at £19,000. This time a wave, and, thank God, a salesclerk saw Blake's arm and tugged the sleeve of Lindsay's jacket. The auctioneer looked across, saw who was bidding, smiled and called, "£20,000."

From then on there were three bidders in the ring, but Lindsay made most fuss about Blake, nodding to him, pointing to him, leaving no one in any doubt, in that area of the room, as to who wanted the *Madonna and Child*. The bidding rose steadily to £32,000, and then one of the others dropped out. The other two went on to £40,000, when Blake dropped out. At £42,000 Lindsay came back, looking down quizzically. "It's against you," he said. "One more?" A nice try but Blake shook his head. Another bidder came in and the painting eventually was knocked down for its reserve of £45,000.

Blake hadn't had a chance to register the impression his bidding was having on those around him, but he didn't have long to wait. While the next rather indifferent picture was being sold, he felt a tap on his shoulder.

He turned to see the "voice" leaning forward. He was a dark, curly-haired man with glasses, still in his thirties. In the heat of the TV lights, he had taken his jacket off. "Was that yours?" he asked.

Now this was a strange question. What did he mean? He could have meant: Did you get that in the end, through an agent? Or he could have meant: Were you selling that painting and bidding yourself to help it reach its reserve? This was uncomfortably close to the truth. The voice was a sharp character, whoever he was. I judged it best to look a bit vague, muttered, "No," in answer to whatever the question might mean and turned back to face the front, once more damp with nervous sweat.

A couple of bids later, however, there was the tap on the shoulder again. I half turned and the voice whispered, "Are you interested in early pictures?"

At this stage Blake hadn't too much of an idea what "early pictures" were, but he nodded and said, "Why?"

"Because," whispered the voice, "I have the best two early pictures in London at the moment."

It was then that Blake saw a way out of his problems. "Who are you, anyway?" he asked rather aggressively. "Do you have a business card?"

It turned out that the voice didn't. He rummaged in his jacket, and asked his recruit if he had one. It was now that the Dunhill expenditure paid off, for Blake drew out his gold-tipped writing pad and sterling-silver Tiffany pen. He could see the voice savor the opulence: he clearly thought that the man in front of him was a potentially wealthy client. Then came the *coup de grâce.*

The voice handed back the pad. On it he had written, "David Posnett, Leger Galleries, 13 Old Bond Street." So that's who he was.

"Do *you* have a card?" Posnett asked.

Blake drew one from his (Dunhill) wallet and said, "I'd been meaning to have a word with you, after the sale, Mr. Posnett. You see, you've just been talking about me. But I assure you I do exist." And with that he handed him an "A. John Blake" business card.

Posnett stared at it for a while, looking puzzled. But, in the end, he permitted himself a smile. "You mean you actually did buy the Corneille de Lyon and the Joos de Momper?"

Blake looked enigmatic. Then moved to get up. "I'm afraid my leg's hurting; I think I'll stand at the back for a while. If I may, I'll come into your gallery next Tuesday or Wednesday." And with that he struggled to his feet, picked up his cane and hobbled off to the safety of the back of the room, where he spent the rest of the sale.

For the time being catastrophe had been averted and Blake's name was still spreading. But Posnett was as bright as a Bronzino. We weren't out of the woods yet.

5

Blackening Blake's Name

WHEN WE HAD FIRST THOUGHT UP the idea of John Blake one of the reasons we decided he should be a dealer-cum-buying agent rather than any other kind of person in the art world was that Andrew Purches thought it would be easier that way to make him out as dishonest. At the end of the day Blake had to be a man who would consider buying a stolen painting. More important, he had to be the kind of person to whom stolen paintings were offered. It so happened that the crisis over David Posnett turned into one of the best opportunities we had to publicize Blake's more dubious activities.

At first it was difficult to decide how to make Blake dishonest. We couldn't be too blatant about it. In the end we evolved three methods.

The first was Don Langton's idea. While Blake bought and sold paintings on others' behalf, the money he "earned" in this way should be put into gold bullion. It was Langton's view, and the rest of us agreed with him, that Blake's dealing in gold would suggest to others that he was indeed a bit "shady." William Whelan, who was, after all, a dealer himself, explained that in Britain, at that time, the buying and selling of gold was strictly controlled. In theory the Bank of England was supposed to know exactly how much of the metal was in the country at any one time. British residents were not allowed to import it and could buy and sell only from other British residents. However, a Kruger-rand, the size of a quarter, was then worth £236, making bullion an easy and profitable thing to smuggle. If Blake was known to be interested in bullion, we figured that many people would suspect that he smuggled the metal from time to time.

When I outlined the plan to Whelan one day over lunch at the Reform Club in London's Pall Mall, his reaction was enthusiastic. "I must say," he chuckled, "it'll help reduce the boredom for a while."

The plan was for Whelan to visit the sales during the London season that year and lose no opportunity to talk about John Blake with anyone who would listen. He was to say that Blake was a dealer who had suddenly appeared on the scene and dealt in gold coins at, well, an unusually high rate. An added flourish was that Blake always paid in cash. Whelan, although a coin dealer primarily, also had one excellent client who collected paintings with coins in them; in fact, almost every decent painting of this type which comes onto the London market is usually knocked down to Whelan. So it was not at all odd that a coin dealer should have been seen at Sotheby's and Christie's.

The second part of our plan made use of picture restorers. This was another of Andrew Purches' ideas stemming from his unparalleled understanding of the natural history of the art world. Restorers, he said, are very useful gossips. They work by themselves all day at what is often a solitary trade but they have to go around several galleries picking up and dropping off paintings. This lifestyle makes them avid talkers when they are with other people. Nothing could be more natural than for a picture restorer to casually ask in a gallery during one of his regular visits, "Who is this John Blake? He's given me a couple of very good pictures [a restorer would never give away more than that], has always paid in cash, on the nail, and seems in a dreadful hurry."

This arrangement had several things to be said for it: besides spreading doubts about Blake's honesty, it also served the function of spreading Blake's name and adding to the store of pictures he had apparently bought.

Don said he knew the very people who would be able to help. A few days later he took me to Mayfair and introduced me to what must be the most colorful family of picture restorers any-where—the Hahns of Albemarle Street. The Hahns have their own gallery, almost opposite Agnews, and the restorers' floor is above it. Paintings were propped up against the walls, spread over trestles, the smell of surgical spirits was everywhere. Sidney, Paul and Julia Hahn were hard at work, brushing, wiping—and gossiping away at the tops of their deep, East End voices. They must have been audible across the road at Agnews.

Most flamboyant of all was the old man himself, Sidney, who defied Oscar Wilde's maxim that only dull people are brilliant at breakfast time. Sidney was sitting in a corner, by the window overlooking the street; he had on a gleaming white lab coat, held a palette in one hand, and a big cigar was jammed in his mouth—in the corner, so as not to prevent him from speaking. Although it was not yet ten o'clock, a huge whiskey and water stood at his elbow. He called across the room as soon as he saw us. "Come," he croaked, pointing to his easel, "tell me how you love my pic-ture." (I checked later: it was a crib from Sam Goldwyn.)

The Hahns were old friends of Don's and we were made very welcome; in no time we both had large whiskies and Don explained why we had come. They heard us out in silence and, although I think they thought the scheme was a shade on the bizarre side, agreed at once to help. They would mention Blake's name and hurried manner of dealing in hard cash when-ever they could.

The final touch in subtly blackening Blake's name was also the simplest. Don Langton's background made it perfectly natural for him to do the rounds of the Bond Street and St. James's gal-leries asking dealers if they had done business with John Blake, and if they knew where he lived. The sight of an ex-policeman making inquiries about Blake was almost certain to arouse doubts about his credit worthiness and/or his honesty. The implication was bound to be that there was something not quite wholesome about the man—exactly the image we wanted. Don made his round several times.

So, as the final sale of the season approached, we judged that

Blake's false identity was as near complete as we could make it. We had dealers, picture restorers, policemen and William Whelan feeding rumors into the art world about Blake's dishonesty. With the aid of dealers and the auction houses Blake was made to appear a wealthy man with hundreds of thousands of dollars to spend on paintings. And we had Andrew Purches, whose link with us was not known, attending sales and exhibitions, listening to gossip to learn how Blake was viewed by others, to see whether this carefully constructed false identity was actually getting across.

After the main Sotheby's auction, scheduled for 11 July, the old master galleries would shut up shop for August and the dealers would go on vacation. There would be little else we could do in Bond Street or on Madison Avenue. At some point very soon, therefore, we had to make our next move and approach someone who we knew was less than honest. That pointed to the London dealer in Siviero's secret file, the man who had been offered the Caravaggio. By now I also knew that there was all sorts of gossip about this man, about how clever he was, how tricky and, by implication, how shady. The Christie's sale had given me an idea how I might contrive an introduction to him. But, before I could try out my plan on Andrew, there was that dangerous loose end to tie up: the clever Mr. Posnett had to be fixed.

THREE DAYS after the Christie's sale, John Blake called Posnett. It was a Monday. Would Mr. Posnett be free to see him the following afternoon at, say, four o'clock? "Indeed, yes," said David Posnett, "I shall look forward to it."

Just before four the following afternoon, Blake was limping up Bond Street from Piccadilly when he heard his name called out. It was Posnett. Blake shouted across the street that he just had to see Van Haeften first but would be back soon.

In fact I had spent quite some time with Johnny and Rafael Valls since the Christie's sale on the previous Friday, filling them in on the near catastrophe that had occurred that morning. All agreed that I had made the best of a bad job and that I had to follow through with a visit to Posnett at the Leger galleries. It would look suspicious otherwise.

Johnny and Raf had also been able to fill me in on the two
early paintings that Posnett was so proud of. One, said Valls, was
by Bernard van Orley, a Dutch painter of the sixteenth century,
and could be identified by a rather hairy dog in the foreground.
Posnett, Raf checked in his records, had paid £39,000 for it a
year before at a sale at Sotheby's. The other painting was in a
similar vein but even better, except that it was ascribed, rather
vaguely, I thought, to the "Master of the Antwerp *Adoration*."

"Master of this" or "Master of that" are terms first used by
Bernard Berenson, possibly the most famous critic in the history
of art scholarship, the friend of Proust, whose views on art
pepper the pages of *Remembrance of Things Past*. When a single
artist is regarded as responsible for a painting or group of paintings, yet remains anonymous due to a lack of information, he is
given an identity. Berenson hit on the trick of taking a particular
characteristic of the artist's work and naming the "Master" after
that. Thus there is the "Master of the *Bambino Vispo*" [the
Lively Christ Child] or the "Master of the Castello *Nativity*" and
so on.

Raf and Johnny had shown me the catalogs of last year's
Sotheby sale with a picture of the Van Orley in it, and recom-
mended that, before my meeting with Posnett, I do some homework on this painter. So over the weekend I had spent some time
in London's National Gallery looking for their only Van Orley (it
was on loan to a gallery in Hull), and then had gone on to the
Witt, where I found that Van Orley was at his best doing por-
traits and in his tapestries and that his major altarpiece, *The
Trials of Job*, dated 1532, was in Brussels. I also read that Van
Orley had several powerful patrons, including successive regents
of The Netherlands, Margaret of Austria and Mary of Hungary.
Finally, I read that the painter was, at one time, known as the
"Raphael of the North" but that this spoke "rather more for
Raphael's fame than it did for northern judgment."

My last-minute visit to Johnny's gallery was for a final look at
the Van Orley in the old Sotheby's catalog to make sure that I
recognized it when I saw it. This meant that I announced myself
at the Leger galleries twenty minutes late. As I climbed the stairs
to the second floor the boy at the door called Posnett from his
back office and he met me in the main gallery. To begin with my
intention was to keep the conversation away from John Blake, so

as we both slumped into the sofas thoughtfully provided I began my attack.

"Mr. Posnett, the art world says of you that you are very clever, very rich, very honest and a terrible gossip. I know from my experience at Christie's last week that the last bit is true. I hope that, if we do business, my affairs will not become the subject of that gossip."

Posnett was thrown. He recovered by replying to the charges, one by one, ticking them off on the fingers of his hand. "Clever—well, I would hope so. Rich—I am afraid not. In fact, I've come in 'specially to see you today after organizing the building of a new wall at home. Honest—well, what do you mean by honest? A gossip? Let's just say that, although art is my life, I get a lot of fun out of it. I enjoy the absurd side."

I had won the first round. We spent the next five minutes talking about Posnett, not about Blake. In turn this enabled me to keep the initiative for, after a while and with just the merest hint of impatience, I was able to say, "Now, are you going to show me some pictures?"

Posnett got to his feet and went over to stand by one of his two best-displayed paintings. "This is the one I particularly wanted you to see," he said, pointing to what I recognized as the Van Orley. There was the shaggy dog in the foreground. I took out my magnifying glass and limped across.

"What are you calling this?" I said at length.

"I'm calling it the 'Master of the Antwerp Adoration,'" said Posnett. So he had changed the Van Orley's attribution.

I looked at it for a while, then walked across to the other picture, the one that had been called a "Master of the Antwerp Adoration" when he had bought it.

"I like this much more," I said.

"Yes," said Posnett, "it's more expensive, too."

I resisted the invitation to talk about prices, but said instead, "Have you anything else for me to see?"

"What are you interested in?"

"Early Italian for myself, Caravaggisti for clients."

Posnett led the way to the back of the gallery where many pictures were stacked. For a while we flicked through them. I was shown a terrible Federico Zuccaro, the inevitable Guardis, but eventually we came upon a Niccolò di Pietro Gerini that I genuinely did like. It showed Jesus crowning St. Catherine with five saints/cherubs looking on. The clothing was painted in white, gold and scarlet (except for Christ's robe, which was deep green). Delicious. The picture was pulled out and stood on a viewing easel.

My aim, however, was to keep the initiative. This was my first close encounter with a real expert and I couldn't get into any conversation too deeply. Before long, therefore, I suddenly broke off examining the Gerini and went back to the picture with the shaggy dog, which I again scrutinized closely. Posnett followed and we stood together in front of the picture. After a pause, I said, "This is the Van Orley that was knocked down to you at Sotheby's last year."

To say that Posnett was shocked would convey little of what happened in the seconds that followed. His hands went to his face, his mouth sagged open and he walked away.

"Correct," he said at length. But then, recovering himself: "Only I don't think it's a Van Orley. It's too good."

"Too good for the 'Raphael of the North'?" I said pompously, trying to appear knowledgeable.

But Posnett was clearly impressed, still reeling mentally, so I pressed my advantage. "What are you asking? And remember, since I know where you got it, it stands to reason that I know how much you paid for it."

"I paid £39,000 for it," said Posnett quickly, "plus the buyer's premium; plus I've had it cleaned and restored. I'm asking £52,500," he finished in a challenging voice.

I still had to keep moving quickly so now I switched my attention back to the Gerini. "And this," I said, taking out the Dunhill writing pad and the Tiffany pen, "How much is this?"

"£60,000—but to you, £52,000."

I wrote the amounts down, rubbed a little spittle on the picture and played my trump card. "I'd like to get my restorer to have a look at this," I said. "May I use your phone?"

"Who is it?" said Posnett. "We'll get him for you." He was playing right into my hands.

"Paul Hahn. I expect you have his number."

Indeed they had. Paul had been briefed, of course, and knew that my end of our conversation was being overheard in Leger's.

The phone was in the main office, where everyone could hear what I said.

"Paul? John Blake here, hello. . . . Very well thanks. . . . Listen, those two pictures of mine that you've had for a while—any chance of me taking them to New York on Monday week? . . . One will be ready? . . . Okay. . . . What about the other? . . . I see. . . . Well, I suppose that will have to do. Now look, I'm around the corner from you at the moment, at the Leger gallery. . . . Yes, that's right, with David Posnett. . . . There's a picture I like and I'd like your opinion, do you think you could? . . . Oh, you could . . . good . . . as soon as you can then . . . thanks. 'Bye."

Almost the entire staff of Leger's had listened to this exchange. I hoped that both Posnett and the recruit he had had with him at Christie's the week before had forgotten entirely that they had once believed Blake to be a buying-in name.

It took Paul less than five minutes to walk around from Albemarle Street. When he arrived he shook hands with me as familiarly as he did with David Posnett. He took his time scrutinizing the Gerini and then he and I strolled out of the gallery together and turned down Bond Street toward Sotheby's. Ostensibly the two of us were discussing the state of the painting.

WE JUDGED that our little maneuver had been successful. But Johnny and Raf also thought that we now had a good chance to consolidate the rumors about Blake. Posnett worked for one of the big old master galleries, was much grander than Johnny or Raf, was widely known in the trade and was, without doubt, a very useful gossip. If, therefore, Blake were to suggest a deal that was basically dishonest, or a bit shady, there was every chance that Posnett would turn it down—but tell other people about it. Three days after he had visited the Leger gallery Blake telephoned Posnett and invited him out to lunch the following week. The venue was Wilton's, a stylish seafood restaurant in Bury Street, often frequented by art dealers; it was an ideal setting for another, carefully planned maneuver.

For the average person Wilton's is unbelievably expensive (lunch for two then could cost anything from £50 to £80). But that made it perfect if John Blake was to appear as a man of sub-stance.

When Posnett and Blake met at the restaurant the next week, Blake was carrying a black leather briefcase, locked. What Pos-nett didn't know was that Willie Whelan was sitting at the bar of Wilton's tucking into his second gin and tonic. His instructions were to wait in the bar until he saw Blake and Posnett settled, then find a table where he could be seen by Posnett. In any case, it couldn't have worked out better: Blake and Posnett were seated in full view of the bar so Willie simply ate his lobster where he was.

Blake and Posnett ordered fresh asparagus followed by cold salmon, washed down with a 1971 Chablis. Posnett was far more deferential than he had ever been before; perhaps he sensed a deal. Blake said he had proposed lunch because he felt he had been "somewhat brusque" at their earlier meeting and because he had three questions he wanted to put to Posnett.

Posnett admitted he had been thrown a little by Blake's ap-proach, but didn't mind really. What were the three questions?

First, said Blake, could he have a color transparency of the Gerini to take to New York on the following Monday?

"You may have it this afternoon, if you wish."

Blake then asked if Mr. Posnett could lean a little way across the table and "take a look at this." He had by this time made a show of unlocking his briefcase. As Posnett leaned forward Blake opened the case a fraction to reveal inside several packets of £20 notes, £25,000 in all. Blake gave Posnett barely time to take in the packets of money. You don't flash bank notes in those quanti-ties too widely, but Blake had another reason for closing the briefcase sharply.

What the case actually contained was a very amateurish at-tempt at "flash money." This had been prepared by Don Langton and Willie Whelan around the corner from Wilton's about an hour before and consisted of piles of specially cut Croxley script writing paper, topped and tailed, as it were, with real £20 notes. They were packed in "£1,000" bundles and wrapped in what looked like official bank plastic envelopes but were in fact sub-standard bacon wrappers that were too high in sulphur content to be used for food. Willie Whelan had spotted this dodge some time before and always stored his money in that way. It worked splendidly—the bacon wrappers looked very realistic and Posnett was taken in.

"I arranged our meeting for today," said Blake, relocking the briefcase, "because I knew I would have this cash on me—I am closing a deal later this afternoon. I deal quite a lot in bullion, Mr. Posnett, Krugerrands and sovereigns mainly; everyone prefers it if I pay cash. I wanted to show you this because my next question is, if we were to do business and I paid you in cash, would you make some allowance?"

Posnett frowned questioningly, though he must have known what was meant.

"I know you don't own the Leger galleries, Mr. Posnett, but I know you are the senior person there, apart from old man Leger. You could easily knock something off a particular painting I was keen on, take the money in cash from me, and then tell old Leger that you had sold it for somewhat less . . ." Blake's voice trailed off as he emptied the last of the Chablis into Posnett's glass.

Blake wasn't really interested in Posnett's answer—he had played his dishonest gambit and that was the point of the exercise; but, to his credit and for the record, Posnett said no, he wouldn't make allowances, even for cash. He was honest and that was that.

Blake's final question was designed to keep Posnett off balance. Blake said he had heard that Posnett had been mixed up in a scandal over some fakes and asked for the Leger gallery's version.

In the early 1970s the Leger gallery had acquired four pictures by Samuel Palmer, one of Britain's most famous nineteenth-century watercolorists. The pastoral landscapes were of the artist's "Shoreham Period" (1826–35) and has been described as "the moment of perfect balance between inner and outer vision." However, doubts were expressed about these pictures a few years later, and they were eventually shown to be fakes produced by a Mr. Thomas Keating, whose girl friend had sold the pictures to the gallery.

It was bad enough having a major London gallery duped in this way and it was unfortunate that the directors of the gallery, Mr. Posnett included, stuck to their attribution even when it was challenged by none other than Sir Karl Parker, for seventeen years curator of the Ashmolean Museum in Oxford, which houses one of the finest Palmer collections in the world. But what set the art world alight was the fact that the Palmers were only the tip of the iceberg: after they had been exposed Keating confessed that he had flooded "2,000 to 3,000" other fakes on to the market—including Rembrandts, Goyas, Constables, Degas, Renoirs, Turners and Reynoldses. Moreover, Keating claimed that some galleries had acquired his pictures knowing them to be "pastiches" and had themselves added signatures of the artists concerned.

Posnett's version left a few gaps in the story, of course, and he made light of his own involvement. But he admitted now (which he hadn't done at the time) that he had been taken in. Blake, trying to appear a roguish man of the world, smiled at Posnett as he came to the end of his story and quoted Mark Twain: "One of the most striking differences between a cat and a lie is that a cat has only nine lives." Posnett finished his wine but looked uneasy.

Halfway through their cold salmon, a figure suddenly lowered over Blake and Posnett: it was Willie Whelan. "I thought it was you," he said to Blake, as though he happened to be lunching at Wilton's by accident. "Am I going to see you later today?"

"Yes, of course," replied Blake, who then introduced the two men. "By the way, Willie," he added as an afterthought, "I have that money for you, right here. Why don't I give it to you now?"

Excusing themselves to Posnett, Blake and Whelan retired to the front of the restaurant, where, making sure they were just *in* the dealer's view, Blake handed over the "£25,000" in cash to Whelan. Loudly, they exchanged farewells, Whelan left the restaurant and Blake went back to join Posnett.

That encounter had gone well. Posnett was clearly agog at John Blake's opulent, rather flashy style. However, just as Blake was sitting down he noticed at the back of the restaurant and behind Posnett a good friend of Peter Watson's. It was David Stephen, a large bear of a man who had earlier been political adviser to David Owen, when Owen was Labour Foreign Secretary. Watson and Stephen had once worked together and it was a pound to a penny that, if he finished his lunch first, Stephen would stop by at Watson's table to say hello. Posnett was near the end of his salmon, but even so Blake wolfed down what was left on his own plate, kept the dessert very simple, bypassed the courtesy of a brandy and shunted Posnett out of the restaurant before Stephen had a chance to finish his coffee. A near thing.

OVER HAM SANDWICHES at the Phene Arms, Andrew and I discussed my plan to approach Siviero's suspect London dealer. Andrew thought that the final Sotheby's sale provided the last opportunity of the season to do so and that we were now as ready as we would ever be. In the days preceding the sale Blake had gone through what were now familiar motions, looking over the works offered, spitting on several and taking copious notes. Van Haeften, Valls, Paul Hahn and Ciechanowiecki had all played their part, too, obligingly recognizing Blake in the viewing rooms and stopping to chat with him at the tops of their voices. Andrew Purches, of course, *never* acknowledged Blake. His role was to follow me around, but at a distance. He was to chat to as many of his friends and acquaintances in the art world as he could and, where possible, bring the conversation around to Blake. We needed to know if my disguise was making any impression.

From Andrew's inquiries it seemed that Blake *had* been noticed—several dealers were aware of his name. But one encounter Andrew had was particularly encouraging. While Blake had been engrossed in conversation with Ciechanowiecki at Sotheby's one day, Andrew had bumped into a friend, one of the smaller dealers with a gallery in Pimlico. "Who is the man with the bow tie and cane?" Andrew had asked. "I haven't seen him before."

"Bit of a mystery," said the Pimlico man. "Apparently wealthy —or he has good clients. What with that limp and the floppy bow tie, we've taken to calling him 'Zoppo.'"

Andrew had looked up "Zoppo" later. There was no suggestion of dishonesty in this nickname—more of cruelty, really. Marco Zoppo was a fifteenth-century Bolognese painter influenced by Bellini. But *zoppo* is also the Italian word for cripple. . . .

So Blake had been noticed—and there was no suspicion that he was in any way a fake. It was a pity that the Pimlico man did not appear to think Zoppo was shady, but—well—we couldn't have everything. We agreed it was time to act. In any case, perhaps by the time of the Sotheby's sale, Posnett's gossiping would have begun to spread.

Another reason why we became convinced it was time to act arose out of my meetings with two directors at Sotheby's. Peter Wilson, the managing director, had been in on the plot for some time and, as befitted a man who used to be in military intelligence, had given it his blessing. But about a week before the sale

I had also seen Derek Johns, then head of the Old Masters Department and the auctioneer on 11 July. Johns had indicated that a number of substantial order bids had been received and there was a good chance that Blake would have some pretty important pictures knocked down to him, including, perhaps, the Canaletto, which was expected to go for close to £100,000. Johns wouldn't say who the order bids were from but I later learned that one, at least, was from Norton Simon.

Simon, a self-made American businessman-turned-art collector, caused a splash in 1972 when he admitted that a bronze sculpture of the god Shiva, which he had acquired from India, had indeed been smuggled. "I have spent between $15 million and $16 million in the last two years on Asian art," he said, "and most of it was smuggled." Had he known, Simon wouldn't have minded our "arrangement" that summer. In fact, I am sure he would have enjoyed it.

With such a successful sale in prospect, neither Andrew, Don nor I thought we would ever have a better chance of approaching the suspect dealer. The plan was simple, but depended totally on Sotheby's cooperation.

Patrick Lindsay, at Christie's, had given me the idea when he had pulled out the seating plan for their big sale, the one where Blake had been placed in front of Posnett. All around where Blake was positioned we had seen the names of the other London dealers—Colnaghi, Agnew, Wildenstein, Leger, McGill. Well, McGill* was our man.

My idea was simply that, if Sotheby's would play ball, Blake and McGill could be seated next to one another for the duration of the sale, a couple of hours at least. Then, if Blake really did "buy" some first-class works, McGill couldn't help but notice. The two men might even get to talking, just as Posnett and Blake had talked at the Christie's sale. It seemed to us as foolproof a way for Blake to meet McGill as we could devise. But would Sotheby's agree?

Tantalizingly, Johns could give no definite answer. It was rather late in the day, he said, to make such arrangements. Some of the sales tickets had already gone out with seat numbers on them. He would do what he could but we wouldn't know definitely until Blake arrived on the day in question.

For the sale Van Haeften had two bids for Blake and Feigen

promised three but wouldn't make up his mind until an hour before. He arranged to meet Blake in Bond Street outside Sotheby's at 10:45 on the eleventh.

It was a fine summer day and Blake was at Sotheby's dark green door on the dot. Feigen wasn't. Ten-fifty came, still no sign of Dick; 10:55—could Blake leave it any longer? Regretfully he decided he couldn't—the major sales always start right on time. Blake made his slow way up to the auction room and found his seat, halfway down the center aisle. Next to him, on his right, was a young Dutch dealer; but across the center aisle, directly opposite, sat a very garrulous, loud-spoken (but not loud-mouthed) Irishman who also wore a bow tie. Howard McGill.

Johns appeared precisely at 11:00 and mounted the rostrum. He is a good-looking man with vivid blue eyes and wavy blond hair set off by the camel-colored suits that he often wears. Like the other auctioneers before him, he registered where Blake was sitting, glanced around the room smiling and the sale was on.

The Canaletto came up early—it was lot 10—and sure enough, when the bidding started at £25,000, Johns was looking hard at Blake. It rose swiftly to £60,000, slowed, but then at about £80,000 speeded up again as Richard Green, one of the main London dealers, entered the contest. By £90,000 only Green and Blake were left and the bidding rose inexorably to £100,000. Green obviously sensed that the Blake fellow had a limit of £100,000 "plus one" for, after Johns had made Blake bid £110,000, Green called out £115,000 (the bidding would normally have gone straight to £120,000). The fact that Johns accepted it (auctioneers don't have to) showed that the other bidder's limit had been reached.

So Green got the Canaletto, but at least Blake had been seen bidding for a major "first-league" picture, willing to spend £110,000. He hoped McGill had noticed. He also benefited from a coincidence: lot 11, the very next set of pictures, was his first bid for Van Haeften. He had been given a limit of £10,000, plus one, and although he didn't get it—the paintings, a pair of flowers in a vase, went for well over his ceiling at £17,000—he was seen to raise his hand. He was clearly an active, if so far unsuccessful, buyer.

Things were happening fast, moreover, for all of a sudden Blake noticed that Feigen had slipped into his place, just two

seats away, and was passing across a slip of paper. This gave simple instructions to Blake to bid for Feigen on two lots—and gave
his limits. Great news—if it were not for the fact that one of the
lots was one of those he was already handling for Van Haeften,
and Feigen had given him a different limit (a rather higher one).
Using Feigen's bid would have given Blake more chance of getting the picture, but he judged it somewhat unethical to pull out
in this way. So Blake sent back a note saying that he was already
bidding on lot such and such for Van Haeften.

Feigen duly backed out, in view of this, but McGill was beginning to wonder what was going on. Feigen's note passing was not
part of the plot but it couldn't have been better timed in drawing
Blake to McGill's attention.

Blake then noticed that Johns, the auctioneer, was staring hard
at him again. The painting was an early Italian landscape, with a
pair of lovers and a pilgrim, by Domenico Caprioli. It became obvious, as the bidding rose through the twenties, that the reason
Johns was staring so hard was that there were two bidders for this
picture and they were sitting next to each other: *Blake and
McGill*. What a stroke of luck. The bidding rose through the
thirties with Johns inclining his head just a fraction between
bids; it slowed at around the £40,000 mark and, with McGill
eventually dropping out, the Caprioli was knocked down loudly
to Blake at £43,000—the most expensive picture he had ever
"bought."

The next lot was a Brueghel (which went for £60,000) so
all eyes were on it. But over the next few bids Blake could feel
that McGill's eyes were on him. Eventually, after a few more
bids, the Irishman leaned across and said, in a deep loud voice,
"Mr. Blake, you just bought a very beautiful picture."

"Yes," said Blake sanctimoniously, trying to keep his eyes on
Johns, "I think so too."

Before McGill could say more another lovely early Italian picture had been raised to the easel, a *Madonna and Child* by
Pseudo-Pier Francesco Fiorentino. Once more Johns was staring
at Blake. Blake stared back and this time the Irishman stared at
him too—trying to see how he was bidding.

Forty-five seconds later this picture was knocked down to John
Blake—for a staggering £60,000. In seven minutes he'd "spent"

£103,000 and been ready to spend a £110,000 more. McGill was silent.

But not for long. "Are you a dealer, Mr. Blake—or a collector?"

"Both," whispered Blake, trying to quieten the man. He fished out his business card and handed it across.

McGill seemed to scrutinize it for ages, then began scribbling on a sheet of paper torn from his notebook. He handed it to Blake, who looked down to see an address in West Eaton Place, Belgravia.

"I'm having a few friends over for drinks tonight, Mr. Blake," he croaked. "I'd like you to come."

WHAT EXTRAORDINARY LUCK. Our planning could not have paid off better. An accidental introduction to McGill was the best kind of all. It could raise no suspicions. A Dubliner living in London, McGill is one of the legendary figures in the art world, an expert on Italian paintings who, like one or two others, seemed to attract notoriety.

I was, however, of two minds as to whether I should go to his cocktail party. Was I ready for such a close encounter? On the one hand, I couldn't hope to keep up a conversation about art for more than a few minutes, and my experience with Posnett, in maintaining the initiative, might be difficult to repeat. On the other hand, unless I saw more of McGill, I would never be able to approach him about the Caravaggio—or other stolen works, come to that.

I decided to compromise. John Blake would go—but in black tie. That way he could pretend he was going on somewhere else for dinner; it would make Blake seem a popular, social man and it had, after all, been a last-minute invitation. It would make it all right for Blake to stay for just one drink. He could see what kind of man McGill was and how best it might be to develop the relationship.

But Blake was very nervous that evening when he knocked on McGill's door just after seven. The other guests were all in the art world—dealers, experts from the auction houses and a restorer or two. But, as it happened, the conversation turned not around art but centered instead on religion and medicine.

The others were talking about Veronese when I arrived. The

Venetian painter had been called before the Inquisition in the late sixteenth century and accused of heresy, of putting animals and (Protestant) Germans in a *Last Supper* he was painting. Veronese had given a good account of himself, saying he felt free to put into his pictures what he wanted, though in the end he changed the title of the picture to a secular one. This was dangerous ground for me but I was fortunate in having recently worked on an article for the London *Sunday Times* about the Bollandists, another manifestation of the Jesuits based in Brussels and whose self-imposed task it is to check out the lives of saints. This involves investigations of all alleged miracles and it always proves an absorbing topic of conversation. For the moment, art was safely forgotten.

Also McGill's wife, who was a doctor, held us riveted with some stories of Richard Selzer's, the witty and compassionate Yale surgeon who writes for *Esquire* magazine. One I recall her telling that evening was about Selzer's treatment of a diabetic woman who was blind and came to him with a big black ulcer on her ankle. He described it as a "Mississippi Delta brimming with corruption." The woman couldn't see it, but she could feel the pain it caused and for a year Selzer tried hard to cleanse the corruption. At last they gave up; the gangrene had won. Selzer had to amputate.

On the day of the operation, he was tense, sad. He was not unused to amputations but somehow the courage of this blind woman had affected him. She was anesthetized and fell asleep gracefully. He uncovered her leg. And there, just below the knee and above the point where the bone was to be sawn, she had blindly drawn a face, upside down so he could not fail to see it as such. It was just a circle, two eyes, two ears and an upturned mouth. And below, in an untidy scrawl, the words: "Smile, Doctor."

After that things might have gotten sticky but for the delightful habit which the McGills shared. Whatever sentence "Gillie," as his wife called him, began, she would finish. Whether this stemmed from chronic absentmindedness on Gillie's part I cannot say, but he would start along these lines: "Have any of you tried that new—" "—restaurant in Conduit Street?" Sally would add. "Very good," Gillie would start again, "only you must go—" "—downstairs," Sally would join in. "Upstairs is much too crushed." All this appeared quite unconscious on their parts but the rest of us found it hilarious, so much so that half an hour passed quickly without any discussion of paintings.

Nevertheless, it was just as well I had decided to leave after one drink because the house, although magnificent, was full of pitfalls for John Blake—what looked like a Botticelli over the mantelpiece; a reddish portrait, possibly a Tintoretto, up the stairs; and I think a Rubens in the hall. It was the most gorgeous private collection I have ever seen, the more so as it was a small, lived-in house, and the pictures were "used," as it were, every single day.

McGill accompanied me down the stairs as I left for my "dinner engagement." At the bottom he gripped me by the arm and drew me to one side to show me his small but exquisite Brueghel. "We must talk," he said, in that gargling voice that some old people acquire later in life. "You are a very attractive man, Mr. Blake. Give me a ring."

I wasn't sure whether Blake's "attraction," as McGill put it, lay in the size of his wallet, in the fact that his taste in pictures appeared to coincide with McGill's or in something else I preferred not to think about. Still it seemed that we were off to a good start. I didn't have a clue about how to broach the subject of the stolen Caravaggio with him, but in general we were going in the right direction.

As it happened, it was McGill himself who helped move matters along. Before the sale at Christie's I hadn't noticed him and he certainly hadn't noticed me. But two days later, at the Bonham's sale of old masters, we bumped into each other again.

Compared with Sotheby's and Christie's, Bonham's salesrooms, almost opposite Harrods in Montpelier Street, retain a family atmosphere. The auction room is much smaller, there are no electronic scoreboards for the prices and the painters auctioned there are rarely household names. I had no bids that morning: Johnny and Raf were not interested and Feigen was already back in New York verifying his Claude. I was there just for appearances' sake and by now I felt that I knew the ropes well enough to get noticed without having to bid.

The informality at Bonham's is such that many dealers wander about while the sale is in progress, and are even allowed to inspect a picture on the easel as it is being offered. In theory this is to allow for last-minute bidders to check a work. But from my point of view it meant that, two or three times during the sale, I could limp up to the easel, in full view of the rest of the room, and scrutinize a painting with my magnifying glass. At this time a Landseer profile of a dark-colored charger had been reported stolen in London and many of the dealers were—jokingly, of course—on the lookout for it at Bonham's.

McGill saw me before I saw him. I was just returning to my seat after one of my forays to the easel when he called out, "You're not bothering with that one, are you?" I recognized the throaty voice immediately. "I'm under instructions," I said, and sat down next to him. I then turned, looked to the back of the room and nodded pointedly at no one in particular.

"Got an agent bidding for you today?" he asked.

"Yes," I said. "I only want three fairly reasonable pictures . . . but my clients want them badly." I implied by this that I had rivals who I didn't want to alert by bidding myself.

We sat in silence for a while watching the sale. He bid, unsuccessfully, for a fourteenth-century Italian primitive that I admired, then I made to move: "Must talk to my agent at the back," I muttered.

Again, just like three nights before, he put his arm on mine. "Mr. Blake, I'd like to talk to you . . . I have a question to ask. Can we meet after the sale?"

I didn't know what to do. Once again there was the dilemma of taking the relationship further with the risk of getting in over my head in a conversation about art. I decided I had no option. "I'm seeing someone in the bar of the Hyde Park Hotel at twelve-thirty. I could meet you there at one."

He nodded. "At one, then." I slid away, hovered at the back of the hall for a while, where I was supposed to be talking to my agent, and then left. McGill watched me go, and waved.

The Hyde Park was fairly busy when I arrived at ten to one, but I found a seat in a corner of the bar where I could see the door. I ordered a tonic water with ice and lemon; McGill would, with luck, think there was gin in it. He was on time, saw me immediately and ordered a glass of wine from the bar before he sat down.

"Everything go okay this morning?" I asked.

"No," he growled. "Everything was too expensive."

I smiled. Knowing what he had spent on pictures in the past, I thought it ironic that he should find anything too expensive.

The wine arrived and, while he was reaching in his pocket, I intervened. Already I was nervous to keep the initiative. "What was it you wanted to ask me about?" I said softly, paying the waiter.

"Thank you," McGill replied, lowering his eyes to indicate the wine. There was a pause while he took a drink; then he said, "The Caprioli . . . I'd like to buy it off you. How much to make you part with it?"

It was a good job I'd stuck to tonic. What could I say? That it wasn't mine to sell? I couldn't; that would blow the whole thing. I had to carry on with the deception but that meant . . . that meant I had to refuse his offer. But wouldn't that seem odd, especially if he offered a lot more money than I had paid for it? A refusal carried with it the risk that our "relationship," such as it was, would be over, too. I stalled. "Why do you want it?"

"That's my business." He was suddenly quite fierce and made it seem as though I had no right to ask. I felt I had blundered. "Will you sell? How much do you want?" He was pressing again.

If there was one moment in the life of the entire project when I thought quickly, when I acted as people *do* act in movies, it was during that drink in the Hyde Park Hotel. An idea came to me. I had no idea whether it would work, nor did I know then whether it might endanger the whole conspiracy. I had known McGill for just a few days and there was no reason why he should trust me. On the other hand, he appeared to like my company, believed for the moment at least that I was a dealer, and he was, according to Siviero, a step forward toward the Caravaggio or another treasure. If I could give him no satisfaction over the Caprioli, I might never see him again.

To say that I carefully weighed the pros and cons is just not true. To say that I thought through what I did with the speed of light is even less true. I had an idea and plunged ahead, hoping for the best.

"You can have it," I said. "But I don't want any more than I paid for it."

That caught his attention all right. He sat up. I went on before he had a chance to speak.

"I want some information." I judged now that I should keep

talking, get it all out before he had time to stop me. "I travel a bit, America mainly, but Italy as well. I heard in Italy that you were once offered Caravaggio's *Nativity*, the one that was stolen from Palermo. I was also told that you turned it down. All I want is the name of the man who offered it to you. Tell me that and you can have the Caprioli for £43,000. Plus the buyer's premium." It was done. I breathed out. I took a drink, wishing I'd had gin in it after all.

He had averted his eyes as I spoke and now shook his head. For a short while he didn't say anything. Whenever I am tense, waiting for an exam result or an injection, say, at the dentist's, I don't always sweat or feel my heart pumping. Sometimes, for some reason, I chew on the inside of my cheek. That's what I did now.

"Who told you all that?" McGill said after a while. He didn't really expect an answer. Siviero's secret file in Rome had been vindicated. Had McGill *not* been offered the painting he would have been protesting much more by now—but he just sat there in his chair as if he had been winded.

What was he thinking? Perhaps that he would have to check me out, that there was more to this Blake fellow than met the eye; perhaps he was trying to work out for himself who had told me.

I waited. My glass was empty, as was his. The bar was emptying too as people went in to lunch. If I was to get an answer to my question I didn't expect it there and then. We had been led to believe, by Siviero especially, that Blake would be thoroughly checked out before any information came his way, that master art crooks are a special breed—sophisticated, intelligent men, with excellent sources of information.

Life isn't always like the textbooks, of course, especially where strong-willed men are concerned. Successful businessmen, successful crooks, successful art dealers are alike in one important respect: they have good judgment and are quick to use it. There isn't always time for the textbook approach, to check your options, do the necessary research and anticipate all possibilities before making a move.

Looking back now, on that drink in the Hyde Park, I believe that McGill was sizing up whether or not to trust me. He knew he was taking a risk but he was letting his instincts speak to him.

I was gambling on *my* instincts: that he would feel Blake was a bit of a hustler, like himself, that they spoke the same language, cut the same corners, bent the same rules—whatever metaphor you like. But his reaction would be instinctive, not intellectual.

"When can you bring me the picture?" he said. I was right.

"Monday. It's at the restorer's," I lied. "He's away till then."

McGill shifted in his seat. "All right. But I'd be grateful if you didn't tell anyone I told you . . ." He paused as I shook my head. "You want a dealer in Naples. I don't know his address exactly, but he lives in a villa on a cliff up the Posillipo. His name is Baratti—Vittorio Baratti."

6

The Heroin Connection

IT IS TIME NOW to introduce a couple of new characters. So far we have been concentrating on the activities of John Blake in the salesrooms of London. But parallel with this, another part of the plot had gone ahead in New York. Siviero felt that, for two reasons, an approach from there was the most plausible.

In the first place, as Lord Duveen said in the early part of the century, "Europe has the art, America has the money." That is still broadly true today so far as old masters are concerned. Given that, and Italy's particular abundance of art, the most well-trodden conduit, for legal or smuggled paintings moving around the world, had to be from that country to the U.S.A. Second, one didn't have to be a specialist to know that the criminal links between Italy and America were much, much stronger than between Italy and the U.K. The Mafia has never gained much of a toehold in London.

After the events of July, I had a third reason for wanting to pursue the project in New York. Following my meeting with

McGill in the Hyde Park, I sent him a card from Manhattan to say my restorer had been taken ill but that I would be back in contact immediately on my return at the end of August. That maintained the illusion that McGill was still going to get the Caprioli, and might keep him from asking too many questions about Blake, for a while at least. But I could never go back to McGill again. He had been helpful, I hoped, in passing me down the trail to the Caravaggio; but we couldn't now use him as a lead to other stolen paintings. That London bridge had been burned.

My task in New York was essentially twofold. I had to get to know the art world; and I had to delve into the underworld. I needed to know if they had links with each other and whether they had counterparts in Italy.

As you may imagine, researching the art dealers was considerably easier than studying the criminals, but again I was particularly fortunate in being helped by a special person, Detective Robert Volpé, the New York Police Department's one-man art squad. I met up with him in Manhattan a few days after the Bonham's sale and my close encounter with McGill.

Volpé could not look less like a cop. In fact, at that time he rather resembled Salvador Dali, the Spanish Surrealist painter. Volpé (the name is Italian and means "fox") is a painter himself, slightly Surrealist in style. But what made him so much like Dali were his white suits, his bold, striped, double-breasted blazers and, best of all, his magnificent waxed moustache, long, dark and curly.

He had had a fairly rough time in the force since the art squad had been founded. A lot of publicity had come his way, and the fact that he was a painter as well as a policeman had provoked all sorts of jealousies and sarcastic rivalry among his colleagues.

Volpé grew up in the raw streets of south Brooklyn. Born in 1942, his parents were third-generation Italians, and it was therefore entirely natural for Robert to become a "greaser" in the black leather, rock-'n'-roll gangs of the 1950s. However, he managed not to get too involved with any one gang by virtue of his ability to paint the gangs' insignias on their leather jackets. That gave him acceptance among the blacks (the Chaplains and the Bishops) as well as among the whites (the Jokers and the Eldorados).

Perhaps it was this marginal position of his, but he admits now that he grew up actually liking the police. "It was an era when they were called bulls, not pigs," he recalled. He always wanted to be a detective and entered the Police Academy in 1964. Eventually he found himself in narcotics, where he was introduced to undercover duty. His job was to work the "flower power" discos of the late 1960s with a policewoman, looking for marijuana, cocaine and, later, heroin.

In 1971 Volpé was instructed to join the art squad, then in process of being formed. When I met him, he had already had nearly eight years among the museums, galleries and auction houses of New York. I first visited him in his office on Old Ship Street in lower Manhattan. It was festooned with paintings, exhibition posters, curious little inventions to hold his pens, flowers and greenery. He also had a cat.

The squad's first major success had occurred in 1972 when the Museum of Modern Art reported the mysterious loss of a number of prints by Toulouse-Lautrec, Pierre Bonnard and Edward Hopper. Working with another detective, Marie Cirile, Volpé soon found that prints were missing from other museums and libraries in New York—the Metropolitan Museum and the Brooklyn Museum—though until he asked, neither institution was aware of its losses. Since both museums and the library kept strict records of everyone who used their print rooms, it did not take Volpé too long to narrow a list of suspects down to one.

Volpé and Marie Cirile eventually arrested their suspect when he turned up again at the Metropolitan Museum and was observed shuffling a set of Dürer etchings and two Canaletto cityscapes into a black, artist's portfolio and then sealing it with masking tape.

He was held on the steps of the museum, but before he could be brought to trial, while out on bail, prints of all kinds, including a Rembrandt and a Degas, started turning up in the mail at several other museums in the city which didn't even know at that stage that they were missing. It was a spectacularly successful recovery and the ensuing publicity put Volpé on the map. Since then he has become something of a celebrity in the New York art world: he is often seen at openings and private showings at galleries on Madison Avenue or at the Metropolitan Museum; and he

has even had an exhibition of his own, "The Volpé Room" at
Bloomingdale's department store.

Lately, however, he has shunned publicity, fearing that his
face has become so well known as to hamper his undercover
work. In one recent instance, involving the recovery of a Byzantine icon worth $200,000, the thieves were so well organized that,
when they offered it to Volpé, who was posing as a dealer, an
elaborate police backup system was needed to ensure his safety.
The thieves were all armed. Volpé was very nearly recognized by
one of the gang because his picture had appeared in the newspapers a few days before after having made an earlier recovery. He
was able to draw his gun just in time—but only just.

As Don Langton used to do in London, Volpé works closely
with a number of dealers in Manhattan who not only tell him
when they see anything suspicious, but also play a more active
role—rather like Andrew Purches. I was anxious to be passed on
to Volpé's contacts of this kind. In the first place, I had a series of
names that I wanted to try out on them. Second, I needed to im-
merse myself in the gossip of the art world in Manhattan, just as
I had done in London, to find out who might be less than honest
and who, therefore, John Blake ought to get to know. Third, after
my meeting with Howard McGill, I had a rough plan worked out
as to how John Blake could get to know Vittorio Baratti, the
dealer from Naples who had offered the Caravaggio to McGill.
For this I needed the help of an adventurous New York dealer.

That was some way off, however. I was going to have to get to
know Volpé much better before he would give me his contacts. I
would also have to give him something in return.

This I was happy to do because I had my long list of names
from Siviero's secret file and I was naturally anxious to see
whether any of them meant anything to anybody in the New
York art world. I judged that I could not take the list around all
the galleries: this would have been to publicize the project too
much, and, presumably, if anybody did know one or more of the
names on my list, they would have had good reason of their own
not to admit it to me or to anyone else.

Instead I showed my list to Volpé. Unfortunately, the names
meant nothing to him. Next, I tried Tom McShane, the FBI agent
in New York who looked after art theft. I had met him at the conference in Delaware where I had met Don Langton. Nothing.

Then I contacted McAward Associates, a private detective agency on Lexington Avenue.

I had been introduced to Jerry McAward some months previously by a mutual friend. He had started in the business after the army, where he had bunked next to a "supposed left-winger" and had been asked to keep an eye on him secretly. Success with that bit of prying had led to an undercover job with the FBI where for years in the 1950s McAward had posed as a card-carrying Communist. Later he testified against the Communists for the bureau and then left to found his own agency.

I wasn't sure I approved of Jerry's snooping in the past, but I have to admit that he would make the ideal private eye on television. He has gritty good looks, a bit like the younger Hemingway, and, with his droopy moustache, showed more than a passing similarity to Dashiell Hammett.

The reason I contacted Jerry was that he had told our mutual friend that an increasing amount of his work was coming from respectable businesses who wanted to know whether a prospective partner or investor was connected with the Mafia. It was becoming common in New York at that time for organized crime to infiltrate a legitimate business and suck the blood from it later. McAward had a burgeoning Mafia suspect file and through him I paid $400 for the official (but confidential) Justice Department "Organized Crime principal suspect list." There are in fact three of these lists, some arranged alphabetically, others by "family." In all they run to forty-six pages. But the lists I bought were no help at all. There was no overlap with Siviero's list. Nothing.

Finally, I showed the names to Charles Koscka, an agent in the U.S. Customs Department who specializes in the smuggling of art and antiquities. I had already met "Agent Koscka," as he invariably calls himself, at the conference on art theft at the University of Delaware. He had rushed off after his speech on art-smuggling techniques to be with his wife, who was about to have a baby. I had thought this was touching and assumed that it was their first child. Though Charles was somewhat bald, with only a few wisps of red hair drawn across his shiny skull, he seemed quite young to me, no older than his mid-thirties. I was wrong. He was in his late forties, and the child his wife gave birth to shortly after the Delaware conference was his *eighth*.

Charles was—is—an extraordinary man—and very likable; cheerful, polite and fiercely moral. With that balding head, he was a real-life Kojak with a keen sense of right and wrong. Many people may not realize it, but in some countries—certainly in the United States and in Britain—the Customs and Excise Investigation departments are extremely tough outfits. Their powers are generally greater than those of the police (that is, they can act on less evidence) and the individuals themselves are usually of higher quality: tougher, sharper, better-educated and often far more intent on enforcing the law because they do not have to live among the community they police, as ordinary officers do.

Charles was just such a type, though not a crusading zealot. He was most interested in the project and offered an enormous amount of practical cooperation. The first thing he did, after he was convinced that our plot was real, was to throw open his access to the criminal records available on the customs and excise computer in the United States.

It took a few days. I had exactly thirty names on my list, but not all of them had dates of birth attached. This was a hindrance, Charles groaned, since many criminals had similar names. But eventually he found some available computer time and we ran the names even without dates of birth. By now I had drawn so many blanks in New York that I didn't hold out much hope.

Charles called one afternoon toward the end of July, but I was still out at lunch. I returned his call around three. He was matter-of-fact: "We're in luck. One of your names checks with one of ours. A heroin smuggler called Giuseppe Catania."

IT WASN'T MUCH but it was enough to be excited about. It held out the possibility of a link between the New York underworld and the Sicilian art thieves. I wasn't too happy with the fact that Catania was a convicted heroin smuggler but—well, I had always known that we might have to risk bad company. For the time being, I tried to put it out of my mind.

According to the computer records, Catania was a "major drug trafficker" who had featured in four cases in the New York area, all in 1973 and 1974. Since he had come out of prison he had either been quiet or had not been caught. I immediately filed an application for transcripts of the trial hearings in the District Court of New York—but was told that would take time. In the meanwhile Charles put me in touch with Tony Boccachio, an officer of the Drug Enforcement Agency. Boccachio was the officer who had handled Catania's cases and was well acquainted with him.

We met in the department headquarters in Manhattan, on West Fifty-seventh Street, overlooking the Hudson River and the West Side Highway, a pure New York landscape but hardly beautiful. Boccachio, a dark-skinned Latin type man with a luxuriant black moustache, was attached to the Conspiracy Group of the New York Eastern District, which covers Brooklyn and Queens. He was fast-talking and wisecracking with a colorful vocabulary. He would have made a perfect character in his namesake's *Decameron*. Certainly he had no shortage of tales of adventure and deception.

He was very informative. Catania, it turned out, had a nickname: "Pino." He was now in his late forties or early fifties, a small, dapper man who wore tinted spectacles. He spoke English and Spanish fluently, in addition to his native Italian.

As Boccachio talked on my heart began to sink. It soon became clear that Catania had been, and presumably still was, mixed up with organized crime in a very big way indeed. (This added to the flavor of the tale of course but, now that things appeared to be falling into place, "things" began to look a little menacing.) Pino, I learned, spent a lot of time in Brooklyn but didn't live there. He had his own haberdashery and shirtmaking business in Mexico City. How much this was a legitimate business and how much a front Boccachio couldn't say, but what was clear was that Pino's presence in Mexico City made him a perfect conduit for drugs entering the United States from South America. Pino had actually admitted driving from Mexico City to New York with fifty kilograms of heroin (worth $30 million on the street), which he had sold in Brooklyn.

He had started, apparently, by smuggling silks from Europe into Mexico City, where he had developed "connections" at the airport. This had drawn him to the attention of the drug smugglers. He had become involved with drugs, cocaine at first, then heroin, via a fugitive from Europe who introduced him to the Cotroni family in Montreal. My heart really began to do tricks at this point since I knew by then, through Jerry McAward and the Mafia suspect lists he had sold me, that the Cotronis were the

Mafia family who run Montreal (in fact, they apparently had links with Louis Martin Maurice, the Quebecois who featured in the book *The French Connection*). Vic Cotroni was head of the family but I was told that Catania had worked closely with Frank, Vic's brother.

Catania had helped the Cotronis smuggle narcotics into both Montreal and New York. The drugs he smuggled overland by car he had delivered to someone called Carlo Zippo, who owned an import-export business in Brooklyn called Brazitalia. The conspiracy seemed to involve no less than twenty people in all (at least, that was the number on the indictment when I got it much later from the court). Catania was cited as being involved in illegal acts in New York, Montreal, Mexico City and Rio de Janeiro.

Later, we would send the other nineteen names from the indictment to Siviero in Italy, to see if they meant anything to him. Long before that, however, one other name that Boccachio threw off struck my ear. One of the men in the Brazitalia case was called Giuseppe Tramontana. He was a Sicilian, a "garage mechanic" according to his passport, but he had been charged with heroin smuggling in the past.

Tramontana: I was sure I had come across that name before, but I couldn't place it. "Tell me more about Tramontana," I said to Boccachio. "What else have you got on him?"

He thought. "Not much . . . except . . . except that he had his own way of smuggling heroin. He used it successfully on at least three or four trips, that we know of."

"Oh, yes. What was that?"

"Picture frames," said Boccachio. "He hid the stuff in those antique gilt picture frames. You know, the type you get on those old Renaissance religious pictures. Tramontana always brought the stuff in with religious pictures."

The possibility raised by this agonizingly incomplete snippet, that the Caravaggio was here in North or Central America, was tantalizing. The suggestion that the theft of the painting might, in some round-about way, have a link with international trafficking in narcotics was even more mouth-watering. The idea that Catania, the "dapper, well-dressed con man" as Boccachio described him, was actually at or near the center of all this seemed just too good to be true. And from what Boccachio said, the gang might have been involved with other art thefts as well.

It made a kind of sense. If you smuggled drugs inside the frames of stolen paintings you would double your earnings at no extra risk. The scenario was so enticing that it almost made you overlook what kind of men these characters were. Almost, but not quite.

Boccachio sketched in other parts of the picture as he knew them. Catania's contact at Mexico airport was a man called Jorge Asaf y Bala, who was a diamond dealer as well as everything else. Asaf y Bala saw the stuff into Mexico City through the airport and sold it to Catania. Catania was responsible for the shipment overland to the United States and it was he who sold direct to the Cotronis. Catania had also been involved with a notorious drug dealer, well known to police in New York, who was killed in Mexico City a few years ago.

The main thrust of what Boccachio had to say was that Catania was so involved in drug trafficking that he probably had links with all sorts of people. He emphasized that drug smugglers started out in a variety of ways—as pickpockets or cat burglars, selling stolen articles of jewelry. One—a Frenchman called Richard Berdin—had even started as an art thief. But, like most who graduate to drugs, he had done so because the money was better.

Catania had made money all right. "He's very big on horses," said Boccachio. "He has a large stable in Mexico, and a real big house. I did hear that he wanted to open a restaurant but I'm not sure he ever did." Boccachio wasn't at all surprised to learn that Catania could be an art thief. "If you go and see him," he advised, "don't be taken in. Pino's a very good actor—he cries easily and could convince you he's starving even with a loaf of bread under his arm. You'll kind of like him, until you remember what he does."

Boccachio had one more surprise for me that afternoon. I had shown him my list of Caravaggio suspects, all thirty names. None, except Catania, had meant anything to him at first. But, just as we were winding up, he looked at the list again.

"Zuccheto." (That was the last name on my list—they were alphabetical.) "That name rings a bell. Zuccheto, Zuccheto . . ." He disappeared down the corridor talking to himself. He had gone, I supposed, to look for a file. He was away some eight or nine minutes. When he came back he was smiling.

"Got it," he said, sitting down. "Zuccheto is an alias for Tommaso Buscetto. Buscetto is the fugitive I mentioned, the man who introduced Pino to the Cotronis."

I didn't know what to think. It might have been a coincidence but . . . Zuccheto was a suspect, a one-time art dealer in Palermo who had bought land in Sicily, where there was an old acropolis. Antiquities from the acropolis had disappeared soon after and Zuccheto was believed to be expert at smuggling materials *out* of Italy.

Was Buscetto (alias Zuccheto) any relation to the Palermo dealer of the same name? There was no evidence, but if we put together Zuccheto, Catania and Asaf y Bala, we had the perfect chain of people who could smuggle something out of Italy and into New York via Mexico City. And we also knew that Tramontana (I still hadn't placed that name) used pictures to smuggle drugs; so this "gang" was used to pictures.

I now had *two* promising leads to follow, one through London and McGill to the dealer in Naples, the other via Catania and the heroin connection in Mexico City, back directly to Sicily.

7

Summer
Among the Fakes

THINGS WERE MOVING FORWARD on the Caravaggio front as well as we had a right to expect. However, natural prudence told me not to put all my eggs in one basket. The Landseer, the two Goyas, the Rembrandts, Renoir's *Sous-bois* and El Greco's *Jesus Salvador* were still missing, out there with the hundreds of masterpieces looted by the Nazis—all waiting for John Blake.

For the time being there was little I could do to advance the conspiracy. The art worlds—in London and New York, in France and in Italy—enjoy a long summer break, when the dealers and museum curators go off to the sun to combine relaxation with a little on-the-spot research not too far from the shores of the Mediterranean, and polish up their romance languages.

I used the weeks of high summer that year to study. I found out what I could about Caravaggio, his *Nativity* and about how it came to be stolen. I read books, academic articles and newspaper clippings about art theft. I visited other art squads in Paris and Germany. I made sure, as best I could, that I had an above-average idea of what was missing at the time and I looked at the circumstances in which a number of stolen pictures had been recovered. I also delved into the dubious world of art forgery and faking. If, in my disguise as John Blake, I was ever fortunate enough to be offered an old master that was supposed to be stolen, and I called in the police or customs officials to make an arrest, and it then turned out that the painting was a forgery, I was going to look a bit fake myself.

That summer yet more wonderful paintings had been added to the list of masterpieces that were missing. El Greco's *Mary Magdalene Before Christ on the Cross* had disappeared from the Church of St. John in Saarbrücken, Germany; two Renoir portraits had gone, one from Buenos Aires and the other from the Florida home of Stavros Niarchos, the Greek shipping millionaire, who was offering a reward. A Van Gogh was missing, a Modigliani and a Matisse. At the very time I sat down at my desk a Del Sarto, *Portrait of a Shepherd Boy,* was stolen from a collection in Santa Ana, California. In the next few months a Holbein, a Brueghel and a self-portrait by Sir Anthony van Dyck would all disappear.

These paintings, all by household names, were, however, only the tip of the iceberg: Each year 44,000 works of art of all types were disappearing *from Italy alone.* Enough to fill a medium-sized museum and far too many for any one organization to keep track of all the losses. For example, the *Bollettino* of the Italian Carabinieri, which comes out annually, lists on average just under three hundred stolen works, far fewer than are taken. Unlike publishing, with its mammoth Books in Print, or shipping, with its Lloyds Register, there is no master list, no comprehensive source, that will conveniently tell the policeman, the honest art dealer or the journalist whether a work is stolen, still less where it has been taken from.

To make matters worse, I soon found out that, from my point of view, the three lists of stolen art that *are* published all have serious shortcomings. The Carabinieri's *Bollettino* is a shiny red booklet that contains details of stolen sculpture, coins, antiquities and furniture as well as paintings and it has one great strength: about 90 percent of its entries are illustrated on glossy paper, an indispensable aid to identification. But besides its incompleteness and the fact that it deals exclusively with Italian stolen art, the drawback of the *Bollettino* is that it comes out only once a year. Art thieves in Italy know they have several months to dispose of a stolen work before it appears in the Carabinieri's published record.

The second list I found out about is perhaps the best known to the general public: Interpol's dossier of the twelve most wanted works of art. This is revised from time to time and, when it is, it usually makes news. At that time, works included on it were Rembrandt's *Portrait of a Rabbi,* taken from a museum in San Francisco months earlier, Picasso's *Woman with a Sheep's Skull* and a harbor scene by Van de Velde. But Interpol also issues other bulletins with details of less sensational stolen art works which come to its notice. The shortcomings of this list stem from the fact that Interpol depends in the first place on national police forces to provide it with details of thefts. This produces enormous delays—even worse than with the Carabinieri's *Bollettino*—so that the details on the Interpol list are often well over a year old before they are circulated. Another drawback is that it is rather inaccurate. In one entry I consulted there were as many as four errors: the Christian name *and* the surname of the artist were misspelled, the dates of his birth and death were wrong and the surface on which the picture was painted was given as canvas when it should have said board. This last could be quite an important error for dealers on the lookout for a particular stolen work.

The third source of stolen art I familiarized myself with was a booklet called *Art Theft Archive,* later renamed *Stolen Art Alert.* This is produced by the International Foundation for Art Research, a nonprofit organization with offices in the Explorers Club on East Seventieth Street in New York City. The strength of this bulletin is that it is issued monthly, is international in scope and carries lengthy articles about particular art thefts as well as lists of stolen works. From my point of view, however, *Art Theft Archive* had two major drawbacks. One, it had not begun publishing until January 1979 so, by definition, could not hope to refer to the mass of art stolen before that time. Assuming it took a little while for stolen works to dribble back onto the market, this meant that if I was offered any stolen works at all they would probably have been taken before the *Art Theft Archive* began publishing.

Second, the *Archive* contained relatively few illustrations. The importance of photographs in this context cannot be exaggerated. With old master paintings especially, the number of compositions, though not small, is not infinite either. Nearly all pre-nineteenth-century painters did their *Madonna col Bambinos, Sacra Conversaziones,* Depositions and their Entombments; Supper at Emmaus, the Mystic Marriage of St. Catherine, and *Baccanale* are themes which most old masters depicted more than once. Then there are the vaguely worded compositions: *Capriccio,* Landscape, Portrait of a Man or Portrait of a Woman. When, therefore, you come across a verbal description of a picture in *Art Theft Archive,* it is quite likely to read: *"Portrait of a Woman,* Italian, seventeenth century," or, *"Biblical Scene,* by Bernardo Cavallino (Neapolitan school), oil on canvas, eighty by sixty-five centimeters." What hope would John Blake, would *anybody,* have of spotting that such a work was stolen if it came his way? A photo is essential.

Faced with a painting that might be stolen, but which was not in any of the lists, my task would be far more daunting. I would either consult the Witt Library or, if one existed, a *catalogue raisonné* of the artist. The Witt is supposed to have a complete record of the works of most artists; a *catalogue raisonné,* by definition, includes all known and accepted works by a particular painter, sculptor or craftsman. First, therefore, one had to find the said work. If it wasn't in the Witt, or the *catalogue raisonné,* then the chances were that the work was a fake or by a follower of the alleged artist. But even if it *was* in the Witt or the *catalogue raisonné,* that was just a beginning. That simply gave the whereabouts and owner of the picture *at a particular point in time.* For example, the *catalogue raisonné* on Van Gogh by De la Faille was compiled in 1927. Should one be offered a Van Gogh in mysterious circumstances by someone who won't tell you where he got it, the only thing one can do is go back to De la Faille, find out if the painting is there and, if it is, refer to the owner of the painting in 1927. That person may have died by now and bequeathed it to someone in a different country. He or she may have sold the painting, or have auctioned it and not known, or not remembered, who bought it. The picture may have changed hands several times. Because of this it can take months, years, to trace a picture. Often it is impossible.

With a painter who doesn't have a *catalogue raisonné*, the problem is even more formidable. One *may* find, in the Witt, details of an exhibition the picture was shown in, or a catalog record of when it came up for auction. Again, these provide a starting point. But the museum where the exhibition was held may be honor-bound to preserve the anonymity of a lender, or the auction house may choose not to reveal who bought a particular painting. Once more, tracing a work to check if it is stolen is exhausting and often fruitless. But there may be no alternative.

The more time I spent in the Witt that summer the more I realized just how many first-rate paintings were scattered around the world in unlikely and inaccessible places. With a sinking heart, I began to see that, even if I *was* offered a painting that was actually stolen, I might never know, never be able to prove it.

Somewhat deflated, I moved on to study the circumstances in which stolen paintings had been recovered. I was able to track down about 115 cases where some details about the recovery were available. In about 10 percent of recoveries I found that the thefts were inside jobs—museum employees, greedy curators or, in the case of private collections, ex-servants. Tip-offs and smart auction-house personnel, vetting their own forthcoming sales, accounted for another 10 or 12 percent. Apart from that, what seemed to betray most art thieves who got caught was their own impatience. Almost a third of the stolen art that was recovered was offered to dealers in the same city or the immediate vicinity from which it was taken. Moreover, 40 percent of it was offered for sale within six months of the theft. All this told me was that the amateurs got caught while the professionals got rich. My analysis did reveal that 20 percent of (recovered) stolen art made its way to New York, so I was on the right track there. Then I turned to the subject of fakes.

I HAD NO IDEA, until I did, that art faking was so widespread or that the study of it is almost a branch of scholarship. Yes, I knew about Hans van Meegeren, the Dutchman who had sold a fake Vermeer to Hermann Goering, one that he—Van Meegeren—had turned out himself. I felt it very unjust that he was sentenced to prison for his genius—and not altogether surprised that it killed him. And I had noted earlier in our conspiracy that Tom Keating, whose forged Samuel Palmers had duped David Posnett, had faked a number of other artists and turned out 2,000 Rembrandts, Goyas, Turners, Reynoldses, Renoirs, Constables and Degas. It soon became apparent that as many masters had been faked as, I already knew, had been stolen.

In English, the standard work on art forgery is Otto Kurz's book *Fakes*, which examines archaeological objects, prints, glass, furniture and tapestries as well as paintings. I was agog as I read through it from cover to cover in a sitting. I learned that a paper published in 1929 had given a "chronological chart of pigments" which explains when certain colors first came to be used. This can obviously be critical when dating a particular work. For example, neither Prussian blue nor zinc white were used before the eighteenth century; cadmium yellow and cobalt blue didn't come in until the nineteenth century. This knowledge was used in one important test at least, with a *Laughing Cavalier* supposedly by Frans Hals. In Holland an expert had attested that the picture was genuine but chemical analysis revealed that cobalt blue and zinc white were present on the canvas—both unknown at the time Hals was alleged to have painted the picture in the seventeenth century.

Then I read about what you might call the natural history of cracks. Most people take the cracking of paint as an indication of age. Quoting Icilio Federico Joni, a celebrated Italian forger, Kurz says that forgers often bake a newly finished painting—and then place it in a refrigerator or the cold night air. The paint is unable to follow the swift contraction of the panel or canvas and cracks. Then there is a special forger's varnish which actually guarantees to contract abnormally when it dries. Glue will also break up the paint and the glue is usually easy to remove with water after it has caused the right amount of "aging." A more devilish method involves making a painting damp, then scoring on the back of the canvas where you want the cracks to go with a bradall or similar pointed instrument. The canvas is afterwards rolled backward and dried: the cracks will be found just where they are wanted. Cracks on panel, in order to appear natural, must go with the grain of the wood, whereas cracks on canvas usually radiate from a central point. Provided the canvas is then fixed to a panel with good glue, says Joni, the forgery cannot be detected, unless, as is sometimes done, an attempt is made to make the cracks stand out by rubbing soot into them.

The most common kind of forgery, I learned from Kurz, is the alteration to an existing picture. Many of these alterations are not forgeries as such, but involve the painting out of ugly bits or parts of a composition that go against the taste of the day (such as nudity, inevitably). Of course, one of the simplest, yet most important, alterations that can be made to a painting is the addition of a signature. According to Kurz, Dutch pictures are particularly susceptible to this type of addition since early Dutch painters were more likely to sign their pictures than, say, early Italians. It followed that Dutch paintings without signatures invariably had them added. A number of apocryphal names have apparently been added to Venetian and Bolognese school pictures, "Franco Bolognese" being one to look out for. If the authorship of a painting is suspect, says Kurz, look up the work of the pupils of the alleged artist. Many unscrupulous dealers will scratch out the name of the lesser known pupil and substitute that of the stylistically similar, better known and, therefore, more valuable, master.

But, says Kurz, better than a familiarity with the methods of the forger is a knowledge of the forgeries that have taken place. This may be an unusual aspect of art scholarship, but it is scholarship nevertheless and someone like Blake would have done his homework. I thus examined Kurz's breakdown of the types of forgeries in painting. It was a long list.

Hieronymus Bosch. This early Surrealist painter was widely forged in Spain in the sixteenth century (Bosch's own dates are c. 1450–1516). According to Don Felipe de Guevara, a Spanish connoisseur of the time, countless forgeries were made and smoked in chimneys "to give them a genuine and antique appearance."

Raphael. It is known that a certain Terenzio da Urbino (who died in the 1620s, about 100 years after Raphael) passed off his own paintings as the master's, who also came from Urbino. Terenzio hunted for old panels and dirty frames and, according to the painter/biographer Baglione, Terenzio at least once tried to pass off a *Madonna* as a Raphael. He was found out that time, but none of his other fakes has yet been identified. Raphael drawings have been widely forged, first by Denys Calvaert, a Bolognese painter, then again in the eighteenth and nineteenth centuries and finally in a batch of twentieth-century fakes which included collectors' marks and "restored corners" to the paper.

Dürer (1471–1528). Towards the end of the sixteenth and early in the seventeenth centuries there was a rash of Dürer copyists and many new pictures were "compiled" from his works. These forgeries are harder to identify because Dürer's monogram was also forged and stamped on the fakes. Luca Giordano, a seventeenth-century Neapolitan painter, also faked Dürers though no doubt it wouldn't be a total tragedy if one's Dürer turned out to be a Giordano.

Giorgione, Titian and Other Venetian Masters. Pietro della Vecchia (1605–78) was born ninety-five years after Giorgione died and twenty-nine years after Titian. Nevertheless he was well known as the "ape of Giorgione" and he copied all the other Venetians as well. At more or less the same time Sebastien Bourdon and Jean Michelin in France were creating as much havoc with their copies of Annibale Carracci and the Le Nain brothers. The French fakers, it is known from accounts of the time, used methods very similar to Joni to age their pictures, such as chimney soot and rolling the canvas to produce cracks.

Italian Primitives. The beauty of this type of painting is that there is no need to produce a legitimate masterpiece. The magic mellow shine of that gold-leaf background with scarlet just peeping through is all that has to be reproduced. No one expects a Giotto or a Duccio.

The suspicious signs to look out for with Italian primitives, I learned, are: woodworm holes that are too conveniently placed—at the edges usually—so as to give the appearance of age without destroying the image. This indicates the picture was painted *after* the holes had been made and that the "inconvenient" ones have been filled in. Broad, uneven brush strokes are another giveaway: this is a modern technique. Primitive Italian paintings are strictly religious works and the masters who produced them cut no corners; so, in a triptych, say, if the panels are uneven, or the boards of the three panels do not match, this is not an engaging sign of primitive antiquity but almost invariably a sign that the work is fake. Further, saints not properly attributed are a suspicious sign: in genuine paintings the saints are distinctive, their identities always known. Early masters had too much veneration for saints to paint anonymous crowds of them.

Gentile Bellini. These forgeries tend to be portraits and to have a bold outline and crude features. Usually, they are not identified as any particular person in Italian society because, more often than not, the head has been copied from a religious Bellini and moved out of context.

Vermeer. "There is perhaps no other painter with so large a percentage of forgeries among his officially recognized *oeuvre.*" So says Kurz, adding that Vermeer was forged long before the Goering/Van Meegeren affair.

He says that the forgeries of Vermeer's work are very good and all one can do is remember that originals by this master are rare and that the fakes usually comprise ordinary Dutch landscapes into which Vermeer's famous scheme of blue and yellow have been spliced.

Corot. In the early part of this century especially, the silvery manner of Corot's landscapes spawned many "imitations." His gray tones and blurred outlines were easy to copy, giving rise to the joke among art connoisseurs that "Corot painted 2,000 pictures, 4,000 of which are in the United States." One Dr. Jousseaume, a Frenchman who died in 1923, left 2,414 "Corots," including 1,000 sketches in *détrempe,* a kind of gouache. Corot *never* worked in *détrempe.*

Van Gogh. Between 1925 and 1928 more than thirty hitherto unknown Van Goghs appeared on the art market. They included self-portraits, flame-shaped cypresses, the sower in a sunny meadow, sunflowers—all typical themes. Experts certified them as original and they were incorporated into the official Van Gogh catalog by De la Faille, published in 1927. Only when an exhibition was held in Berlin a year later, and the new pictures were seen side by side with others, did doubts arise. Before long, all of the new paintings were traced back to Otto Wacker, a Berlin dancer and art dealer. He said he had bought them from a Russian in Switzerland but refused to identify this man. No one believed Wacker.

Yet the forgeries were good, the faker having caught Van Gogh's style of bold strokes, using a thick build-up of paints. More to the point, in the confusion created by Wacker's trial some of these forgeries slipped back into the master's official *oeuvre*. They are still around.

KURZ'S BOOK appeared in 1966, and for the discovery of more recent fakes I had to look elsewhere. I found that the practice was —is—continuing unabated. Rubens, Van Dyck and Renoir seem particularly popular among modern forgers, though the list of others is quite long.

Rubens and Van Dyck. In 1971 it was found that thirteen of the most prized paintings in Genoa, Italy, were fake: nine Van Dycks, three Rubens and a Titian. Scholars discovered that these pictures had been given to the city by the Piola family, who made their living in the seventeenth century by copying the masters. Three years after that discovery, in 1974, an alleged Rubens (*St. George*), a Guercino and a Lucas Cranach were withdrawn from sale at Sotheby's in London as soon as the paintings arrived from America. The staff at the auction house was convinced that the pictures were not genuine.

Renoir. Apart from Tom Keating's fake Renoirs, another appears to have turned up at Christie's in the mid-sixties. Mr. Harry Spiro, an American art collector, bought a pastel, *The Bathers*, and he paid £2,520 for it. But soon after he got it home for a close look he had his doubts and wrote to Christie's. Incredibly, they wrote back to say they had their doubts, too, although they had given the picture a full attribution in the catalog. Yet another fake Renoir, *Girl with a Parasol*, turned up at a New York gallery on Madison Avenue in 1968. The only clue as to who might have been responsible for these forgeries came several years later when, in 1974, 4,000 paintings were sequestered by Rome police and seven persons arrested after an inquiry into the Italian black market in forged pictures. The works included paintings allegedly by Goya, Renoir and Velásquez; another thirty people were warned that proceedings might be brought against them. They included gallery owners.

Fragonard. In 1978 it was discovered that upwards of thirty drawings assumed to be by Fragonard, the eighteenth-century French artist, which had fetched up to £20,000, were fake. North American museums and well-known old master dealers admitted they had been taken in. The pictures were mostly traced back to a Paris firm, M. and Mme. Higgons. These fakes had forged collectors' marks and false inscriptions on the back—and here again acknowledged experts had been foxed.

Utrillo and Vlaminck. "*L'affaire Petrides,*" as it was known in France, rocked the art world in the early 1970s. Paul Petrides, a one-eyed Cypriot tailor, had made a fortune in Paris in the 1930s, at first making suits for artists, then forming a friendship with, and later controlling, the painters Utrillo and, to a lesser extent, Vlaminck. For many years Petrides controlled the Utrillos coming onto the market and compiled the official Utrillo and Vlaminck catalogs. However, in 1974 Petrides—then one of the wealthiest and most prestigious dealers of modern paintings in Paris—was charged with dishonestly handling nineteen pictures that had come from four burglaries. The trial didn't take place until February and March 1979, so it was fresh in my mind. Among the paintings Petrides was charged with handling, knowing them to be stolen, were four Renoirs, three Vlamincks and two Utrillos. Petrides was given four years and a $100,000 fine for his part in *L'affaire.* The trial revealed that Utrillo, toward the end of his life in the late 1940s, was so addled with drink that he would put his name on almost any painting placed before him— even on photographs of paintings. God knows how many fake Utrillos there are.

Modern Masters. One set of very successful fakes came to light in an unusual way. During the Second World War, the Marien- kirche, a Gothic church in Lübeck, Germany, was badly damaged by Allied bombing. Restoration began in 1948, when it was found that the heat produced by incendiary bombs had caused the whitewash to peel off the church walls—and revealed fragments of ancient paintings. The Marienkirche didn't reopen until 1951, but then, in a great ceremony of pomp and prestige, it was announced that the walls of the choir were covered with rows of giant saints and wild animals of the thirteenth century and those of the nave displayed similar figures a hundred years younger. Paintings such as these, preserved in perfect condition, existed nowhere else in Germany, and such was the impact of the revelation that stamps were produced to mark the event, showing the larger-than-life saints.

Dr. Dietrich Fey, the restorer who had masterminded the renovation of the church, was honored and feted—and that's where things began to go wrong. For Fey did not share these honors with his assistant, Lothar Malksrat. Yet it was Malksrat who had actually done most of the donkeywork in the preceding years and he soon grew to resent being left out of the limelight.

Eventually, he caused an even bigger sensation than the re-opening of the church. In 1952 he confessed that the twenty-one "early" saints in the Marienkirche had in fact been painted by himself. He revealed that all that had been found of the thir-teenth-century originals were a few sandals and bare feet and he even named the book on medieval painting from which he had copied his "masterpieces." As if this were not enough, Malksrat also disclosed that, in the service of Fey, he had, in previous years, produced scores of pictures in the style of modern masters. The painters he had forged included Rousseau, Vlaminck, Cha-gall, Degas, Matisse, Cézanne, Gauguin, Rodin and Kokoschka. Fey, he said, had pushed these onto the open market.

Fey and Malksrat were both given prison sentences as a result of their activities in the Marienkirche. But of greater long-term significance are those modern fakes. The church saints couldn't walk off the walls and so pass into currency as originals. But all the other pictures Malksrat turned out did—and they are still out there.

It goes on. As a final example, in 1975 five people in Italy were arrested (and eleven more sought) in an investigation by Milan police into an international ring of art forgers who sold paintings in Italy and abroad. The inquiry had begun after a complaint from a New York gallery. Eventually, the police seized five hun-dred pictures, including alleged works by Picasso, Kandinsky, Bacon, Ernst, Sutherland, Magritte and De Chirico. Despite their success in seizing so many fakes, it seems highly likely that there are as many forgeries from this gang still on the market. One of the forgers, a woman who trained as a restorer and was a special-ist at turning out Kandinskys, admitted she was paid 150,000 lire (about £75) per painting and that they went onto the market for ten times that amount.

I WAS RELIEVED to find that Caravaggio was not featured among the forged artists. But it seemed that almost every other painter of note had been faked at some time or other. Though engrossed

by the colorful activities of the forgers, I was by no means sure I
had done John Blake a favor. If I was ever fortunate enough to
be offered a picture in dubious circumstances, the chances were
that it would be a fake, not stolen; and even if it *were* stolen, I
probably wouldn't be able to prove it. Hardly the kind of ending
to the project I had envisaged at the start.

August became September and September turned into October. The cricket season was over. With the onset of autumn the
gloom I had begun to feel while I was studying the fakes seemed
to descend more closely around me, like the autumn leaves I
could see from my desk. I took small comfort from a sentiment I
came across late one night when reading a book by my namesake,
Edgar Watson Howe: "A good scare is worth more to a man than
good advice."

8

The Nativity: How It Came to Be Painted —and How It Came to Be Stolen

IN OCTOBER 1609, Michelangelo Merisi da Caravaggio, the celebrated Italian painter, was sitting at a table, drinking in the Hosteria del Ciriglio near the docks in Naples. It was a warm, sticky evening and he had opened the neck of his rough shirt almost to his waist. The white, somewhat sour Neapolitan wine had brought a beaded ring of sweat to his hairline. Suddenly the light from the doorway was blocked as a group of men crowded into it. The painter was startled to recognize one of the men and fear immediately darkened his already swarthy features.

The other man was a Cavaliere di Giustitia, a fellow knight of the Maltese Order. Caravaggio had insulted him some months before and as a result had been imprisoned in the castle at Valetta. He had managed to escape but this was an act which counted as desertion from the order. The knights from Malta had chased Michelangelo across Sicily. Now, they had caught up with him. The painter reached for the large sword that he always carried at his side—but it was too late. The men were upon him and his screams could be heard even aboard the *feluccas* in the docks as his assailants hacked away, leaving him for dead, dripping in blood and with a terrible wound from one side of his face to the other.

The cuts didn't kill him outright—but the terrible wound on his face made Caravaggio barely recognizable and he never properly recovered. A short while later he was arrested when a ship he was aboard put ashore near Port 'Ercole. The arrest was a mistake, but by the time the muddle had been sorted out the ship had left, taking his belongings with it. Caravaggio set out to follow along the beach, but *malaria perniciosa* was then endemic to the area. He caught a fever and died.

It was not a fitting end to the life of a great painter—but it wasn't surprising. More than any other old master, Caravaggio had lived the life of the bohemian artist. He drank, he gambled; he argued endlessly; he was constantly being arrested. He had no time for artistic theorizing and made no preliminary drawings for his works; instead he simply brushed them straight onto the canvas or panel. He was arrogant and sarcastic and was at one time sued for libel by a fellow painter.

He would buy fine velvet clothes and not change them until they had fallen into rags. For many years, morning and evening, he used the canvas of a portrait as his tablecloth.

But though he made many enemies his brilliance was widely acknowledged and he counted cardinals and dukes among his friends. Even the pope commissioned a portrait from him. Caravaggio's approach to his art—conveying miraculous biblical episodes through vividly real but otherwise ordinary people—revolutionized painting. His early death only means that those pictures left to us are even more valuable than they would have been had he lived longer, to paint more.

MICHELANGELO MERISI DA CARAVAGGIO was born in September 1571, the son of fairly well-to-do parents. His father, Fermo Merisi, was a stonemason. In the village of Caravaggio, near

Milan, it was traditional for the men to become craftsmen of one kind or another, going sometimes as far afield as Rome. The village was then only a few miles from the important intersection at Treviglio, where the east-west road from Milan to Verona and Venice crossed the road from Bergamo, winding south to Parma, Bologna and Florence. It was relatively easy to get around. So Michelangelo Caravaggio had a good opportunity to travel and enrich his eyes with works of art by the masters who worked in the region.

Very little is known about Caravaggio's early years. One story has him working as a hod carrier for a builder and discovering his passion for painting when he started mixing plaster for frescoes. But it may have been invented. He *did* become apprenticed in 1584 to Simone Peterzano, a Bergamesque painter who claimed to have been a pupil of Titian's. But it is by no means certain whether Caravaggio did the full four years with Peterzano that his father had contracted for. One account states that he had to leave his apprenticeship after a brawl and flee to Venice, for safety's sake. But there is no hard evidence.

What does seem likely is that he spent some time in his early teens traveling in Lombardy, where there were paintings—by Giorgione, Titian, Veronese, Lotto—which may have had an early influence on him. Other great painters—Parmigianino, Bronzino and Del Sarto particularly—held no lessons for him. Bronzino's graduated shades of color and the soft blues and subtle changes in tone so popular with Del Sarto were banished from Caravaggio's powerful renderings. "All prettiness and vanity" were dismissed and, according to Pietro Bellori, Caravaggio's seventeenth-century biographer, he regarded blue as a "poison among colors."

We don't know when he traveled to Rome, or why. But he was in the papal city by 1588, when his apprenticeship with Peterzano was due to end.

One episode of his early years in Rome is worth mentioning: a report that Caravaggio suffered from an illness and was treated. No one seems to know what this illness was (though there was a plague in 1591), but in view of what seems to be his almost pathological behavior in his later years, it could be that this illness had something to do with it. At any rate, he spent some time convalescing.

Caravaggio's life becomes somewhat better documented around about 1590; by then he was working in the studio of a painter who was so successful in his own day that he was knighted—Cavaliere Giuseppe d'Arpino. D'Arpino's own pictures were very elaborate affairs and Caravaggio couldn't stand them. He soon decided to strike out by himself. A certain Monsignor Petrignani provided him with a room—it was hardly a studio—and Caravaggio began to turn out many pictures. The younger painter enjoyed this work more, but though he was prolific he was not successful. The arrangement eventually bore fruit, however, through the good offices of an art dealer named Valentino who had exhibited paintings by Caravaggio and finally succeeded in selling several of them to Cardinal del Monte.

Cardinal Francesco Maria del Monte was a civilized man. The official representative of the Grand Duke of Tuscany in the College of Cardinals, he lived in Rome in the Palazzo Madama, one of the palaces belonging to the Medici. The cardinal had become a kind of ecclesiastical minister of the arts in Rome and was an active patron. He recognized the genius in Caravaggio and also saw that the young man was capable of being his own worst enemy. As well as buying Caravaggio's pictures, therefore, he took him in and became his protector; he gave him a room to paint in, a roof over his head and food in his belly.

Caravaggio had still to reach the peak of his talent, but the years of hardship were now over. The tragic circumstances that were to overtake him were not produced by external conditions, but by his own tempestuous character.

THE FIRST MENTION of Caravaggio in Roman police records comes on 25 October 1600. That day he was involved in a fight between two other painters, Onorio Longhi, a friend, and Marco Tullio, who was passing and took certain rude words Longhi was then speaking as meant for himself. Caravaggio was convalescing at the time and he had to have a boy carry his sword for him. Nevertheless, he separated the two fighters.

A month later sees the first complaint lodged against Caravaggio himself. He is alleged to have attacked yet another painter, Girolamo Sampa, with a stick and with his sword. Three months after that, in February 1601, he was prosecuted for a sword wound he had inflicted on the hand of Flavio Canonico, a former sergeant of the guards. There was "no danger to life, but with a permanent scar."

From then until he was forced to leave Rome in 1606, Caravaggio crops up in the police records with depressing regularity. Barely three months would go by without his being jailed for throwing stones at the police, insulting a corporal or, once, wounding a notary in the head during an argument over a girl. His brawls in 1605 alone made for five separate entries.

Two features of these brawls stand out. In the first place, there is no record of them at all until 1600, when Caravaggio was already twenty-nine. He had emphatically *not* been a juvenile delinquent. Second, none of the brawls was for personal gain. Much of his best work had already been done and, in spite of the disappointing public reception of his altarpieces, he had a faithful and rich clientele among the more sophisticated notables of his day. Money was not a problem. No, the brawls were usually petty, impulsive acts against minor police officials, former landladies, vague acquaintances.

Nothing much is to be gained by retrospective clinical diagnosis—but in fairness to the painter there are grounds for the suspicion that the illness from which he was convalescing when first mentioned in police records had something to do with the relatively late onset of what certainly seem to be pathological acts. If so, it might help explain the way his short life was to end.

Not that all his misdemeanors were violent. In fact, the most publicized at the time was the complaint brought against Caravaggio and his painter friends Onorio Longhi and Orazio Gentileschi by a fourth painter, Giovanni Baglione. Baglione complained that, out of envy, Caravaggio and the others had libeled him in a series of satirical and obscene verses which they had distributed among other painters in Rome.

The trial threw a great deal of light on Caravaggio's character. In cross-examination he denied writing the verses, but described Baglione's paintings as clumsy. Other painters called to give character references described Caravaggio's arrogance; even though they were friendly toward him they were annoyed, for instance, that he would never raise his cap to them until they had done so to him—indicating that he thought he was their superior.

Up to and during the trial Caravaggio (and the others) were

kept in prison. After fifteen days, however, Caravaggio was released on the stipulation that he would not leave his house without written permission. That seems to be the last anyone heard of the affair; there is certainly no record of any proper verdict being handed down.

By now, however, Caravaggio's temper was becoming notorious and nobody was surprised when, six months later, he was in jail yet again for assaulting a waiter who taunted him over some artichokes that had been served. Caravaggio had flown into a rage and emptied the plate of scalding vegetables over the unfortunate waiter's head.

That year—1604—was bad enough. He was in jail three times. The next was even worse: he was in either the governor's or the senator's jail no less than five times. It may have been that some personal crisis was approaching or that, if he had some residual illness after his convalescence, his condition was deteriorating.

However, in May 1606 his career in Rome came to an inglorious end with yet another of his outbursts.

It was a Sunday, 29 May, and Caravaggio, as was his habit, went to the Campo Marzio to play *palla a corda,* a kind of tennis. He played a doubles game with Onorio Longhi as his partner against Ranuccio Tomassoni, a well-bred young man from Terni, and Captain Antonio, a soldier from Bologna. Ten scudi were staked on the result—not a large sum. But, by all accounts, the result turned on one point and there was an argument over whether the ball was inside or outside the line. Ranuccio was given the verdict, whereupon Caravaggio hit him with his racket. In no time a sword fight broke out.

It was a long and bloody brawl: the captain was slashed across the mouth, Caravaggio was stabbed in the throat and his left ear. Incensed and frightened by the blood all around, Caravaggio lunged wildly at Ranuccio and cut him through the stomach. To everybody's horror, the young nobleman collapsed and died instantly.

Caravaggio ran off to hide in a friend's house, but the captain was so severely wounded that he couldn't escape. He was arrested and taken to prison, where he told of Caravaggio's part in the affair. The painter was not arrested immediately but was visited by the clerk of the criminal court, who questioned him but could get Caravaggio to admit nothing. He was forbidden to leave the house on penalty of a 500 scudi fine.

But Caravaggio knew that he had to get away: his exploits were too well known for any magistrate to believe his denial. So a day or two later the painter who was preeminent in Rome left the Holy City, never to return. It is no exaggeration to say that he spent the rest of his short life on the run.

He went first to the Sabine Mountains, south of Rome, where he lived for a while under the benevolent protection of Duke Marzio Colonna. There he was beyond the reach of the pontifical courts but could still keep in contact with his friends in Rome, who tried hard to gain him a pardon (the murder was not premeditated and the painter had been wounded). But the pardon didn't come and Caravaggio busied himself painting a *Magdalene* and a *Christ at Emmaus*.

He must soon have grown tired of waiting for his pardon—and he would have needed cash, too—so he moved farther south, to Naples. There, lucrative commissions awaited and he painted many works. The most beautiful was *The Seven Acts of Mercy*, now in the Chiese del Monte della Misericordia in Naples, but he also painted the *Flagellation of Christ*, which was recently restored and can be seen in San Domenico Maggiore in Naples. Both are fantastically detailed, vividly real, and betray, as only Caravaggio could, the deepest understanding of Christian humility.

In the *Flagellation* Christ's body is pictured as strong, muscular —fit. But this only makes the contrast with the pain felt on his face harder to bear. In *The Seven Acts of Mercy* the faces of the angels—pale, smooth, innocent—contrast vividly with the unattractive features of the earthly creatures below, each obsessed with his or her predicament. It is a marvelous composition.

Around this time—1607—a large new church was being built in Valetta, Malta, and it seems likely that the Grand Master of the Knights of Malta, Alof de Wignacourt, a French nobleman, had heard that the famous, not to say notorious, Caravaggio was in Naples and invited him to come and decorate the church. Caravaggio leaped at the opportunity, the more so since he saw a chance to win a knighthood from Wignacourt and so get even with his old master and rival, Cavaliere d'Arpino. This may explain why his first paintings in Malta were not for the church but portraits of the grand master himself.

Wignacourt was so pleased with these that Caravaggio was indeed given the Cross of Malta and became a knight. He was officially received into the order as Cavaliere di Grazia (Obbedienza) in July 1608, and the records show he was favored with a gold chain, two Turkish slaves "and other signs of his [the grand master's] esteem for the painter's work."

For a time it seemed that Caravaggio's fortunes were on the mend. He was now a *cavaliere*, was able to live in abundance like a nobleman and he even found the inspiration for a superb composition, the *Beheading of St. John the Baptist*, in the Valetta cathedral.

The ugliness of the Biblical episode, in a simple setting, conveys perfectly the Christian horror of the story, and the draftsmanship, as usual, is faultless. St. John is forced to the ground by an executioner's muscular arm, straight as a rod. You *feel* the saint's head on the hard stones.

However, the familiar, tempestuous Caravaggio would not lie hidden for long. He got into a quarrel, this time with a superior in the order, a Cavaliere di Giustitia, and now found himself in a different prison, the castle at Valetta. Incorrigible as ever, he then proceeded to escape from the castle one night—the only person ever to do so—and fled to Sicily. It was a fatal mistake.

To the Maltese Order of St. John, escape constituted desertion, which was a capital crime. The order was convened especially to consider the painter's case and he was expelled, "thrust forth like a rotten and fetid limb from our Order and Community." It didn't end there: the order was instructed to follow him, seek him out—and kill him.

Caravaggio went to Sicily, first to Syracuse, where he painted the *Burial of St. Lucy*. But he had to leave Syracuse after yet another brawl with a schoolmaster and he moved on to Messina. There he painted two superb pictures, the *Ressurection of Lazarus* and the humble and miraculous *Nativity* for the Church of the Cappuccini in Messina. This painting was later criticized because both the Virgin and the Child are together on the floor, but once again this overlooks Caravaggio's message: that the Bible story is essentially about miraculous events happening to ordinary people.

During the summer of 1609 Caravaggio left Messina and went to Palermo. There, in the church of the Oratorio of San Lorenzo, he painted his *Adoration of the Child with St. Francis and St. Lawrence*. It is an unusual painting for Caravaggio: it almost seems that the events of the preceding months were beginning to catch up with him. It is still a Caravaggio but it is as if he had begun to doubt his own vision. The peasants watching the event are in the old, familiar style. They are ordinary, balding, tired, rather shabby people lost in wonder. But Mary particularly is a more stylized figure: her features are regular, smooth, her skin is like marble. There is even an angel descending from on high. Some sort of change appeared to be coming over Caravaggio.

This, of course, is the *Nativity* we were after. (It is known as the "Palermo *Nativity*" rather than by its full title.) Its special place with regard to Caravaggio's psychological state, and its stylistic difference, meant that it was doubly valuable and that it was doubly important to return it. The painting combined religious and artistic interest unusual even for Italy at that time. Whoever had stolen it had taken more than an object; he had deprived the world of a sign of change in the mind—the somewhat unstable mind—of a great man.

The Palermo *Nativity* was one of Caravaggio's last paintings. We do know that after he had finished it he returned to Naples, still hopeful of a pardon in Rome, and while there may have completed a *Salome with the Head of St. John*. The date of this is uncertain but he could have painted it without a commission in the hope of placating the anger of the grand master.

If so, the ploy didn't work. Caravaggio spent the last months of his life on the run from three separate sets of people: the police in Rome, the knights of the Maltese Order and the friends of the late Ranuccio Tomassoni and Captain Antonio.

It is most likely that the men who slashed his face at the Hosteria del Ciriglio that October day in 1609 were knights of the Grand Cross; but they just might have been friends of Ranuccio and Antonio. After all, the gash they left Caravaggio with—from one ear to the other—was the same as he had inflicted on Antonio after the tennis match. . . .

If so, it was a bitter irony—but not yet the last his unruly life had to deal him. On 28 July 1610 an *avviso* [notice] was published in Rome which read, "Word has been received of the death of Michelangelo da Caravaggio, a famous painter, eminent in the handling of color and painting from life."

Another *avviso*, published at the same time, announced that he had been granted a pardon by His Holiness the Pope.

THREE HUNDRED AND FIFTY-NINE years later, on the morning of 19 October 1969, Maria Gelfo noticed a cat run into an open door in the Oratory of San Lorenzo near the center of Palermo. The place was crawling with cats—that didn't bother her. What *did* make her think twice was the open door. She and her family lived across the courtyard from the chapel and she and her sister Amelia were the oratory's official caretakers. They kept the keys, and when a visitor wanted to see the beautiful seventeenth-century chapel somebody in the family would let them in and show them around. She knew that the door should have been locked. Curious, but not unduly perturbed, she followed the cat inside.

The chapel is built in the most exuberant Baroque style. The windows are rimmed with carved stone runnels and flocks of marble cherubs turn capers along the walls and peep around corners. Still, the chapel is small, almost on a domestic scale and it is dominated by the altarpiece, Caravaggio's huge, eight foot by seven foot, painting of the *Nativity*.

Maria Gelfo had always loved the *Nativity*, with its warm, cozy, shadowy simplicity. But that wasn't why she stared on the morning of the nineteenth. She stared because it had gone.

Someone had hacked the *Nativity* out of its splendid frame with a razor blade. Fragments could be seen hanging from the gilt frame. Appalled, Maria shouted for Amelia. Neither of them had heard anything suspicious during the night, but they soon realized how the thieves had entered. There were no bars on the chapel windows, and they had simply forced one of the two shutters which give on to the street. The street is in fact little more than a narrow alley in the heart of old Palermo, near the docks. The door was easy to open from the inside and the thieves must have just walked away in the dead of night, leaving no trace.

Maria and Amelia rushed to phone the police, but from that day until I started looking for stolen paintings, just over ten years later, no one except the criminals had seen it. It had vanished and, apart from the Nazi lootings, had become the longest-missing old master.

Only once had anybody in official circles heard even a whisper in connection with the painting. That was a few weeks after it had been taken when word was passed to Siviero via the police in Sicily. The theft, ran the message, had been set up in return for what he had done to the Mafia over the *Ephebus* in Foligno.

ON THAT OCCASION, Siviero had used all his wiles to trick the Mafia out of a unique bronze, a statue of a boy, dating from the fifth century B.C. Known as the *Ephebus,* the statue was the only surviving example of pre-Christian Sicilian-Greek workmanship and this is what made it worth more than $1 million on the open market.

To get it back, Siviero had first obtained the cooperation of a well-known Florentine dealer, Amadeo Ricardi, who had himself sailed close to the legal wind a number of times. Siviero convinced Ricardi that it was his turn to side with the police authorities. Then Siviero's few trusted police colleagues in Palermo put out the word that Ricardi's gallery on via Lago Maggiore was not to be trusted. . . .

After a few weeks the bait was bitten, and Ricardi received a visit. A few inferior pieces were offered to him but eventually he was offered a sculpture that sounded like the *Ephebus.* However, Ricardi was genuinely infirm and so suggested that his "nephew" actually go to Sicily to see the figure and negotiate for it. The "nephew" was, of course, Siviero.

A price was agreed, as well as a venue for the exchange— Foligno, a smallish agricultural town in Umbria, near "the city of birds and silence," Assisi. Siviero's trap worked perfectly—the bronze was recovered and six arrests were made. Almost perfectly, anyway, for the old man's hand was shot through in the last-minute struggle; and, when the thieves appealed their twenty-five-year sentences, they were reduced, incredibly, to between eighteen months and four years. In a matter of months some of the gang were out of prison.

Shortly after that the Caravaggio was taken. It was the Mafia's way of exacting revenge. And this time, it was whispered, Siviero would not see the stolen work of art again. Ever.

9

Undercover in Italy

DURING THE SUMMER, my hopes had reached the point where I was certain we were on the edge of cracking the whole business. Zuccheto had smuggled the painting out of Sicily, Asaf y Bala had brought it into Mexico, Catania had been the man behind it all and might even still have the Caravaggio in Mexico, where no one thought of looking.

When I returned to New York, in the middle of October, all the court transcripts were waiting for me. There were four juicy cream-colored folders bulging with photocopies. I never read them and haven't to this day. By that time Siviero had provided us with Giuseppe Catania's date of birth. It was very disappointing. *His* Catania was about twenty years younger than the man in the files: there was no way they could be the same person. I felt naïve and stupid. A simple check had destroyed the whole edifice.

There are three ways of bearing the ills of life, said Charles Caleb Colton: "By indifference, by philosophy, and by religion." Wrong—you can also get lucky. Two days after the Catania fiasco

I was scheduled to meet Bob Volpé, to go over my "progress." By now I was itching with impatience to get back on the McGill-Naples trail, or to discover more about the New York art underworld, so I could maybe make progress there. To make matters worse a cache of important old masters worth $3 million had just been recovered in Boston. The paintings had been stolen in Maine in 1978 and included Brueghel's *Harvest,* Rembrandt's *Portrait of a Lady,* El Greco's *St. Matthew,* Van de Velde's *Salute on a Calm Sea* and Van Goyen's *River Scene with Sailing Boats.* The pictures had been just thrown on to a vacant lot because the insurance company refused to meet the thieves' demands. That meant there were now five old masters less for John Blake to recover.

Volpé and I had breakfast at a coffee shop at Eighty-second and Madison. He must have taken pity on me that morning because, after I had finished describing my disappointment, he immediately offered to introduce me to one of "his" dealers—i.e., one of the regular art dealers who not only kept a lookout for him for stolen art but occasionally played a more active role as well. The equivalent, in effect, of Andrew Purches in London. I had been anxious to make contact with someone like this for several months, ever since I had first thought up the plan to contact Vittorio Baratti, the Neapolitan dealer who had offered the Caravaggio to McGill. Two days after our coffee-shop meeting, Volpé introduced me to Robert Steffanotti.

Steffanotti may have played much the same role for Volpé as Andrew Purches had done for Scotland Yard, but there the similarity ended. Where Andrew was—well, untidy, casual and dark—Steffanotti gleamed brightly, a neat, shiny professional ensemble of fashionable suits, the latest, small-collar shirts and unusual woolen ties. His gallery, on West Fifty-seventh Street, gleamed also: it was airy and specialized in modern art and photography. After Volpé introduced us, Rob Steffanotti and I went around the block for a Japanese lunch to discuss my search in more detail. He had studied art history at Yale and knew something about Italian paintings. At one stage he had run a very big gallery but had overextended himself and gone bankrupt. He was now working his way back up the ladder again.

This was the first Japanese meal I'd ever had that I'd liked and Rob and I got on well. I had told Volpé the bones of the plan I needed Rob for—to go to Italy on our behalf—and Rob had let it be known in advance that he was interested. So we had several Japanese beers and I outlined my idea in detail.

Our central problem was to introduce John Blake to Baratti in a way that would not arouse suspicion, and there were other complications. In the first place, Blake needed an introduction to Baratti from someone Baratti knew or had had business dealings with. Second, Blake needed to know, not just about art, but about Baratti's art, the pictures he had in his gallery: Blake needed to know who they were by, who would be interested in them, what they were worth and so on. Only in that way could he appear a genuine dealer. And last, he had to be seen to be wealthy, so that Baratti would not have the slightest inkling Blake was an imposter and the Neapolitan would consider offering him an expensive painting, even one that was stolen.

The plan I had worked out, I now put to Rob. Did he know Naples? He said he knew Rome better but that he did have one good contact in a Naples art gallery. What I hoped was that Rob would go to Naples, having alerted his contact that he was coming, and contrive through this man an introduction to Baratti. We would provide Rob with a certain amount of money, enough for him to buy a small picture from Baratti, to set up a "business relationship." In visiting Baratti's gallery to view the painting and to collect it after he had bought it, Rob was also to have a good look around, find out what paintings Baratti had and what he wanted for everything. He was then to report back to me on the contents of Baratti's gallery so that when John Blake visited Naples a couple of months later he would appear properly professional.

There was one further refinement. Since the Catania fiasco we could no longer assume, as I had done over the summer, that the Caravaggio had left Sicily. Since Naples was so near to the island, we reasoned that it made sense for Rob to go on to Palermo and nose around the art dealers there. By now I had a number of other names from Siviero, including art dealers in Palermo who were believed to be less than honest and might be useful conduits to the painting. So Rob agreed to follow the same procedure and buy into a business relationship with any dealer in Sicily who appeared to be crooked and find out what else was on offer so that Blake, visiting Sicily after him, could appear knowledgeable.

We would pay Rob's fare and provide him with a sum of money to spend on works of art in Naples and in Sicily. Back in New York, he was, of course, free to sell them and keep the profit. If he bought dud pictures, he would either make a loss or not be able to move them, in which case we would both lose out. If he made good buys, he would make a profit and we would get our money back and have pushed the story forward at no net cost. It seemed as fair and sensible a deal as the circumstances would allow. Rob agreed and prepared to fly to Italy as soon as he could. However, he could not leave straightaway, and before he did a curious twist in the affair occurred that had a profound impact on our plans.

A FEW DAYS AFTER WE MET, Rob was offered several Italian paintings which, he had reason to believe, were stolen. A man, an Italian and a friend of a friend, had turned up at his gallery one morning with three color photographs. The pictures on sale, this man said, were a Raphael, a Veronese and a Pomarancio. A stolen Raphael or a Veronese were, of course, too good to miss; especially now that one of my leads to the Caravaggio had proved a dead end. I persuaded Rob not to tell Volpé for the time being but to introduce me to the people offering the pictures.

It was a Thursday morning when John Blake limped into the New York Furniture Exchange at 200 Lexington Avenue. At that time, Italcraft had showrooms on the sixteenth floor, and as Blake entered the "gallery" his footfall triggered a two-tone gong. Italcraft imported all kinds of Italian arts and crafts into the United States, mainly for use in hotels. The walls of the showroom were lined with bright, cheap paintings, heads of girls, snow-covered trees, yachts. Cheap "Venetian" glass, mock Rococo commodes with yellow lacquer, gilded and painted with flowers, and eighteenth-century writing desks, inlaid with imitation ivory, occupied the rest of the space.

Two men appeared. One, introduced as Vincent del Peschio, was fat and balding, a calm rather cheerful person. The other, Achilles Renzullo, was taller, thinner, swarthier, with a moustache and a slight stoop.

It was difficult to know who was in charge (Blake never did find out) but, after he was shown to a chair, Renzullo disappeared—"to the bank" he said—and was gone twenty minutes. Both men spoke excellent English and Blake and Del Peschio passed the time discussing Italcraft's business. The company, it appeared, brought a container into America from Italy every month loaded with pictures, lamps, glass, furniture, even carpets. Hotels bought the pictures by the score: none cost more than $25.

When Renzullo came back he had a small package under his arm, a sheet of wrinkled red and silver Christmas paper wrapped around a piece of board. Unceremoniously, he laid the package on a desk and opened it. Inside was a wooden panel nearly an inch thick and measuring no more than eighteen by twelve inches. On it was painted a small boy and the head of a lamb against what looked like the red folds of a dress. Two things struck Blake immediately. First, the painting could not possibly be a Raphael, could it? The quality of the picture was just not good enough. The figure of the boy was imperfectly drawn and the nose of the lamb was so pointed it made the animal seem almost like a goat. A second point was that the picture was obviously a fragment taken from a much larger painting. There was no sense of composition, the folds of the dress just carried on to the edge of the board and past it, so to speak. Anyone who knew anything about Christian iconography would have known that St. John (who is usually shown with a lamb) would never have been painted alone, in this way and at that age. As a young man, yes, but as a baby, no. It had to be some fragment from the bottom of a much larger picture.

In turn, this told Blake two further things. It wasn't a Raphael —that much was certain. No one in his right mind would carve up a Raphael in this way. No one would accept just the fragment as a Raphael without having some idea where the rest of the picture was. And second, all this seemed to suggest that Renzullo and Del Peschio did not know much about painting. But no sooner had Blake thought this than he realized he might be on trial. Perhaps they were testing him.

Therefore, he carefully went through the rigmarole Van Haeften had taught him a few months before at Christie's. He picked up the picture and examined it. He took out his black metal magnifying glass and looked over this "Raphael." The child's eyes were very nicely painted and he spent some time inspecting them. He wet his finger slightly with spittle and rubbed it gently over the paint. He turned the board over and looked at the edges and the back. There was nothing much to see.

This ritual completed, what to say? He paused, took out his Dunhill notebook and scribbled a few lines with his Tiffany pen. Raising his head, Blake said, "It's not a Raphael."

"It is!" they chorused as one. "It is. We can get documentation." Over the next few months, Del Peschio and Renzullo particularly would say of any number of paintings that they could "get documentation." This seemed to Blake only to underline further that this outfit wasn't especially honest: no amount of documentation could make a bad painting good and it was widely known that some academics were only too willing to sell "authorizations" about a picture, especially in Italy.

This wasn't too encouraging. On the other hand, the more he thought about it, the more it seemed to Blake that Italcraft was a perfect front for an art-smuggling operation. It was, to begin with, a legitimate concern, doing plenty of business. It would be no problem to slip a valuable painting in among all the modern rubbish it was importing by the containerload every month. And these two men, Del Peschio and Renzullo, could be just the front men. The real villains might be back in Italy, in safety.

There was silence in the small room as Blake thought. They were watching him.

"When do you say this was painted?" he said.

"In 1517."

Luckily Blake could remember Raphael's dates. "Three years before his death . . ." Renzullo nodded. "It's not good enough to be a later Raphael—and it's just a fragment in any case."

They shook their heads, disbelieving. More silence.

"You know Raphael was widely forged during the seventeenth century?"

They looked at him, saying nothing.

"Terenzi, who came from Urbino like Raphael, was caught trying to pass off one of his *Madonnas*. But others got into circulation."

I was impressing myself but the other two still said nothing.

"Anthing else?" Blake said at length.

They shook their heads. "Nothing here. Only photographs," said Renzullo.

"May I see?"

They looked at each other, a bit shiftily now. Which one *was* the boss?

Renzullo opened a drawer and pulled out a paper bag. Inside were three color photographs, which he handed to Blake. One showed a man in a red robe holding a staff and looking up. A light was shining on his face. The man looked well drawn, but again it seemed like a fragment, as if the subject was a soldier or a saint at the Crucifixion, looking up at Christ.

"It's a Veronese," Renzullo said.

Another big name, but again Blake was instinctively skeptical. It was so obviously a fragment. The other two, it was claimed, were a Zuccaro and a Pomarancio. Unlike the "Raphael," these paintings were not in New York but still in Italy. There was, however, "no problem" in getting them to America. This was interesting because, if the paintings were real, Renzullo, Del Peschio and their friends were breaking Italian law. Such paintings could be exported only with the government's permission, and in the case of a Raphael, a Veronese or Zuccaro, this permission would almost certainly not be given. Either the Italcraft people were dealing in fakes, of one sort or another, or they were smugglers.

Blake didn't stay much longer but limped away, promising to "think it over." He took the photographs with him.

THE FIRST THING I DID was to give Renzullo's name and Del Peschio's, and Italcraft's, to Charles Koscka at customs to see if they had criminal records or associations. "Negative," came the disappointing reply.

Meanwhile, Rob's plans were coming along. He had decided to go to Rome first. He had colleagues there who could provide him with introductions in Naples and, we hoped, he could get himself plausibly introduced to Baratti through that network.

But Rob couldn't go to Italy until after Christmas, and by this time Blake had had quite a few dealings with Renzullo and Del Peschio at Italcraft. They had what seemed like an inexhaustible supply of paintings—though most of them were not very good. Colored photographs turned up at their showroom almost weekly. Blake's aim at this point was to keep the Italians interested—but at arm's length. A plan was beginning to form in his mind, but it required Steffanotti to go to Naples and Sicily first.

Blake went back to London. He told Renzullo it was for the November sales, the other big event of the art year. He called Italcraft from London, just to maintain contact and to make it seem he was an international figure to whom the cost of a transatlantic phone call mattered hardly at all. Blake also kept them interested by saying that he was planning a trip to Italy in the not-too-distant future and hoped then to travel to Parma, where their contact appeared to be. Blake could then look at their cache of paintings for himself.

The November sales came and went without Blake "buying." We could not go through the same elaborate subterfuge we had employed in the late spring and early summer. In any case, the object of our deceit had been attained. I didn't want to bump into McGill again and my attention had now shifted from the art world in general to Baratti and Italcraft in particular. This time a different pretense was used to convince Renzullo and Del Peschio that Blake was a wealthy man.

With the help of a printer friend, George Darker, a fake newspaper clipping was made to represent the "Court and Social" page of the London *Times*. On this page—alongside a diary of events attended by the Queen—are shown betrothals, religious and university news, and salesroom news. The fake cutting took some real university news (new professorships mainly) and church appointments and juxtaposed near them a short article, by-lined "By Our Salesroom Correspondent" and headed "Six Figure Sum Paid for Del Sarto 'Sacrifice.'" The article reported in passing that a Mr. A. J. Blake had spent £110,000 on Andrea del Sarto's *Sacrifice of Abraham* at the previous day's sale at Sotheby's. Interviewed after the sale, Mr. Blake was quoted as saying that the picture would go to a client of his in Los Angeles after it had been cleaned in London. A photocopy of this clipping was then sent to Steffanotti, together with a covering note on fake headed notepaper as if from a friend of Steffanotti's in London. (The photocopy got around the problem that there was nothing on the reverse side of our fake clipping as there should have been if it was real.) Steffanotti passed it on, in a gossipy way, to Italcraft.

When Blake subsequently called Renzullo, again to keep in

contact, the Italian congratulated him on his purchases at Sotheby's. Blake pretended to be mystified as to how Renzullo had received this intelligence—and the Italian smugly refused to tell Blake what he already knew. But it appeared that Renzullo had believed the deception and had no doubts about Blake's worth.

Christmas came and went. The fifty American hostages were being held in Iran and Ayatollah Khomeini was threatening to "try" them. Lord Soames was governor of Rhodesia, soon to become an independent Zimbabwe. Starvation in Kampuchea had become an issue. Steffanotti left for Rome in the second week of January. He would be gone for over two weeks, and while he was away Blake let it be known to the Italians on Lexington Avenue that he was very keen to visit Italy soon so that he could look at the canvases they had on offer.

By now, in his conversations with them, Blake had also begun to introduce the notion that he was less than honest. Whenever he could, without making it too obvious, he made it known that he didn't care where a painting came from, as long as he got a good price for it. In return, Renzullo and Del Peschio made it clear that they could deliver works wherever Blake wanted them: New York, London, Marseilles, Mexico—he only had to name it. It was clear they were accomplished in the transportation of artworks. Whether what they had on offer in Italy was stolen or faked—well, that remained to be seen.

When Steffanotti returned from Italy, he had a lot to say—and one or two surprises. Rob had started in Rome, where he knew a stamp dealer. This man had referred Rob to a prince and a count in Naples. When in Naples a couple of days later, Rob had been invited to a cocktail party at the count's and there, to his delight, had met Baratti—the man we were after. He and Rob got on very well and Rob was invited to Baratti's house to look at his paintings.

The gossip on Baratti in Naples was encouraging too. According to the prince and others, Baratti was mixed up in all sorts of shady goings-on, and was believed to be a member of the local *camorra*, the Naples version of the Mafia.

Rob didn't see anything he wanted at Baratti's, but he did see two pictures that Blake might like later, on his trip. They were still lifes, one of fish, the other of birds—pigeons. They were small oils, nicely done in plenty of color and they had been recently cleaned. The irony was that Baratti claimed they were by Cara-vaggio. It wasn't true, of course, but it was a nice try. He wanted $25,000 for the pair. Rob thought they were worth it and that he could make a reasonable profit on them if he sold them in New York. He didn't mention Blake to the Neapolitan, of course.

Baratti also told Rob quite openly that he could "negotiate" the "export" of any painting he wanted. As we have seen, this is illegal in Italy—so it was an admission by the Italian that he would carry out illegal acts.

That night Rob caught the ferry from Naples to Sicily. In Palermo, he stayed at the Villa d'Igeia, one of Europe's most in-teresting hotels. It is an elaborate, flamboyant building, overlook-ing the Mediterranean, an old edifice of pillars and arches fes-tooned with greenery like something out of a Guardi or a Tiepolo *capriccio*.

In Sicily Rob did not discover any more links along the Cara-vaggio trail, but he did buy five photographs, pictures of young, naked boys posing among the Greek ruins of the island. They were the work of the German homosexual photographer Baron von Gloeden. When Rob returned to New York I had to admit he had done his job well—save for those pictures. I was by no means certain I wanted the project associated with such "art." I was therefore anxious for Rob to sell the photographs as soon as possi-ble. However, he said he wanted to hold on to the pictures for a few months, to give them time to appreciate; he seemed confident he could make money on them, so I had to admit that made sense. Besides, we had the rest of the plan to be going on with.

WHILE ROB HAD BEEN AWAY, I had been thinking about John Blake in Italy. In order to approach Baratti in Naples about the Caravaggio, Blake would first have to do business with him. It occurred to me that since Renzullo and Del Peschio were always bragging about how easy it was for them to transport pictures out of Italy, it might be an idea to pay them to smuggle the prelimi-nary painting I hoped to buy from Baratti. That way the Neapoli-tan would think I was well organized and at least a bit corrupt. Renzullo and Del Peschio would see that I really did have con-tacts in Italy. And, provided I could keep within my budget,

Blake would have done business with both. That might lead to the Caravaggio via Baratti, or other stolen paintings via Italcraft.

Renzullo and Del Peschio were pressing Blake to go to Italy, to look at the paintings they had on offer there, but it seemed somewhat risky to meet *both* the New York Italians and Baratti on the first trip. If Blake had to introduce Baratti to Renzullo, I wanted the latter to think that Blake already knew the Neapolitan. That way Renzullo would think Blake a regular visitor to Italy and familiar with Italian dealers. Also, I had no idea how long negotiations with Baratti would take and it struck me as obvious that if I seemed in a hurry, as I might appear if my "transporters" were in town, that would affect the price he would try to exact from me. Besides, natural prudence made it seem sensible to check out the setting before the crucial part of our plan was put into effect. Tedious as it seemed, I decided that Blake must pay a visit to Mr. Baratti *before* the trip to meet Renzullo's colleagues. Though it was expensive to fly to Naples just for this trip, it had to be done.

Just before Blake left for Italy, in March, Rob wrote to Baratti telling him how much he had enjoyed meeting him, and thanking him for his contacts in Sicily who, he said, had sold him "five works." He added that he hoped to find a buyer in New York for Baratti's still-life Caravaggios, but, meanwhile, he was introducing a friend of his (Blake), a dealer from London who would soon be in Naples. Steffanotti wrote that he had done a lot of business with Blake, who was interested mainly in seventeenth-century paintings.

A week after I judged Baratti had received Rob's letter, Blake telephoned Naples from London. This was ostensibly to make initial contact but also to check how well Baratti spoke English (Rob had said it was "passable"), and whether he would be in Naples the following week. Blake, trying not to appear too deliberate, said he would be in Naples on one of three days. Baratti said he would be expecting him.

I didn't fly straight to Naples but stopped off in Rome to see Siviero again. At this stage he was against the way our project was proceeding. He still wished we had used a real dealer for the whole deception. There seemed no way of convincing him that it couldn't be done. We met for coffee at his offices just off the Piazza Venezia. He said that he knew about Baratti—that is, he had heard of him on his travels in Naples, would not be surprised if he had Mafia connections, but could add nothing to that. It was my plan to go on to Sicily, since I was so close, to at least make contact with the handful of dealers in Palermo. Siviero said he had his suspicions about two of them—and he gave me their names. Rob had heard stories about one of these dealers, too.

I arrived in Naples by train. From time to time we had given some thought to the question of whether Blake would be followed, and although we never took this really seriously we did take some precautions. This was one reason why I had not flown directly to Naples—there are only a few flights from London every week and it would have been easy to pick up Blake at Naples' airport and follow him from there, had anyone wished to do so. Blake wasn't expected at Rome, and there were many more flights anyway. There are, of course, trains from Rome to Naples almost hourly, so it would have been extremely unlikely for anyone to bother to tail Blake from the Naples' railway station.

Blake had to stay in one of the best hotels in town, so I chose the Excelsior, which overlooks the bay and the Castel dell'Ovo. Once settled, I called Baratti and arranged to visit him at eleven o'clock the next morning.

It was a beautiful day as the taxi drove up the Posillipo hill to the west of the city center. Blake was dressed in his usual double-breasted English suit, striped English shirt, dark, spotted bow tie—and was carrying a black cane. He was very noticeable in the Neapolitan sunshine. To get to Baratti's apartment I had to scramble down a path under some trees. He met me outside his door. Sporting a heavy beard and long hair, he wore a navy-blue double-breasted blazer, white shirt and striped tie.

Baratti greeted me warmly and took me inside. After the glare of the bright sun, it took my eyes a while to adjust to the gloomy interior. When I did I could see that it was crowded with works of art. Like many dealers the world over, Baratti worked from home. He no doubt found it profitable not to have a shop but to deal only with other professionals who knew what they wanted. That meant he would rarely make a *coup* but that he had a steady trade with people who came to him for specific things.

In his hallway Baratti had sculpture, oils, bric-a-brac, icons, medals and small pieces of china. To my untutored eye most of it seemed junk—coarse, shabby, often incomplete fragments. However, I took my time. I couldn't afford to miss anything and I didn't want him to think that I was interested only in two particular paintings. I took out my Dunhill notebook and my silver Tiffany pen and began to make notes.

The next room was better. It was a small sitting room with a number of small oils on the walls. These were of much better quality, especially one, a *modello* of a madonna and child and, next to it, a still life of apples and flowers. I spent some time looking at these, using the tips Johnny van Haeften had taught me: I rubbed my finger over the pictures with a little spittle on it to see what it might look like if cleaned; I looked behind the *modello* for what I could find.

After a suitable interval, I looked at Baratti and smiled. He then showed me through into his main room, a long narrow dining area which gave out onto the terrace overlooking the sea. Here, high up, were two still lifes, one of fish, the other of birds. The "Caravaggios"—he still had them.

I allowed my eyes to widen as I recognized these pictures and indicated that I woud like a closer look. Baratti, whose English was not as good as Rob had said and only a little better than my Italian, pointed to the terrace. I followed him out and he showed me to a bench. It was by now eleven-thirty and the sunshine was piercing. On the terrace, however, it was interrupted by a huge vine and a few pieces of broken sculpture. The view was marvelous and Baratti invited me to sit while he went to fetch the pictures. He brought them out and placed them at the foot of a sculpture. He then disappeared again.

It was clear that both pictures had been cleaned recently. The features of the animals were clear and the backgrounds, though dark, were distinguishable as the interiors of shops. Books and planks and drapery were all evident. The paintings were horizontal oblongs and not large, say eighteen inches by two feet. They were not framed.

Baratti reappeared, this time with a bottle of wine and two glasses. He arranged a chair next to me and opened the bottle—it was an Italian sparkling wine, every bit as delicious as champagne. We sat with the paintings at our feet, overlooking the Bay of Naples, the wine by our elbows. Only then did he say softly, "Caravaggio." Baratti certainly knew how to do business. I expressed my surprise, saying they did not appear to be in Caravaggio's style, and that, so far as I knew, Caravaggio had never painted fish or birds in his still lifes, but only fruit and flowers. Baratti was insistent, however, and went on about some Italian authority who had said that Caravaggio had painted many still lifes that were no longer attributed to him. He pointed out the lighting effects, saying that the use of chiaroscuro was in Caravaggio's style. This was a stroke of luck for me since I was then able to say that in the Friedlander *catalogue raisonné*, the accepted authority on Caravaggio, there were only sixty-six accepted works, and that these two were not among them. He shrugged, as if to say "Take it or leave it." But I was scoring points.

I finished my wine; he refilled the glass. Then I got up and went back into the room to look at some of the other paintings. I had him bring three other canvases out into the sunshine, a tavern scene, a weak *Conversion of St. Paul* and a *St. John the Baptist* as a young man, the latter two pictures by unknown painters of the Neapolitan school. Baratti had by then put the "Caravaggios" back in the dining room, but I made him bring them out again for a second look.

Only now did I ask the price: $25,000, he said, for the pair. So he hadn't come down since Rob had visited him. On the other hand, neither had he increased his price.

I said that I wanted time to think about it, that I was leaving for Rome the next day and suggested meeting at my hotel that evening to carry on our discussions. This was intended to do a number of things. First, I wanted to get him to the Excelsior to rub in how wealthy I was; second, I wanted to put him off the track because in fact I was headed for Palermo that night on the ferry from Naples—an easy way to be followed; and third, I hoped he would think I wanted him on my home ground, as it were, to do business. He said he had a dinner date that night, but could come around beforehand—at, say, seven o'clock. Since the ferry left at ten, this was ideal. He telephoned for a taxi and I left.

That evening Baratti and I met in the Excelsior bar. I had by then considered my plan carefully. My long-term aim, of course, was to return some weeks later, buy a picture from Baratti and then have the New York Italians smuggle it to Manhattan for me. That way I could establish a business relationship with Baratti *and* with Renzullo and Del Peschio. So I didn't actually want to buy anything on this, our first meeting, but I did want to make him think of me as a real businessman.

What I planned was to make him an offer for his two "Caravaggio" still lifes but it would be an offer he would turn down. That is to say, I would make him a very low offer—just high enough to be credible but low enough for him to be certain to refuse it, even after I had increased it in a (sham) effort to bargain. In this way a business relationship of sorts would have been established and, although no money would have changed hands, I could come back to him again. There was also the possibility that, when he saw I was not going to be beaten up in negotiations just because I had come a long way and didn't want to return empty-handed, he would respect me more and, the next time around, might be more accommodating in his prices.

So, after we had settled with a drink (as I recall, he drank scotch that night), I made my offer. Since he was asking for $25,000, I reasoned that he might settle for $20,000, just possibly $18,000. My top offer, therefore, was going to be around $16,000, safely below what I thought he would accept. And so I started at $12,500, exactly half what he was asking.

He simply shook his head at this and laughed, as if to say "You are being ridiculous." He took a drink.

It was in my interest to keep things moving slowly, so I lifted my briefcase onto the low table between us and opened it. Inside were many pictures of paintings, mainly by Italian artists, that I had been given by our dealers in London, and which I now pretended I had bought in Rome and other Italian cities. They were just lying in my briefcase underneath the pictures of his Caravaggio still lifes, which he had let me have that morning. I now started to examine these once more.

After a while I "allowed" myself to be driven up to $14,000. Again he shook his head and again he took a drink. I ordered more whiskey (I was drinking scotch, too) and noticed that he had acquired a fairly fixed smile on his face, and a somewhat distant look in his eyes. When people make an effort to appear relaxed and smiling, they are usually tense inside. I judged that Baratti was preparing to lower his price the next time I raised mine.

I waited until the drink had arrived and then obliged. "$16,000," I said.

He pursed his lips, still smiling, inclined his head to one side and said, "$23,000."

As far as I was concerned, of course, my objective had been completed. Even in haggling once, we had a relationship. Baratti would remember me, would remember that I had managed, by however little, to negotiate with him, to beat him down a bit. All I had to do now was make sure we didn't end up with a deal.

I shook my head, not realizing then what a mistake I was making. I had misjudged the psychological balance of the negotiation because I took my time over my next offer, and just as I was about to say $17,000," Baratti spoke again: "$22,000."

We were getting a little close for comfort. And Baratti had been very clever. In conceding when he had, he had achieved two things: in the first place, it was now once again my turn to give way; second, we were now close enough for a deal to look possible. To begin with, when I had offered $14,000 and we had been $11,000 apart, I could have offered a small increase—$500, say—safe in the knowledge that either he would agree to a real bargain for me or we would still be miles apart whatever concession he made. But now I would have to increase my offer by at least $1,000. We were in a serious negotiation and anything less would look suspicious. An experienced bargainer would know that, in my position, I had to offer just enough to entice the other person down. I was, effectively, trapped; and, it seemed, in danger of acquiring these paintings for a price I couldn't afford.

I had no choice. "$17,000," I said. If he came down to $20,000, I was in real trouble. In proper negotiations dealers who are only $3,000 apart can always work something out.

I was growing tense and had begun to chew on the inside of my cheek. But now Baratti behaved curiously. Instead of coming down to $20,000 and therefore making a deal of around $18,000 to $19,000 virtually certain, he must have judged that I wanted to buy the pictures far more than he wanted to sell—because he now came down by only $500, to $21,500.

If it was his intention to force me up to $20,000 and above, he could not have been more wrong. His miserly drop was an invitation to me to stick at $17,000.

Of course, it may have been that he had thought I was beating him down too much and he was trying to put me off; but I don't think so, because after another pause, and more of his forced smiles, he came down again, by another $500, to $21,000.

But, just as a moment before I had suddenly found myself in a real negotiation despite my intention to avoid it, now the chemistry between us had gone. Whereas we had once been in contact with each other, giving and taking, now we were as far apart as we had been at the start. I was off the hook and I felt perfectly safe in sticking at $17,000. Baratti sensed the change, too, for he sat back, took another drink and visibly relaxed. He had made up his mind that $21,000 was his limit and he now knew no deal was possible that night.

From my point of view, of course, it had been an invaluable, if nerve-racking, fifteen minutes. We had made real business contact even though no money had changed hands.

We sat for a moment without speaking. I then looked at my watch to suggest that our meeting did not have long to go but added, "Signor Baratti, I expect to be back in Naples in a few weeks. I may call upon you?"

"But of course . . . I look forward . . . Now, I must go."

We stood and shook hands. "Good-bye, Mr. Blake. Till next . . ." I watched him weave his way through the lobby into the street outside and into his car, a somewhat rickety Renault. I sat down again, exhausted. There was just time for another whiskey before I had to leave for the Palermo ferry.

IN PALERMO I FOUND THE ORATORIO SAN LORENZO. It was locked, but I persuaded the caretaker woman to allow me in. The place smelled of wood and damp, and was altogether depressing. Recovery suddenly seemed much further away. I flew back to London via Milan in a much more sober mood than when I had left Naples.

BACK IN LONDON my bleak mood persisted. A Van Dyck, a *Holy Family with St. Anne and an Angel*, had been stolen from Imperia, in Italy; no fewer than twenty-five paintings by Joan Miró had disappeared from a collection in Paris, and Lucas Cranach's famous picture of *Lucretia*, the one in which she wears nothing but a dagger and a necklace, had gone from Stockholm. Two

Teniers had been taken in London, and four Dalis from Barcelona. Five very valuable old masters had been taken from the Palace Museum in Gotha, East Germany, including Holbein's *St. Catherine*, Jan Brueghel's *Life on a Country Road*, yet another Van Dyck, a *Self-portrait* and Frans Hals' *Portrait of an Old Man*. (I also learned, with interest, that two paintings by Lothar Malksrat, the German who had faked the Lübeck saints, had been stolen from Kampen, in West Germany. There was a kind of justice in that.) The world's art thieves were as busy as ever, but John Blake, it seemed to me, was missing all the action.

On the other hand, a Tintoretto looted from the Dresden art gallery during World War Two had turned up in New York, where it was seized by FBI agents. The painting, entitled *Holy Family with St. Catherine and a Donor*, had allegedly been exported from Russia by a family emigrating to Israel. A Tel Aviv art dealer, Rajmond Vinokur, had offered it in Europe (unsuccessfully) before bringing it to New York, where he had also had difficulty in passing it off until he was led to an undercover agent. . . . John Blake had missed yet another masterpiece, but at least they were still coming out of the woodwork, and being recovered. That revived my spirits a little.

I had been back in London a few days when Renzullo rang. He said he was going to Milan in a few weeks and asked if I could join him there. He had several paintings to show me, he said, including a Bassano, a Tintoretto and a pair of Magnascos. No, he didn't have photographs, I would have to travel there to see them for myself. This was getting frighteningly expensive. If the paintings were real, especially the Bassano and the Tintoretto, the chances were that they would have been stolen—and that might be relatively easy to check. The memory of the Dresden Tintoretto was fresh in my mind, of course. I said I would call back.

I consulted my lists of stolen art. In this case the Carabinieri's *Bollettino*, volume 4 (for 1974) and 7 (for 1977), produced the goods. The earlier volume recorded that a *Portrait of a Man*, a large oil on canvas and possibly by Tintoretto, had been stolen from a private house at Oderzo, near Treviso, on 20 November 1973. The portrait showed a bearded, broad-shouldered nobleman with closely cropped hair and with fur edging on his robe. The same bulletin also recorded that a medium-sized canvas by Jacopo da Ponte, known as Bassano, and entitled *The Presen-*

tation of Jesus in the Temple, had been stolen, also from a private home, at San Remo, near Imperia, on 17 July 1974. This was a busy painting, with many figures and angels clustered around the infant Jesus, who lay on a swaddling cloth in the center. The later bulletin recorded another Bassano, *Il ricco Epulone* [The Rich Feaster, from Luke 16], as stolen from a private house at Lesmo, near Milan, on 12 November 1976. This, too, was a large busy picture with musicians, pets and the remains of what looks like a most enjoyable party. There were four Bassano painters, over three generations, but the second-generation Jacopo da Ponte, known as Jacopo Bassano, was the best. He was a pupil of Bonifazio's in Venice in the early 1520s. The figures in his paintings are robust and stocky and I had learned that he usually painted at least one of them with the soles of his or her feet toward the spectator, as a kind of trade mark, which is very helpful to art historians.

Bassano lived quite a few years before Caravaggio, but his technique and his use of ordinary people, light and shade were so similar to the later painter that I could claim an interest in him.

Other thoughts struck me: both Bassano and Tintoretto had strong links with Venice; and all the paintings were taken from homes in northern Italy, not a million miles from Milan, where I was supposed to meet Renzullo. I wondered to myself whether the "gang," if there was one, specialized in stealing Venetian paintings from private houses. Perhaps that *modus operandi* might give Siviero a clue as to whose brain was behind the thefts.

Since my research seemed so hopeful, I phoned Renzullo back after three or four days and said I was prepared to meet him in Milan. I was excited but played down my feelings on the phone.

We arranged a rendezvous for the third Sunday in April, at noon, in the foyer of the Milan Hilton. (At this, my mind went back to that gang who had been arrested in 1977 for passing off thousands of fakes. They had always operated from luxury hotels in northern Italy.) I said that I would be flying out from London on the Sunday morning but in fact I took the elementary precaution of traveling on the Saturday and staying elsewhere in Milan overnight—just in case anybody was thinking of tailing me.

Sunday was a beautiful sunny day. We met as arranged. Renzullo had two men with him, one who would do the driving and another, called Giancarlo, who was a small, fair man with angular

features, several broken veins in his cheeks and who, in Alexander Chase's words, treated the whole world as though it was an
ashtray. Despite his "rough" appearance, it appeared at that
stage that this man ran the Italian end of the operation. He did
not speak English and, in fact, never appeared as cosmopolitan as
Renzullo.

We all climbed into a green Citroën and drove south, out of
Milan. We headed for a small town outside Parma called Sorbolo.
This journey revealed yet another example of the hidden dangers
of the project. Renzullo may not have known as much about art
as Giancarlo, but even he knew that Parma was the home of Correggio. I didn't. At least not then, and it was a matter of luck that
my ignorance wasn't exposed. A real art dealer, of course, would
have known all about Correggio, how he was a pupil of Mantegna, influenced strongly by Andrea del Sarto, and how the ceiling of the dome in Parma cathedral, which Correggio decorated
with concentric circles of flying figures, was the subject of a celebrated sixteenth-century joke when a local canon described it as
"a hash of frogs' legs."

"You bargain as well as Correggio, eh, Mr. Blake?" said Renzullo at one point.

I just nodded and looked away, chewing my cheek. I had not
the faintest idea what he was on about.

But I made sure I did my homework on the subject as soon as I
returned to London, where I found out that Correggio was a notorious miser who actually dropped dead while carting his money
himself from one bank to another. I also made a mental note that,
on all future trips to Italy, I would find out in advance which
towns I would be visiting and research the art history of these
areas so as not to risk being caught out again.

It took about two hours to reach Sorbolo and I was grateful
that, when we did, our first port of call was a restaurant for
lunch. Since Sorbolo cannot be more than four or five miles from
Parma, it was no surprise that we were served Parma ham. What
was a surprise, however, was the quality. Although the restaurant
was clean and friendly, there was no outward sign that its food
was so wonderful. But the ham that day was, quite simply, out of
this world. I have eaten Parma ham in many restaurants in
Europe and North America, but nothing has even approached
what we ate that day.

From the restaurant we all went to Giancarlo's apartment. There he had four paintings for me to see. The first was the alleged Veronese, the photograph of which I had seen in New York. This was much less impressive in the flesh, as it were, than in Kodachrome, and I was even more suspicious when I saw scribbled on the back of one of the photos of this picture in Giancarlo's flat the figure "1500." Veronese was born in 1528.

Giancarlo would not accept my view that the Veronese was a fragment and we moved on quickly to the next picture. This was the *Portrait of a Gentleman* by Bassano. To me this painting looked more like the Tintoretto in the *Bollettino*. The man, bearded with closely cropped hair, faced to the left of the picture, but was extremely well drawn, forceful and lifelike. It was just how I recalled the Tintoretto except that at the top left of the picture were some folds of what looked like a curtain. This was unusual in such a painting, did not exist in the *Bollettino*'s reproduction of the stolen Tintoretto and I suspected that the folds had been painted on more recently to hide something.

In portraits of this kind it was usual to have a window in the background showing a landscape or animals, or even a motto or a coat of arms, something that would help identify the person portrayed. I suspected that this had been covered over in the present case to make such identification harder. If the motto of the man's family were shown it would be that much easier to identify him and, through that, to check the whereabouts of the original and verify whether or not Giancarlo's picture was real, and stolen, or a copy.

I said none of this, of course. Giancarlo's wife had by now brought us some sticky sweet Italian wine and, as is the Italian fashion, everybody was talking to everybody else. The "Bassano" looked like it might be a "disguised" Tintoretto. My pulse raced with excitement—I would check out the painting as soon as I was back in London.

The next picture was a small, early (fifteenth century) oil of the Ferrara school, showing Christ holding a cross and bleeding from a wound in his chest, the blood spurting conveniently into a golden chalice on the ground. It was ensconced in an elaborately carved wooden frame and had, to my eyes, a kind of awkward beauty. However, I recalled to myself how widespread was the faking of Italian primitives, and since it was the wrong period for my alleged interest in sixteenth- and seventeenth-century works, I passed quickly on.

The final work I was shown at Giancarlo's was either a major *coup* for me or an audacious attempt to con me. It was, they said in all seriousness, a drawing, or *bozzetto,* by Leonardo da Vinci himself, a preliminary sketch for his famous *Entombment* in the Vatican. The saints stood around the sarcophagus in various attitudes of wonder, sadness and piety.

Now this picture was, in its way, a good example of how an art dealer, on his travels, may find it difficult to arrive at a judgment. Clearly, the chances were much against the *bozzetto* being by Leonardo da Vinci. In the first place it was an unknown work. It was plausible perhaps that the master had made a preliminary sketch, but this one was incomplete and much smaller than the painting itself. (I had a vague recollection from my reading that Leonardo's cartoons, or sketches, tended to be full-size.) Second, I could not be exactly sure what material this *bozzetto* was on— and, of course, nobody would let me take it away to be analyzed to see if the paper conformed to sixteenth-century standards. Then there was the fact that many of the outlines appeared to have been touched up; the pencil line did not appear to have faded and fuzzed in the same way as the rest of the picture. I assumed it was pencil because that's what I was told it was. Yet I knew from Kurz's book that graphite (the "lead" in pencils) had not been invented until the middle of the sixteenth century—and Leonardo had died in 1519. Finally. Why me? If it *was* an unknown Da Vinci, Giancarlo and Renzullo could do no better than to auction it. They would become millionaires.

I asked them. "Two reasons," said Renzullo. "We are, of course, not absolutely certain it is by the master himself. But even if it is, the Italian Government would never allow it out of Italy. We would much rather have a quiet sale to someone who will 'export' it himself." They were asking half a million dollars.

I was by now 99 percent certain that this picture was a fake but . . . you never know. I took the photographs I was offered and said I would research the *bozzetto* before deciding what to do. (I would, of course, show them to Siviero as soon as I could.)

That was all there was to see at Giancarlo's. I had been offered two pictures allegedly by first-class artists, both probably fake, though one might just have been "disguised." I was learning how the illegal traffic in international art operates.

However, the day wasn't over yet. We left in the Citroën for another address, on the outskirts of Parma. This was both a flat and a workshop and again I was shown four paintings. One, which showed peasants singing and playing the fiddle and an early form of guitar, was supposed to be by Honthorst, a seventeenth-century master of the Utrecht school who, because of his night scenes, was nicknamed "Gherardo delle Notti." Another, showing the Holy Family, was attributed to Cristofaro Roncalli, better known as Il Pomarancio. (Oddly enough Roncalli was one of only three painters contemporary with Caravaggio of whom the latter spoke well. Their good relations didn't last though and when Roncalli beat Caravaggio in a competition to decorate the Casa Santa in Loreto, Il Pomarancio soon had his face slashed with a knife. Caravaggio was, of course, suspected.) The third picture was alleged to be by the Le Nain brothers and showed an old woman with a young girl. These three looked to be, on the surface, perfectly good paintings. True, the features on the Honthorst were somewhat coarse, but not, I would have said, seriously so. The pictures were also useful from my point of view because both Honthorst and the Le Nain brothers are regarded as late disciples of Caravaggio. I couldn't say much about Honthorst, and less still about Pomarancio, but I was more hopeful about the Le Nain.

There were three Le Nain brothers: Antoine, Louis and Mathieu. All three were elected members of the Academy in France at its inception (in 1648) but the problem with their pictures is that although fifteen are signed, *none* of the signatures has an initial. The small paintings, often on copper with tiny figures in bold colors, are usually attributed to Antoine; the larger, grayer paintings of peasants are ascribed to Louis and the rest to Mathieu. Louis' pictures are generally looked upon as the best, artistically, which was fortunate from my point of view since what I was being offered was clearly a large picture, of peasants.

I was also fortunate in that I was able to lead the conversation about the Caravaggisti—the Honthorst and the Le Nains— smoothly on to Caravaggio himself. This suited the plot perfectly and I underlined to Renzullo, Giancarlo and the new man, whose apartment we were now in and whose name for some reason I

was not told, how interested I was in Caravaggio himself, and
how I would pay a great deal for any painting of his. I didn't
dwell on this, but merely said I had clients who were particularly
interested in Caravaggio because they thought he was under-
rated and that the value of his paintings would increase more
than others.

I then took the initiative, as I was learning to do, and moved
on to the fourth painting. This was the largest in the room and, in
my opinion, the best (though the Le Nain was good, too).

This picture showed two people—a bulky older man and a
younger male figure to the right of the composition. They were
both seated at a table and the older man was wearing a beret and
holding a piece of paper in his hand; the younger one had a quill
pen. There was something vaguely familiar about the piece of
paper, but, for the moment anyway, I couldn't place it. In the
background to the right could be seen some trees and to the left—
some folds of cloth. Once again, I had the feeling that there was
something disguised by those folds. Renzullo said that this painting was the Tintoretto, in this case, Domenico, son of the more
famous Jacopo and, in Johnny van Haeften's words, "the wrong
little dyer."

The gentleman whose name I didn't know said, when I asked
him, that he had bought the painting at auction in Milan three
years before.

And that was it. Renzullo said they would send me a photograph of the "Tintoretto" and we then drove back to the Milan
Hilton at breakneck speed. I managed to doze for a while—it had
been a hard day being someone else—but between dozes I spent
the time talking to Renzullo. It was clear that I was now regarded very much as a bona fide art dealer. Besides that newspaper clipping, they had, after all, seen me in New York and Italy
and spoken to me on the phone in London. During the journey
Renzullo said that he would like me to meet a colleague of his
who looked after the "transshipment of objects from Italy to New
York." This was the opening I was looking for, but I didn't want
to seem too keen. I said I had my own method of shipping works
out but that it was growing unreliable and sloppy and that I
might well wish to meet Renzullo's colleague in the not-too-distant future. "But no hurry," I concluded. "Let's do some business
first."

They wanted to know if they could give me a lift to the airport, but the last flight to London had left. I had anticipated this and had booked into my hotel for two nights. I didn't want them to know that and instead said that I wished to be dropped at the railway station. I had a girl friend who was half-expecting me and would meet me there in reply to a phone call. I told them I had to be careful because she was married. They accepted this and at about 8:30 that night dropped me at the main Milan station. I pretended to make a call, drank a welcome beer in the station bar and took a taxi back to my hotel. The next day I returned to England.

As soon as I got back to London, I checked the "Bassano" against the missing Tintoretto (it was already obvious that I had not been offered either of the Bassanos listed as stolen in the *Bollettino*). No luck. The paintings were very similar, so similar that I spent several hours in the Witt Library going carefully through all of Tintoretto's portraits. The men in the two paintings could have been brothers but there was no trace of the Parma picture in the Witt files. Disappointed, I began to research the other paintings.

I had no better luck there either. There was just no sign of the "Pomerancio," the "Honthorst," the "Le Nain" or the small Christ of the Ferrara school, either in the Witt or in any of my stolen art records. I began to suspect that the pictures were not copies but the work of minor artists in the style of the masters to whom the paintings had been attributed. If that were the case, the chances were that the pictures I had been offered were not stolen and that the Italians were merely trying to pass off as "first-league" works paintings that were much less good.

The "Tintoretto," the double portrait, was a different matter—and threw a great deal more light on the transaction. Renzullo had kept his word and sent a photo. I had no luck in the Domenico Tintoretto file in the Witt so I turned back to his father, Jacopo. He had several box files to himself, including one given over entirely to "double and group portraits." Although there were a great many paintings that were similar to the one I had been offered, "mine" wasn't there. I was also able to check in

The Complete Works of Tintoretto, published by Rizzoli in Milan. The picture wasn't a Tintoretto—at least not a known one.

But there was *something* familiar about it. My art scholarship was, of course, fairly rudimentary even by this time but . . . it was that piece of paper. The paper being held by the older of the two men had been folded and was now opened out—the crease lines showed clearly. I had seen a piece of paper creased just like that in another painting: could it be by the same painter?

The first difficulty was to trace the other painting. Here again the Witt came in handy. I had noticed, going through the files, that there were many cross-references to other artists. More pictures than you would think have multiple attributions. In the Tintoretto files there were cross-references to Bassano, Paris Bordone and Titian. I began, therefore, to look through books on these artists' works. Unfortunately, I did it alphabetically, starting with Bassano. Although I had gone through his files recently, I hadn't been looking for double portraits before. It was curious. To me Bassano (1510/18–1592) had never been a big name but I now discovered that he was, with Tintoretto and Veronese, one of the three main masters of the second generation of Venetian sixteenth-century painters. I learned that through engravings he was influenced by Parmigianino and that in turn he influenced El Greco. Bassano is a very rich, bright painter whose figures grew increasingly monumental as he came under the influence of Veronese. I liked Bassano—but I didn't find the piece of paper I was looking for.

I grew fond of Paris Bordone (1500–71), too. He had been totally unknown to me, but I liked his use of unusual colors in landscapes—indigo blue, for instance, and purplish-red. His *Sacra Conversazione,* in Glasgow, is for me a beautiful blend of Raphael, Titian and Giorgione. But again, no paper.

And so I turned to Titian. Not with any enthusiasm, for I didn't believe that the Italians would offer me a Titian and call it a Tintoretto—and a Domenico Tintoretto at that. I flipped idly through a book on the great master's works. And there it was.

Titian's *Bacchanal* (*Andrians*) in the Prado, Madrid. Painted not long after Bellini's death in 1516, it was reminiscent of the latter's *Feast of the Gods* (which Titian had helped finish) but was a much less peaceful, far more rumbustious work.

Some experts believe that the exhausted god in the background on the right of this picture is a self-portrait of Titian—but I was interested in the piece of paper in the foreground. I remembered now that I had seen an article about this piece of paper in the journal issued by the National Gallery in Washington. The paper shows some music notation—which can be read—and the journal carried close-ups of it: that's why I remembered the folds in the paper. (There are a few historians who believe Titian intended the painting to be looked at while the music is being played—that's why he painted the notes so clearly.)

So was my "Tintoretto" a "Titian"? I tried the Witt, starting with the box file on his "double and group portraits"—just like Tintoretto. Yes: there it was.

In fact, there were several photographs of the picture, each with a different title: *A Senator of Venice and His Secretary* said one; *The Duke of Florence and Machiavelli* said another; *Cosimo de Medici and His Secretary* said a third; and a fourth was labeled *Columbus and His Secretary*. There were versions of the picture in England, Denmark and Holland. But there was also a newspaper clipping which explained everything.

In 1961 the English art historian Michael Jaffé noticed a painting at the home of the Duke of Northumberland at Albury Park near Guildford in the south of England. Jaffé knew that the picture had been copied many times and knew also that Bernard Berenson, the famous American art historian, had at one stage attributed it to Domenico Caprioli.

On seeing it now, however, Jaffé felt instinctively that this Albury Park picture was the original and, further, that it was a Titian. So he did some research. From the golden wheat sheaf, pomegranate and coronet shown hanging to the left of the picture (which had been covered with folds in the version I had been shown), Jaffé was able to establish that the prelate in his beret was George d'Armagnac, the Bishop of Rodez, and that the other man was his secretary, Guillame Philandrier. This meant that the picture must have been painted in the years 1536–39, when d'Armagnac was in Venice as the ambassador of François I. (Titian had been forty-six to fifty-two then whereas the older Tintoretto had been only eighteen to twenty-one.)

Jaffé's researches also showed that the picture was probably in Rome later, where d'Armagnac was created a cardinal, and in Avignon, where he died. The first definite reference to the pic-

ture appears in a letter of 17 November 1624, from Balthasar
Gerbier, who wrote from Boulogne to the first Duke of Buckingham that he had sent to him, for his newly acquired residence,
York House, in the Strand, *Le Tableau du Secretaire de Titian*.
Buckingham was assassinated in 1628 and, in 1635, an inventory
of the inheritance of the second duke, still a minor, was drawn
up. This inventory includes *The French Ambassador Enditing*
[Dictating], by Titian. Evidently, the picture descended to
the tenth Earl of Northumberland, who was in turn an ancestor
of the present owner.

This was a fine example of art history scholarship at work. But
it put the picture I had been offered in its place. I called the duke
to be absolutely certain his picture was still on the wall where it
was supposed to be. It was. I could now be certain that "my" picture at least was *not* an original—more, that it had been deliberately disguised to make identification more difficult. Its attribution had been changed for the same reason.

This subterfuge showed that the Italians, in Italy at least, were
cleverer than I thought. But it also suggested that they dealt not
only in stolen art but in copies and/or fakes, depending how you
look upon these things. Since the "Bassano" also had those
disguising folds, as did the Tintoretto/Titian, the chances were
that it was a fake/copy too.

Whether it was or was not, one thing was certain. The pictures
they had shown me in Italy this time were much better than
what they had shown me before in New York. I told myself not to
be too greedy, not to expect miracles straightaway and to have
patience: the more they saw of me and liked the look of me, the
safer they would feel—so that gradually they might offer me their
better merchandise.

10

Smuggling St. John

RENZULLO CALLED ME from time to time to ask whether I was going to buy any of the paintings I had been shown. To begin with I had to stall, but after my success in identifying the "Tintoretto" as a disguised Titian copy, he grew more circumspect: I was clearly no fool. Later, when I pointed out that the "Bassano" was disguised in exactly the same way as the "Tintoretto" had been, he lost even more face. April turned into May; May became June, and I began to change my attitude. I started to hint that I was growing impatient with being shown pictures that were clearly not in the first league. And I arranged for Renzullo to receive yet another fake clipping showing that Blake had spent $375,000, this time on a Mantegna oil. He called me in London late one night about two weeks after I had sent the cutting to New York. He was clearly impressed.

"Mr. Blake . . . congratulations on your Mantegna."

"What? . . . How did you know?"

"Ahh, I have my means. You have a client for that picture?"

"Yes, I do."

"In England?"

"No, in America. In Los Angeles."

"In L.A.? Will you be coming through New York?"

This was what I was angling for. I was planning a vacation in Los Angeles and to return to London via New York. I wanted to sow the seed of an idea in Renzullo's mind now, and then follow it up in person when I got to Manhattan.

"Yes. I shall be in New York in about a month—and I have a proposition."

"Yes, Mr. Blake. What is that?"

"You and I, Renzullo, we are keen to do business—yes?"

"Of course, of course."

"But we've had no luck so far. Now, I plan to buy a painting in Naples, sometime later this year. I wondered if you—your friends, that is—would help me bring it to America? I would pay you for your trouble, of course."

"Mmmmm. I can't say, Mr. Blake, I don't know. I would have to ask Giancarlo, you know. . . . I don't know whether they will like it in Italy. . . . What kind of painting?"

"An oil. Seventeenth century."

"How big?"

I had no idea. "Medium, you know. Not large."

He was still unsure but I didn't press him. "Look," I said, "there's no hurry. I'll call you from Los Angeles and in any case I'll see you in a few weeks. Ask Giancarlo; ask Del Peschio and let me know."

It was left at that. I went on vacation to Los Angeles and made the check call from there as I had promised. A month passed in the sunshine of Malibu beach and Beverly Hills. At the end of that time I arrived in the Italcraft offices on Lexington Avenue.

Renzullo was there and so was Del Peschio. Renzullo was pleased to see me but for some reason Del Peschio seemed cool and kept in the background. And, in fact, from then on I never saw anywhere near as much of Del Peschio as I did of Renzullo. What I didn't know then, but found out later, was that the legitimate side to Italcraft's affairs was beginning to falter, and whereas Del Peschio was devoting more time and energy to straightening the business out, Renzullo began to think more and more about making a quick killing through illegal art.

We sat down and he got out a bottle of scotch, a gesture of

hospitality that had not occurred before. That day Renzullo seemed swarthier and shabbier than ever. I can't think what possessed Ovid to say that men should not care too much for good looks, that "neglect is becoming." Not in Renzullo, it wasn't. I refused a whiskey, saying that I would drink only once we had done some business. He downed the scotch by himself.

We didn't talk about the smuggling right away. He was excited by something else he had to tell me.

"We have a new source of paintings for you—not in Parma, in Cremona. But they are modern paintings—you want modern paintings?"

I wasn't fussy, of course, provided they were first-division names, and stolen. But I was supposed to be interested in sixteenth- and seventeenth-century works.

"That depends," I said as casually as I could. "I do have some clients who might be interested. What are the pictures?"

"Two Van Goghs, a Renoir, a Vlaminck, a Braque and a Utrillo. Two Modiglianis."

I grinned and whistled. "I think I'll have that whiskey now, please," I said.

"Pretty good, eh? You interested?" Renzullo got out some more scotch while I fished out my pad and pen and wrote down the details. All the names, except Braque, had turned up in my survey of faked paintings; and two Renoirs, a Van Gogh, a Modigliani and a Utrillo were missing at the time.

"Any photos?" I asked, still scribbling.

"No. You have to go there, to Cremona. He won't allow photos."

"Why not?" I asked, still naïvely hoping Renzullo would say "Because they are stolen." No such luck, of course.

"The source is a professor," he said. "These paintings, they came from the Italian Embassy in Buenos Aires and the professor doesn't want it to get about that they have left. That's why they are not being auctioned. Too many people would know where the paintings came from. It would be very embarrassing for his family."

I had been about to ask just that question—why they weren't being sold on the open market. I wasn't sure I believed any of it, of course. But it certainly sounded hopeful, in the sense that there seemed a good chance the paintings were stolen. And one of the missing Renoirs, I remembered with a jolt, had been taken in Buenos Aires. Then Renzullo said:

"They are not framed."

"What do you mean?"

"The paintings have been taken off their stretchers; they are just canvases. They had to do that because they were sent out of Argentina rolled up in the diplomatic bag."

Now I began to itch. This really did begin to sound like stolen art. I had to tell myself to go carefully, not to sound too keen.

"What do you suggest we do?"

"When can you go to Italy?"

"That depends on whether you can meet my request about— transshipment. If you can, then I would like to go at a time when my man in Naples is there."

"If you could make it in late July, early August, then our man from Sicily will be there, in Cremona, I mean."

"Oh yes? Who *is* this man from Sicily?"

"He has an antiquities shop in Taormina. He imports jade and other things from the East—and he has a contact in Alitalia. He is the man who brings things from Italy to New York when we don't use a container."

There it was. They would do it. It had turned out as I hoped. I could kill two birds with one stone, since the smuggler, who, I later learned, was called Concerto Battiato, would meet us in Cremona. I would look at the Van Goghs, the Modiglianis, the Braque, etc. Battiato would then drive back to Sicily taking me to Naples en route. There he would pick up the painting I was planning to buy and leave me in Naples to find my own way home.

But first there was the small matter of money. Renzullo said at first that Battiato wanted $10,000 to smuggle the picture and I offered $2,000. We fenced a bit, he came down to $8,000 and I offered $3,000. That day we left it there. Renzullo said he would talk to Battiato on the phone, since he was the man taking the risk, and would let me know when the Cremona trip was to be organized. I finished my whiskey, said good-bye and limped out. The day after, I flew back to London.

It was about a week before Renzullo called. He sounded excited. "Mr. Blake, I have something very nice for you—a Bellini. You want a Bellini?"

"Which Bellini?" I was praying he wouldn't say Jacopo. That was yet another name in my survey of widely faked painters.

He didn't. "Giovanni," he said. "A *Madonna col Bambino*. It's a beautiful picture."

"Where is it?"

"In Bologna, in a bank. When you go to Cremona you can see it. Giancarlo says it is beautiful."

"When shall we go to Cremona?"

Renzullo suggested a date two weeks later. Once again he suggested we meet in the Milan Hotel at noon and that we would be driven to Cremona from there. This was easy enough for me since it meant that I could once more travel out the day before and stay overnight in Milan at the same hotel as on the previous occasion. "What about Battiato?" I asked. "Will he take my painting from Naples?"

"$5,000, Mr. Blake. Battiato says he will do it for no less, but if you pay $5,000, that's okay."

It still seemed a little expensive to me, but since I was trying to buy my way into their confidence, and since I had to show willingness to do business, and since I was supposed to be terribly wealthy, I acquiesced. I judged in any case that I wouldn't get Renzullo any lower and that to try to do so would spoil our developing relationship, such as it was.

"$2,000, in Italy," I said. "And the rest when the picture gets to New York."

"Okay, Mr. Blake. Fine."

I said that I would have to check that my man was going to be in Naples and that, provided he was, the plan was fine by me. After Renzullo had hung up, I tried to reach Baratti, but did not get through until the next day. He was friendly and said he would be in Naples on the day I planned to be there. We arranged that I should call on him at eleven in the morning.

I spent the intervening days researching Cremona. I didn't want the Parma incident to repeat itself. What part had Cremona played in the history of painting? It turned out, in fact, that Cremona was chiefly known as a center of learning, though there was a Cremona school of painting founded by Giulio Campi, a pupil of Giulio Romano and influenced by Correggio and Raphael. Campi was known for his altarpieces and frescoes in Milan and Mantua, besides Cremona. I also learned that Cremona is chiefly noted for the violins made there by the Amati, Guarneri and Stradivari families. It would not have looked good to have been ignorant of *that*.

More important, I made a discovery that, once again, set my blood racing. Leafing through the *Bollettino* of art thefts in Italy, I found that a Bellini *Madonna and Child* was indeed missing. It had been stolen from the public gallery in Pavia—like Bologna, within easy reach of Parma.

There were three Bellinis, Jacopo (c. 1400–c. 1470) and his two sons, Gentile and Giovanni. Although it is generally regarded as one of the tragedies of Venetian painting that so many of Jacopo's paintings were lost, for me Giovanni Bellini is not only the greatest of the Bellinis, but one of the ten great painters of all time. Giovanni's birth date is unknown, but since he was living away from his father by 1459, it is generally thought that he was born around 1430. Giovanni grew up at the time of the "Paduan moment" in Venetian painting. Padua's important painter was Mantegna and he deeply influenced Giovanni (besides marrying his sister, Nicolasina).

But Giovanni grew (in my view) into a greater painter than Mantegna, with a freer use of line, more liquid color, more space and more play with the effects of light. (It is no coincidence that the Venetian drink consisting of peach juice and champagne is called a Bellini—it catches the light in that city just as Giovanni did.) In many paintings Bellini used color not just for decorative purposes but, for example, to convey the emotional desolation of the dead Christ.

Bellini was a great painter of madonnas, using soft, rich, but gentle colors. His *Madonna of the Pomegranate* in London's National Gallery, for instance, and his Lochis *Madonna*, in Bergamo, are masterpieces of color and emotion. With all this background, I now dared to hope that I was about to recover a perfect example of Venetian art. In fact, one of the most beautiful paintings of all time.

In Milan we met in the lobby of the Hilton as arranged. There was Renzullo, Giancarlo and a tall, elegant, good-looking man wearing a sand-colored suit and those sunglasses which lighten or darken according to the available light. This was Concerto Battiato. He had a smattering of English and seemed very nice and gentle.

We left immediately, but as soon as we had joined the *auto-strade,* we stopped at one of those Pavesi restaurants straddling the motorway and ate lunch. Even though it was a motorway service station, the meal was delicious. Mixed meats (cold), a light red wine with a slight fizz to it, salad, grapes and Gorgonzola cheese. It was perfect and, with the aid of the wine, I began to relax.

Not that I could relax too much, of course. The next hours were to be John Blake's longest test. He was to spend a whole day in someone else's company. After the trip to Cremona and Bologna, Battiato and I were to drive to Naples together. Naples was four hundred miles farther south, a drive of several hours. This would take us well past midnight, and I had no idea what the plans were for sleeping. I didn't ask, but it meant that I had to keep up my disguise and my alter ego constantly until I was back on a plane bound for London.

After lunch, we drove on, chatting idly. I took the opportunity to show off my knowledge of Cremona. For instance, I asked Renzullo whether he or Giancarlo knew if there were any Campi paintings of Amati violins. Renzullo hadn't a clue.

"They were roughly contemporary," I said. "Campi died in 1572, Nicola Amati in 1584. It would be nice to combine two of Cremona's main artists, though a pity the city didn't have any great painter when Stradivari was working, at the turn of the seventeenth century." That very nearly completed what I knew of Cremona, but, fortunately, they appeared to know little more, so my point having been made, I introduced other topics of conversation: our respective governments, football teams, food. Battiato had been to London but the others had not set foot in England so it made my end of the conversation easier. I took care, however, to give them a totally false impression of who I was. I said I lived outside London, was not married, but that I had children from an earlier wife—all statements the exact opposite of the truth. One could never be too careful.

Eventually we came to a village called Voghera, which I presumed was just outside Cremona. Renzullo, who was by now in an expansive mood, drew my attention to the plane trees lining the main street. "In Mussolini's day, every tree had a prostitute standing against it. This town was famous for its prostitutes." He seemed rather sad that that day should have come to an end.

Beyond Voghera we turned off the highway and up a gentle slope covered in vines. The lane curled around the girth of the hill and began to follow the wall of what seemed a rather large estate. Behind us the plain could now be seen as we rose—vines stretched out neatly in all directions. Presently we came to an arch in the wall and turned in. Entering the courtyard was like stepping back four hundred years.

The enclosed area was long and narrow and dominated by a huge tree whose leaves cast hundreds of little shadows across the cobbles and the walls. At one end was a chapel and in front of that a small ornamental garden with low hedges. The main house filled almost one side of the courtyard except for a tall tower toward the end. I later learned that this, now a bell tower for the chapel, was an original Roman construction and literally thousands of years old. The other side of the courtyard was made up of farm buildings and servants' quarters. The far end consisted only of a brick wall with a gate that gave onto the vine slopes, showing as a patch of vivid green in the sunlight beyond. To complete the busy "Brueghel" picture, three women in black sat huddled and talking under an awning, chickens pecked away near the tree and an enormous Alsatian dog barked a ferocious welcome.

Professor Gianroberto Sarrolli appeared. He was a small, stringy man, balding and wearing a dark red shirt and blue linen trousers. He was extremely nervous. Until he spotted Renzullo, he said later, he thought we had come to steal his paintings. He spoke excellent English, having been at one time a lecturer at the City University of New York (CUNY), and he had a somewhat imperious manner—like barristers who are used to being heard out in silence. He liked the sound of his own voice and gave the lie to Eleanor Roosevelt's maxim that no one can make you feel inferior without your consent.

Everybody was introduced to everybody else, including the three old women in black, who turned out to be the professor's mother and two of his aunts. We all moved inside, out of the sun, and were offered a glass of the farm's own wine. This was apparently a singular honor because it was the first bottle of the 1978 vintage—a decent year the professor said—and we were to judge it. He told us it contained three types of grapes in "magic" proportions: Barbera—60 percent; Croattina—30 percent and Uovera

—10 percent. It was dry, almost to the point of sourness as far as I was concerned, and was extremely alcoholic. It went down very well.

Next we were shown around the farm, including the tower and the chapel, which was laid out so that the family from the main house entered into a gallery overlooking the nave, where the rest of the villagers would normally have worshiped. Only when the tour, accompanied by many effusions of praise from Renzullo, Giancarlo and Battiato, was over, and another bottle of wine had been opened, were the women shown out and the paintings brought in.

There were ten of them and, as Renzullo had said, they were unframed and unstretched—just nine canvases and one on paper backed with card: this was the Braque. They were all inter-weaved loosely between sheets of tissue.

Renzullo had undersold the professor's collection. Besides the Van Gogh landscapes, the Braque abstract and the Renoir head of a girl, there was a Toulouse-Lautrec, the head of a woman; two Modiglianis, both heads of young girls; a Vlaminck, a Utrillo and a Sisley, a view of a harbor. Ten modern masters in all. If real, then together they had to be worth millions.

I brought out my magnifying glass. I had to go exceptionally carefully. There was a Van Gogh missing at that time, a Modigliani and a Renoir, which, like the professor's picture, was a head of a young girl. But I knew from my research during the summer that Sarrolli's "collection" consisted almost entirely of pictures by artists who had been widely faked (with the possible exception of Toulouse-Lautrec).

Sitting opposite the professor, I hadn't the foggiest idea at the time whether his Van Goghs were originals or not. The Braque looked good, but here again the style seemed easily forgeable. As for Toulouse-Lautrec and Sisley, I was not at all familiar with their work.

I took my time examining the paintings, turning them over, taking them to the light, scrutinizing the signatures of those pictures which had them. Then we got around to money.

Sarrolli made it clear he wanted to sell all the paintings together. This made it suspicious—all the better from my point of view, but for the moment I didn't press it. He wanted $100,000 each for the Van Goghs, $50,000 each for the Renoir and the

Braque, $20,000 for the Toulouse-Lautrec, $10,000 each for the Modiglianis and $5,000 each for the Vlaminck, Utrillo and Sisley: $345,000 in all. A tidy sum, but nowhere near what they were worth if they were real. To give some idea of the prices he *could* have asked, Van Gogh's *Bouquet of Wild Flowers* was to sell for $2.2 million at auction in New York a few months later; at the same sale, Renoir's *Little Gypsy Girl* went for $1.6 million and Modigliani's *Cornfield* was knocked down for $180,000. Even Vlaminck's *Mount Valerien* went for $76,000. So that made the professor's prices suspicious.

"Have you any documentation?" I said, stalling.

The professor shook his head. "This is all that came from Buenos Aires. I daren't ask since the family must not know I am selling."

I nodded, but that seemed suspicious also. Then I went through the pictures again, dwelling on the Van Goghs and the Renoir, to give the impression that I was more interested in some than in others. I must admit that I was secretly hoping the Renoir was not the one stolen from Argentina but from Stavros Niarchos: then I could get a handsome reward *and* a spectacular end to my project.

Without discussing price any more just then, I stood up. Since Renzullo had said that no photographs were available, I had taken the precaution, this time, of bringing a camera with me. I now asked if I could take photographs of the paintings "to aid my research in London." There was no objection so we trooped outside with the ten pictures. The courtyard was in shadow so we moved into the sunshine on the vine slopes. I hoped to catch Renzullo and, if possible, Battiato, actually holding the pictures— just in case any record was needed as evidence at a later date. I was only partially successful: Renzullo agreed to hold the paintings but the others went on talking about something else and left him to it.

I wasn't at all sure how to continue the discussion on prices, so when we returned to the house, and yet more wine, I asked, "Why don't you sell them at auction, in Milan or New York?"

Did he hesitate? Was that a small drop in his gaze? Difficult to be sure. But then he said, "I want to sell them all at once—and it would be embarrassing to me if my aunt found out that I had sold them. Her husband loved them dearly and wanted them kept together, and in the family. At least if I sell them together, I am keeping part of his wish."

All this seemed pretty thin to me. I asked, "Why are they unframed and unstretched?"

"They came out of Argentina in the diplomatic bag, so they had to be rolled."

I dearly wanted to know why it had been necessary to transport them in this way, but I didn't want to sound too naïve. Instead I brought the conversation back to money. "I will take the photographs, to help my research in London, and let Mr. Renzullo know if I wish to buy the pictures from you. But I cannot, of course, guarantee that the prices I may offer will be acceptable."

He smiled and reached into a drawer, set into the table between us. He drew out what looked like his card—and was just about to give it to me when Renzullo leaped in between and took the card from him. I had wondered what part Renzullo had in all this and it now began to seem he was just the middleman as far as this professor was concerned. In giving me his card, or in trying to, the professor had been hoping to bypass Renzullo and whatever commission he was due.

Renzullo confirmed this indirectly as soon as we were back in the car. He became quite nasty—the only time in our relationship that he had been anything other than perfectly civil.

"Now you know who the professor is," he said. "And where he lives. You can go direct to him. You must promise me you won't contact him direct."

I thought that if they had this little control over the man they should never have introduced us in the first place. But all I said was, "Of course. I do business with you, Mr. Renzullo. If I double-cross you now, we are unlikely to do business ever again. And, in any case, you know I am interested in sixteenth- and seventeenth-century paintings rather than modern ones. Don't worry."

He felt it necessary to repeat himself once more. "You mustn't go straight to the professor. Otherwise . . . well, we know where you live. We shall find you. I have never been to England. It would be nice to go . . ."

It was the nearest I had come to being threatened.

He relaxed, however, and soon the wine began to take effect and we both dozed in the back of the car.

Sometime later I was awakened by a prolonged, rather loud conversation, in Italian, between Battiato, who was still driving, and Renzullo. Seeing me awake, Renzullo turned to explain. It emerged that we were running very late. We were heading for Parma, where we were to drop off Renzullo and Giancarlo, prior to our drive to Naples. It seemed there was no time now to stop at Bologna to view the Bellini. This was exceedingly unfortunate and I made a face, saying that it had been very expensive for me to come to Italy and that I was far more interested in old masters than Postimpressionists or abstract painters.

"Battiato has to be back in Sicily tomorrow night," said Renzullo. "He has a meeting with the mayor of his village."

Awkward. I needed Battiato to smuggle whatever I was going to buy from Baratti. But I wanted to see that *Madonna col Bambino.*

"Do you have a photograph of the Bellini?" I asked.

Renzullo shook his head but said something to Giancarlo.

"There are photographs," Giancarlo said. "But they are kept with the painting, at Bologna."

Then I had an idea. "Can I get from Naples to Bologna?"

"Yes, you can take a train or fly."

"Then why don't I come back to meet you in Bologna the day after tomorrow?"

Again Renzullo conferred with Giancarlo. "Yes, if you get a late train from Naples, you can travel to Bologna overnight and be there early the next morning. We can show you the painting and you can go on to Milan."

It was left like that. For the rest of the journey to Parma, Renzullo, who was now fully awake and garrulous, told me about their organization. It seemed that besides exporting paintings, glass and furniture from Italy to America, Battiato ran an antique shop in Sicily and imported jade and other goods from Hong Kong and the Far East. This was an intriguing development since it was rumored at the time (and subsequently confirmed) that Sicily was one of the staging posts in the movement of heroin from the Far East to America. I wasn't anxious to resurrect the link between heroin and art smuggling, but with Catania still at the back of my mind, it was difficult not to. I looked on the grace-ful and gentle Battiato with a new eye.

Renzullo also became quite open, on this journey, about their smuggling techniques. He said it was simple really. Every month they brought in quite a lot of furniture, including tables of vari-ous sizes. Always, he said, you could find a table with supports running between the legs. Then, it was a straightforward matter to wrap an oil canvas around these supports but under the cor-rugated paper used as protection. If these tables were "lost" in the middle of a container the customs people would never unwrap the paper over the leg supports. It had worked many times.

After that, and I cannot now remember why, the talk turned to politics. I suppose it was because at that time Britain's appalling economic condition was invariably a topic of conversation when-ever two or three people were together. I was surprised to find that Renzullo was a Communist, although Italy has the most ac-tive Communist party in Western Europe. We didn't agree about much, but in my assumed role I don't think Renzullo expected us to. If he thought me an oily, capitalist enemy of the workers (and I half-hoped he did), he didn't show it. It certainly helped to pass the time.

We didn't get to Parma until seven o'clock. After the usual Italianate conversations and good-byes, it was eight before we left. I shook hands with Giancarlo. He had found that if I caught a train from Naples the next evening, I could be in Bologna very early the following morning, a Saturday. Meanwhile, they would have retrieved the painting from the bank, we could have break-fast at the station, in which unlikely setting I would examine the Bellini. A train just before eleven would get me to Milan around one, in time for a flight to London.

As LONG as I live I shall never forget the drive to Naples. Bat-tiato's car was a big, sand-colored Mercedes. By the time we got to the outskirts of Parma, it was clear there was something very wrong with the steering: the wheel was shaking. It took us half an hour, but we found an Italian Automobile Club garage open and the man quickly diagnosed tire trouble. During the day's driving a huge chunk had somehow been gouged out of the left front tire and this was causing the wheel to wobble. A quick change and the trouble was solved—though it did mean that we embarked on our journey without a spare.

It also meant that by the time we slid onto the *autostrade* outside Parma it was four minutes past nine. Parma to Naples is 450 miles. We arrived at the Naples exit from the *autostrade* at 3:08 the next morning—an average of seventy-five miles an hour. But that was only half the picture. It was dark, it was very foggy in places, the *autostrade* was usually only two lanes wide. There were times when we were driving at well over 100 miles per hour and closing on trucks at a terrifying pace. We killed two cats.

My heart was in my mouth most of the time but I did manage to introduce the subject of astrology [*astrologia*]. Koscka and Siviero had impressed on me the importance of checking a suspect's date of birth: it helped so much to distinguish criminals with the same or similar names—as I had found to my cost with Giuseppe Catania.

I couldn't just come out with it and ask Battiato his date of birth in a bald way. So I began by talking about the then current position of the planets [*pianete*], which I had checked, then got around to talking about my own *compleanno* [birthday] and zodiac sign [*toro*]. From there I moved on to Battiato and he revealed that he had been born on the feast of St. Andrew of Avellino—November 10. I couldn't check the year without seeming too obvious, but I reasoned that would be enough to identify him in any criminal records.

At 3:30 A.M. we checked into the Royal Hotel in Naples, just down from the Excelsior and, thankfully, nowhere near as expensive. I crept into bed, weak from fright after the drive. I have not felt the same about motorways or Mercedes since.

Fortunately, I was not seeing Baratti until eleven that morning. Battiato and I breakfasted at about ten; it was a beautiful day and the restaurant overlooked what was by now a familiar sight for me, the Bay of Naples. It was going to be a tricky morning, since Battiato wanted to be off as soon as possible and no later than 1:00 P.M. He had another, no doubt crazy, drive to Sicily, which he said would take five or six hours. That gave me only two hours to conclude my deal.

I arrived at Baratti's on the stroke of eleven. As before, he was

dressed in blazer and white shirt. The chairs and the sparkling
wine were already waiting on the terrace.

Of the $25,000 budget for this part of the enterprise, which
had come out of the publisher's advance, $12,000 had been spent
by Steffanotti, leaving me with $13,000. Since $5,000 was to go to
Renzullo and Battiato for the smuggling, this meant I had exactly
$8,000 to spend with Baratti. This was my dilemma. He had
stuck at $21,000 for those "Caravaggios" on the previous occa-
sion. If he still had them would he let them go for less? Would he
let *one* go for $8,000? That was all I had with me.

The "Caravaggios" were still there. As I limped through to the
terrace, I noticed they were in exactly the same place as they had
been before, high up on the walls of Baratti's dining room. We
sat down and he opened the wine, as on the previous occasion.
For some minutes we made polite conversation. Since I was buying, and visiting him on my own initiative, it was up to me to introduce the business element.

"Those still lifes," I said eventually. "I see you still have them."

He nodded.

"May I see?"

He went to fetch them. I studied them once more, again using
my magnifying glass. He said nothing.

I was in difficulty. Did I try to beat him down—then offer for
just one? What happened if I failed and had to buy something
else? How would I recognize a decent painting worth what I was
forced to pay for it? There was an added difficulty: if he *would*
sell just one of the still lifes but wouldn't accept my $8,000, what
then? If I bid for something else, and had to drop out again at
$8,000, might that not look very odd? He might realize that I had
just $8,000 with me. That would be bad for two reasons: he
would have an advantage over me in any subsequent deal that
morning; second, and more important, a limit of $8,000 was
scarcely in keeping with the image I was trying to give. In international art-dealing terms, it was nothing.

I had, of course, pondered this before I arrived in Naples, and
I thought I knew what to do. I now got to my feet and limped
again around Baratti's flat. He let me go by myself and I scrutinized his paintings carefully—I knew what I was looking for. I
found it in his dining room—and hurried back to the terrace. By
now I hadn't much time.

"Will you sell just one of the still lifes?"

He shook his head. Firmly.

"They are not Caravaggios—you know that?"

He shrugged. He was giving nothing away.

"If I can sell one in London, I'll come back for the other."

He shrugged again, but didn't speak.

I decided to abandon the still lifes. I was reluctant, but if I was going to do so I wanted to move on without mentioning a figure. "That *St. John*—at the far end of the dining room—how much?" What I had been looking for was a religious painting, an oil, not too big, not too small, nicely framed with, as Johnny van Haeften would have put it, "a lot going on." I also wanted a picture with a great deal of light and shade—chiaroscuro. This was the classical Neapolitan school. I had asked Steffanotti in advance and we both reckoned that this mixture would be easiest to resell, and that a Neapolitan school painting bought in Naples stood a better chance than anything else of being what it purported to be. It was a poor substitute for art scholarship, but it was all I had to go on.

"$15,000," said Baratti.

"Christ," I thought, "Now what?" If he was going to be as inflexible about this painting as he had been about the so-called Caravaggios I was truly lost. I began to dislike that ever-present smile on Baratti's face.

I put on a glum expression. "Can we get it out here?" Then, just as he was about to fetch it, another thought occurred. "No, don't bother." I wanted to imply it wasn't worth the trouble. Then I changed my mind again.

It took him a while to get the picture as it was quite high up on the wall and he had to bring some library steps to get it down. That bought more time for me to think, though it was already nearly noon. When the *St. John* was positioned in front of me on the terrace I went through my now familiar routine, poring over the canvas, fiddling with my glass, turning it this way and that. Eventually, I made my offer.

"$5,000."

A long silence. This was new for Baratti. Normally, if he was going to turn something down he did so straightaway. I perked up a bit inside.

"Maybe $13,000."

Interesting. He had dropped by $2,000, signaling, so I thought, that he wanted a deal. I now had two choices: I could increase my offer by $500 or $1,000, to show I was going to be tough, or I could jump by more, say $2,000, as a gesture that I, too, wanted a deal. But that would take me to $7,000, leaving me little room for maneuver.

"$7,000," I said, after not too long a pause, and hoping for the best.

Now he took his time. He refilled our glasses, moved across the terrace and sat on the parapet with his back to the sea. Had I made a mistake?

"$11,000."

The gap was closing, but I didn't have much left in reserve. My turn to delay. I pretended to do some calculations on my Dunhill pad, the Tiffany pen glinting in the sunlight. I decided we were beyond bid increases of $500. It had to be $8,000 or nothing. All I had.

"$8,000."

"$10,000," he came back straightaway.

Under normal circumstances I wouldn't have been doing badly. But in this instance I just didn't have any more money—and we were still $2,000 apart.

I had one more card in my hand, however, and there seemed no choice but to play it. With as much drama as I could muster, I got to my feet, hobbled around the terrace, looked out to sea. One of the hydrofoil ferries was scudding in from Capri, leaving a fresh white wake against the shimmering blue. I moved across to Baratti and sat near him on the parapet.

I took a brown envelope from my pocket and placed it on the stone between us.

"$8,000. In cash. Now. Here it is." The wedge of dollars showed through the pale envelope—green, rich and deep. I looked away, leaving the notes where they were and Baratti to make up his mind.

He took his time. He refilled our glasses yet again and then looked me full in the eye. He must have been asking himself why I had this $8,000 conveniently in my pocket. I hoped he assumed I had brought far more ready cash with me initially, but had already bought other paintings in Naples or elsewhere in Italy. I counted on Byron's dictum when he made Don Juan say, "Ready money is an Aladdin's lamp."

Baratti had the bottle in one hand, resting it on his knee. His other hand he eventually placed on the envelope. "Before it blows into the sea," is all he said, pocketing the packet inside his blazer. "I'll wrap the picture for you."

It was in any case hot enough inside my double-breasted English suit, but with the release of tension I was now awash with sweat around my forehead and down my arms. The wine didn't help, but even so I gulped at it—and helped myself to more from the bottle while Baratti was in the house.

Before long he returned with paper and string and clumsily parceled up dear *St. John.* I felt the need to explain why I was spending only $8,000.

"I would like the still lifes," I said, "but my man who exports things from Italy let me down recently. I am using this painting to test a new route . . ."

He beamed. "If you want, I can help . . ."

"No," I said, holding up my hand. "I want to test my own people. I am buying from other dealers, you know, who are not so well organized as you are. If it works this time, I can come back for more."

He beamed again and handed me the picture, wrapped now in a rather sorry way. "I take you back to hotel—yes?"

He dropped me outside the Royal and I found Battiato completing an early lunch. We returned to his room, where he examined the painting.

It was a little on the large side, he said, but yes he could "export" it for me provided it could be taken off its stretchers and rolled. Rolled—yes, I said; folded—no. He agreed and I handed over $2,000. He had already filled his car with petrol and oil and, after the briefest of farewells, he was off.

I had planned to book my ticket to Bologna for that night; then I could catch up on my sleep in the afternoon. However, when I made a check call to my office, Landon, my editor, insisted that I return immediately. A deal I was handling for the paper, involving several thousand pounds, had run into trouble. This was awkward but I had to acquiesce. Then I had to call Renzullo in Parma. After much difficulty I got Giancarlo and, in my shaky Italian, explained that I had done the deal with Battiato but that

I could not meet Giancarlo and Renzullo in Bologna. I said something had come up in London and that I would call Renzullo as soon as he returned to New York in a few days.

I had already arranged to pay for an extra night at the Royal hotel, since I had anticipated leaving so late. But with an evening to kill now, I had an idea. By this time I could not get back to London that day. There were no direct flights from Naples and it was too late to make the connections in Rome or Milan. I could make it to London the next day almost as easily from Naples as from Rome and it would save money to spend the night where I was. So I called Baratti and invited him for dinner.

It was a marvelous stroke of luck that I was "stranded" in Naples that night. Baratti took me to a restaurant up Posillipo, past his house and then down a winding road to the shore. The restaurant, *Da Giuseppone a mare*, was famous for its view of Naples, Vesuvius and the whole bay, and for its *fegato a Cosa Nostra*, which one cynic had described as a "offal you can't refuse." It was a beautiful, clear evening and, as I recall, we drank the white Neapolitan wine, Greco di Tufo.

Our conversation naturally turned to paintings. He admired Giorgione. I expressed a preference for Bellini—"the light, beautiful women, his textured surfaces—like Cézanne." I trailed off.

He nodded, he liked Bellini too. Then I said craftily, "Of course, for money, I deal in smaller painters—Squarcione, Stanzione, Pesellino—eh?"

"Yes," he nodded. "I also." He knew what I meant. With these artists a dealer stood a better chance of obtaining a picture from an unsuspecting owner, researching it fully and so doubling, trebling, quintupling the price. Not so with a Giorgione or a Bellini.

The conversation was going the way I wanted it to. I poured more wine. "And especially the Caravaggisti—Honthorst, Elsheimer, the Carracci. I specialize in Caravaggisti, in fact. I like chiaroscuro. You know, I still hope for a real Caravaggio someday. I think he is undervalued. And according to Friedlander, in his *catalogue raisonné* on Caravaggio, there are at least ten of his paintings which have been lost. They could turn up. You know one of them, an *Ecce Homo*, was found in Genoa fairly recently. And four of the other missing works, Baratti, were lost in or around Naples. Think of that."

Baratti was still smiling, nodding and eating. I had to push things since I would almost certainly never get a better opportunity.

"Mr. Baratti, I did hear that the Caravaggio stolen—*rubare*—from Palermo was being offered around here. Did you ever hear anything? I would pay a lot for that picture."

He was munching away, amused by my bad Italian, but he managed to speak between mouthfuls. "Yes," he said, "*si . . . sento*. [Yes . . . I hear]."

Careful now. "What did you hear, Mr. Baratti?"

"Someone, a man, came to my home. He asked . . . if I want . . . to buy Caravaggio."

"What did you say?"

"I say . . . *forse* . . . maybe, if I can find buyer. If not, I not buy."

"And did you? Find a buyer, I mean?"

He shrugged, his mouth still full. "No."

"Where did you try?"

"Rome, Milan, Switzerland once."

"Did you see this man again?"

"One more. He came back. I said I not have buyer. He went away."

Care*ful*. "Who was he, this man?"

"He lives . . . *fuori di Napoli* . . . outside Naples; not far—half an hour maybe."

"Can you remember his name?"

Another shrug. "No. It is at home, I can find . . . perhaps."

"Will you ask him for me, Mr. Baratti? I would very much like that Caravaggio. I will give a good price for it." Was I being too obvious? Was I rushing too much, behaving out of character? If I was, I couldn't help it. "Will you ask him, Mr. Baratti?"

"Okay, *si. Provo*. I try."

He was a bit too uninterested for my liking. I had to fire his enthusiasm.

"How much did he want for the Caravaggio, Mr. Baratti?"

Another shrug.

"It could be worth $100,000, maybe more," I said earnestly, confidentially, leaning forward. "Wouldn't you like part of *that*?"

Now he was paying attention. "Mr. Baratti, find that man for me and tell him I want the picture. *Please*."

I left it there. Either it would sink in or it wouldn't. I mentioned it once more as he dropped me off that night at my hotel. "Find the man, Mr. Baratti. I am very interested in Caravaggio."

"Okay, okay," he said, waving from the Renault as he sped off into the dark, back toward Posillipo.

I was asleep in no time that night—not even a late-night limp around the block. The next day was just as sunny and warm and my flight back to London, via Rome, though delayed by ninety minutes, was otherwise uneventful. Because the flight was late, however, I didn't go into the office as I had intended. I called my editor from Heathrow airport, but as often happens in newspapers, yesterday's panic had been superseded by a new one. That morning, at 10:25 A.M., an 88-pound bomb had exploded in the second-class waiting room of Bologna railway station, killing eighty-five people.

Until my plans had changed, and I had been ordered home by my editor, I had arranged to meet Renzullo and Giancarlo that morning in Bologna. At the railway station.

11

The Man from the Mafia

I NOW HAD TO GO BACK to New York to pick up the *St. John* that Battiato was to have smuggled for us. At this time the world's art thieves seemed to have just returned from vacation, like the rest of us, for a rash of thefts hit the headlines. A Rubens, a Van Dyck and Tintoretto's *Portrait of a Man with Fur Coat* had gone from Mexico City; a Stradivarius violin had been taken from Cambridge, Massachusetts; six Toulouse-Lautrec prints and four by Salvador Dali had been stolen in Los Angeles and two Chagall oils had disappeared from Cap-Ferrat in the South of France. John Blake began to itch with impatience once more.

Renzullo was put out that I had not been able to make it back to Bologna in order to look at the Bellini: he thought this somehow showed a tedious uncooperativeness on my part. The fact that we had all avoided possible death or disfigurement as a result wasn't entirely an explanation as far as he was concerned. In his eyes, John Blake had slipped.

Over the phone from London to New York I casually asked if he had any idea when Battiato might be bringing in the painting, since that would affect when I traveled to New York. He replied openly that it would be during the week following 10 August.

I said, "Well, when should I book my own ticket?"

A moment's delay while he consulted with Del Peschio in the background. Then: "Come over around the fifteenth . . . it should be here by then."

I thanked him, arranged to phone as soon as I was in New York, rang off and straightaway called Charles Koscka in U.S. Customs. Charles hadn't heard from me for some months but that didn't worry him. "Hi, Peter. Something about to break?"

I explained that I had arranged for a "dummy run" with the *St. John*. We had agreed earlier that this time around Charles and his team would simply watch the painting come through Kennedy airport to see how the Italians worked. Charles had said that it would make his job much easier if we knew what date the painting was due to be brought in on, who was bringing it and, particularly, which airline or shipping company. I was able to say that one Concerto Battiato would be bringing in the painting on or around 10 August and that, in all probability, he would be arriving on an Alitalia flight from Rome. I was also able to add that Battiato had been born on 10 November, sometime in the late 1930s or early 1940s.

He arrived as planned, entering America via Kennedy airport and Alitalia on the afternoon of 13 August. He gave the place where he was staying as 200 Lexington Avenue, the Italcraft offices, so we had no idea where he actually slept on that trip. Nonetheless, while Battiato was waiting for his bags, Charles' people went to work, found his suitcases and opened them. They discovered that Battiato had selected suitcases which were extra-large and made of stiff canvas. In fact, to the practiced eye, it seemed that Battiato had selected these suitcases especially to smuggle old masters. They didn't unstitch the lining, but the material the case was made from was much the same consistency as a canvas painting; the lid of the case bent and warped under pressure and under handling, making it very difficult to tell the painting was hidden where it was. But we all assumed it was there.

We now knew, or thought we knew, which airline they used, who actually accompanied the pictures and how—technically—

the smuggling was achieved when they didn't use a container. If only it were to be that simple next time around.

I collected the *St. John* from Italcraft's offices on 16 August. Battiato was there when I arrived and there was much hilarity at my expense, since he had been telling them how frightened I had been during the drive south to Naples. Apparently, Battiato's way of handling his Mercedes was legendary and I was not the only one terrified of his speeds.

That day they were understandably feeling pretty pleased with themselves. The picture appeared in good shape although it had been taken out of its frame and off its stretchers. We all drank some Sicilian wine, I handed over the $3,000 I owed them—and they threw in a photograph of the Bellini, which they said still awaited me in Bologna. I promised to research the painting and to let them know very soon whether I would make an offer or, at the least, return to Bologna to take a look for myself. We parted on excellent terms.

Research in the Witt Library and with Johnny van Haeften and Rafael Valls soon established that the picture they had in Bologna was not a Bellini. It was a Bellini-esque composition, perhaps, but, we decided, more probably executed by Beccafumi.

Although Giancarlo had described it as a *Madonna col Bambino* it was in fact a madonna, child and other unidentified saints (possibly Peter and John the Baptist). Close examination of the child showed that its head bore an unusual relationship to its body—the neck was bent at an alarming angle. Bellini certainly had some of the people in his paintings in unusual poses (see, for example, St. John the Baptist in the New York Metropolitan Museum's *Madonna and Child with Saints*), but he was a superb draftsman and we all felt it unlikely that he would make this kind of mistake.

To cap it all, I then learned that the Bellini stolen in Italy had just been recovered. Once again Giancarlo had overplayed his hand: the Bologna picture wasn't a stolen Bellini, just another red herring.

There was no time to dwell on it, for a few days later a call came from Italy. I had, of course, left my "A. John Blake" card with Baratti, with my New York and London phone numbers on it. My ex-girl friend, whose London number I had used, took the call. An Italian, who wouldn't leave his name but was calling from Naples, said he would speak only to Mr. Blake directly. He would call back in two days at the same time—eleven in the morning.

That made it Friday, a very busy time in the weekly rhythm of a Sunday newspaper. But I had no choice. In fact, the Italian came through at 10:30 A.M.—an interesting tactic that I had used several times with Renzullo and Del Peschio in setting up meetings. If you think there is a remote possibility that a private rendezvous will be observed by others, or a telephone conversation taped, you turn up, or call, a little early: that way you hope to catch the other people off balance. It's not a foolproof security gambit, of course, but if you have residual doubts about someone it might just catch them out.

I had taken the precaution of arriving early at my ex-girl friend's flat so she was able to answer the call promptly and pass the phone straight across to me as if it was my office. The Italian introduced himself as Signore Manzu, said that he had heard "talk" about me in Naples and that I was "interested" in "certain paintings." I tried to appear guarded, suspicious, interested but not too keen. All I said was, "Yes . . . that's right."

He said he was coming to London soon and would like to meet me. I said, "Of course," and asked him when he expected to be in town. He would not be drawn—simply repeated the word "soon" —so I asked if he meant in the next month. He said, "Probably," but I had to know so I said that I was leaving for Paris and New York on 20 September (it was then 27 August)—would it be before then? Yes, he said, it probably would be.

I asked him where he would be staying but he was very firm on that: he said he didn't know and added that *he* would call *me* after he had arrived. I replied that I looked forward to meeting him and we hung up.

Now I grew apprehensive. Pretending to be an art dealer in London in front of Signore Manzu was going to be an ordeal quite different from any John Blake had had to endure so far. I had plans, but they were far from watertight.

There had been plenty of time to anticipate this move, but nonetheless the realization that it was about to happen still induced a short period of panic. I could see all sorts of holes in my plan, holes it was too late to repair now and which could wreck the entire venture. Further, I had conflicting advice to fall back on. There was Siviero's, to the effect that you couldn't plan too much and that any disguise less than perfect was bound to be exposed; and the view of Koscka, Volpé and Don Langton, surprisingly in harmony, that criminals were only human, too. They usually checked you out only after they had already decided they wanted a deal. If they wanted a deal they would look for evidence which supported your bona fides and be inclined to overlook, not the inconsistencies exactly, but the "rough edges" in any disguise. A risky piece of reasoning perhaps, but one that they claimed to have tested time and again and which I was inclined to accept. In any case, I had no choice.

The first part of my plan was to establish a convincing base. I had to have a flat. For safety's sake, I couldn't use my own house. A hotel suite might have been more stylish but it would have been almost impossible to "fix," in the sense of arranging it so as to give the impression that Blake had lived there for ages. Too many staff could be bought by Manzu.

The flat could be small, saving expense, since it would have to appear only as a *pied-à-terre* with an office, and used infrequently and irregularly. I would pretend that my main house was outside London. It had to be somewhere fashionable and, if possible, so located as to have few neighbors. It should be some distance from where I actually lived. Andrew suggested that we choose a block of flats with a doorman/caretaker: it would be possible to "fix" him and, if anyone was to check how long Blake had been there, then the chances were that rather than talk to the neighbors, he would try to subvert the caretaker. Since we couldn't hope to "fix" all the neighbors, Andrew's suggestion had some merit.

Another possible weak point could be the real estate agents in the area. They tend to know which among their number helped sell or rent any particular property and it would not have been too difficult for Manzu to find the person who rented the flat to me, and then to bribe him or her into revealing how long Blake had been there. I got around this by using an agent who was a friend and by taking her into my confidence. If approached, she promised to give the impression that Blake was a long-standing tenant and no fly-by-night. Because this behavior was unethical I agreed not to reveal her name or the company for which she (still) works.

There was a final physical requirement of the flat—I wanted a room with a glass door that locked.

Such a flat took a bit of finding (and if Manzu had arrived that week I would have been in deep trouble). But, after four days of doing nothing but look at properties, I discovered something that —roughly speaking—corresponded to what I needed. It was just around the corner from the Royal Albert Hall in South Kensington. It wasn't Mayfair or St. James's, but it wasn't bad. Had I taken it earlier in the year I could have made a tidy profit renting out my view—for the flat was on the fifth floor overlooking, among other things, the back of the Iranian Embassy. This embassy had been, of course, the scene of a notorious siege and dramatic rescue by members of Britain's crack Special Air Service antiterrorist squad.

The flat was perfectly furnished: carpets, busy chintzes, dark mahogany furniture, green flocked wallpaper. It had a small kitchen, a large sitting room with an imitation fireplace and two large, three-seater sofas. There was a sizable foyer, a double bedroom and a small single bedroom with the all-important feature: a glass door. It cost £750 a month and I rented it for two months —just to be on the safe side.

Several things had to be done to convert it into a plausible art dealer's base. First, an office area had to be created. A table behind one of the sofas was converted into a desk. I still had plenty of photographs of paintings and these were strewn over the desk; "A. John Blake" notepaper ("Fine paintings, drawings & prints") was stacked neatly to one side; catalogs of Sotheby's and Christie's old master sales were also stacked on the desk and filled a couple of shelves of the bookcase next to the mock fireplace. This bookshelf was otherwise filled with art books—by Berenson, Fiocco, Veri—and catalogs of exhibitions I had been to during the life of the project—in Venice, New York, Washington and Paris. A small filing cabinet was installed and files invented for imaginary sales and purchases. Letters from dealers in on the project came in handy here.

A major problem was the walls. An art dealer would be expected to have some paintings of his own, pictures which—to put it no higher—would be more than junk. There was little I could do about that. I couldn't borrow pictures from Johnny or Raf or Andrew Ciechanowiecki for an extended period of time; that would be asking too much and they had been more than kind already. And there was no other way I could acquire any suitable paintings. Andrew Purches, who would have lent me some pictures, dealt only in prints and the picture restorers had not heard from me for some time. . . . I couldn't ask them.

What then? I decided in the end to brazen it out and convert the lack of paintings into a virtue. I reasoned that, since the London flat was supposed to be a working base anyway, it would be reasonable, if asked, for me to reply that my own collection of paintings was at my house "in the country." Meanwhile, I would decorate the walls of the flat in two ways. In the first place, there would be a number of paintings, six as it turned out, which would be *by me* but copies—or rather my version—of favorite paintings. I judged this a suitable cover and possibly an interesting enough conversation piece to keep Signore Manzu's mind off the absence of real old masters on my walls. The six paintings I chose were: a detail of Mantegna's *Madonna of Victory*, showing a profile of Federigo Gonzaga; Bronzino's portrait of *Ugolino Martelli;* Del Sarto's *Madonna of the Harpies* (the madonna's head only); Titian's *Ariosto* portrait; Caravaggio's *Supper at Emmaus* (again a detail) and, finally, Antonella da Messina's *Ecce Homo.* Apart from the last two, the pictures were, in fact, not so much my favorites as the famous paintings I found it easiest to copy. As a boy I had once had a success in the "Young Contemporaries" exhibition and a picture of mine once hung (very briefly) in the Tate Gallery.

The Caravaggio was chosen for obvious reasons—to invite discussion of the artist and his work. The Messina was chosen as a conversation piece to lead the talk into stolen art. For this painting exists (or existed) in two versions—and *both* are missing. The first was looted by the Nazis from the Kunsthistoriches Museum in Vienna in the Second World War (but is believed to be still in existence somewhere), and the second, known as *Cristo alla colonna*, was taken from the Civic Museum in Novara, Italy, in July 1974.

The pictures were done in inks and gold leaf and were more enthusiastic than good. Naturally, I did a bit of research on the paintings my versions were modeled on so that I could talk authoritatively about them, should Signore Manzu ask.

The other way I decorated the room was to cover the walls in the corner near the desk with a "research project." This project contained photographs of certain people, dealers in the art world, and next to them reproductions of paintings. Some of the dealers were well known, some were not. A few of the photographs had been taken at auction sales by a photographer friend; others were from newspaper clippings (Norton Simon, for instance, was among them). Some of the paintings were famous, others less so— but all were, at the time, missing.

When I say "missing" here, I don't necessarily mean stolen. Some of the photographs I stuck on my walls were taken from the Carabinieri *Bollettino,* for instance a marvelous *Madonna col Bambino* by Sandro Botticelli, which had been stolen in October 1977 from the Stibbert Museum in Florence. And Paolo Veronese's Mythological Scene, stolen in Rome. Others, like the Del Sarto portrait of a shepherd boy and a madonna were taken from *Art Theft Archive.* And two more, a Correggio madonna and a Bronzino Crucifixion were taken from the *Suchliste,* the list of masterpieces looted from Italy by the Nazis.

But besides stolen pictures, others have disappeared in different ways in past centuries—mislaid, destroyed, misattributed—and genuine dealers often make spectacular *coups* in rediscovering these lost masterpieces. Any standard work on a painter will usually list the master's works that have been lost like this. In Caravaggio's case, for example, the *catalogue raisonné* by Walter Friedlander records a painting entitled *Crowning with Thorns* which the biographer, Pietro Bellori, had mentioned in his *Life of Caravaggio,* published in Rome in 1672. This had stated that the Marchese Vincenzo Giustiniani had ordered the painting but Friedlander noted that when the Giustiniani collection had been auctioned off years later in Paris, the Caravaggio was not among the pictures sold. According to another scholar, a picture in Vienna, entitled *Crowning with Thorns,* by Caracciolo, could easily be a copy of Caravaggio's. So this picture of Caracciolo's copy, which is reproduced in Friedlander's book, also went on my wall opposite the head of a well-known dealer who was supposed to be keen to obtain this painting.

The idea was that the project showed which dealers were interested in which paintings. All the paintings were in some way mysterious. A final touch was that the photograph of the (obviously nonexistent) dealer allegedly interested in the Caravaggio

Nativity was missing from the wall. However, a small piece of torn paper still remained under the drawing pin, designed to give the impression, whenever Signore Manzu appeared, that it had hurriedly been torn away at the last minute to prevent him learning who my buyer was.

The final and most daunting problem, as far as the physical layout of the flat was concerned, was the paintings themselves. I might get away with decorating the walls in the way I proposed, but I had to have some paintings to buy and sell: a genuine dealer would need at least a dozen. (I remembered, with a shudder, how much stock Wildenstein's has.)

I had given this problem quite a bit of thought and decided that, short of stealing some old masters myself, there was no watertight method of getting around this difficulty. There was *something* I could do, but it was risky, very risky. Still, as so often before, I had little choice. This was where the glass door came in.

I bought fifteen cheap oils in and around London's Portobello Road. They were of varying sizes but I gave more attention to their frames than to the subject matter or the quality of the draftsmanship. Some frames were ornate, some were molded just a little; most were oblong, two were oval. Most were oldish but two were fairly new. I also bought two unframed canvases, religious paintings in the Italian style. Together the pictures cost £450.

When I got back to the South Kensington flat the pictures were carefully stacked in the single bedroom, but arranged in such a way that they could only be inspected *end on* through the glass door. Viewed from there, all that could be seen were thirteen frames and the edges of two unframed canvases just peeking above the frames: the canvases clearly had paint on them but not enough was visible to enable anybody to judge their quality or even, come to that, their subject matter. A final touch was that the *St. John* I had bought in Naples, and collected in New York, was stacked—still unstretched—in front of the gilt frames. That at least was worth $8,000 (or, anyway, that is what I had paid for it).

I fixed a fine, white net curtain over the glass door on the inside: the frames could still be seen when viewed through the door but less distinctly. Next I installed a big lock on the door. That was only reasonable if the paintings were as valuable as I was pretending. But the lock also featured in my plans if Manzu should express the wish actually to examine the canvases he thought were inside the frames.

Another lock on the front door of the flat (making three in all) and I was as ready as I could be. There was now just the caretaker to bribe. I didn't do it immediately, but after I had moved in engaged him in conversation a few times so I could find out what he was like. (At this point, before Manzu had turned up, I was sleeping in the flat, leaving every morning in my smart suit, bow tie, slicked-down hair and walking stick, and taking a taxi home—where I changed back into Peter Watson and drove to work. If any of my neighbors observed this strange behavior, they never mentioned it.)

After three or four conversations with the caretaker, I had learned that he was called Mac, that he was widowed, aged sixty next birthday, had served in World War Two and landed in Africa. He had only been working in the flats for "just over a year," which was useful. I also found out that during the siege at the Iranian Embassy, a caretaker at a nearby block of flats, with an even better view of the action and a telephone in the lobby, had made several hundred pounds from the world's press who had used the facilities, including an empty flat to sleep in (presumably illegally).

It was the opening I was looking for. We were standing in the lobby at the time and I asked him if there was somewhere we could talk privately. We went through to the back, out by the dustbins. I didn't tell him the truth, though that might have been easier. I told him I was a journalist, showed him my press card and said that the paper I worked for was trying to recover a collection of paintings looted from the Uffizi Gallery in Florence during the second world war. I told him the collection consisted of twenty-three works, including paintings by Raphael, Bronzino and Veronese.

The reason I didn't tell him the complete truth was partly natural prudence but also because I hoped that my story about the Uffizi theft would appeal to what I assumed would be his anti-Nazi sympathies. Unfortunately, he was one of those soldiers and ex-soldiers who were more against their own top brass than the enemy and he did not respond as well as I anticipated. I had hoped he would be excited by the opportunity to help but all he did was nod.

Despite his cool attitude, I had to press on. I took £100 from my wallet, in £20 notes, and explained what I wanted him to do.

"In a few days, I don't know exactly when, I shall receive a visit from a foreigner, an Italian. He is part of a syndicate of men trying to sell this collection secretly to raise money for Neo-Nazi political groups in Europe [was I overselling?]. He thinks I am a wealthy art dealer, but he may want to check into my back-ground—for instance, he may ask you how long I have lived in this flat.

"If he does ask, all you need to say is that I have been here as long as you have—just over a year. If he asks how much time I spend here, just say, 'Never at weekends,' and that I seem to go abroad a lot. If you can help, and we are successful and get handed on to the next phase in the deal, there's another £100 for you once the Italian has safely come and gone."

Naturally, he now wanted to know more but I cut him short. "No, it's better you don't know at this stage. If you help, and it works, I'll tell you everything when we have recovered the pic-tures." Thankfully, he pocketed the money. I was just about to leave when he said, "What about the other feller?"

"What? What other fellow?"

"There are two of us who work here. What if your Italian talks to Tony?"

At this distance I can understand this transaction from the caretaker's point of view, and I can see why he didn't tell me about the second man until after he had pocketed my £100. There would have to be two of them: it was obvious, when you thought about it. They would need to work a shift system. But at the time I was very angry.

"I can't pay Tony £100 as well. The budget won't stand it."

This was rubbish, of course. Mac probably had a very good idea what I was paying for the flat. However, perhaps because of something inside Mac, something to do with his relationship with Tony, he said, "Maybe he'll do it for £50?"

"Do you think so?" I said, foolishly grateful for this crumb. I realize now that Mac had much more low cunning than I. He had recognized in my anger the possibility of no further cooperation and thus a risk to his own second £100. We agreed on £50 for

Tony and that we would both pretend this was what Mac was getting. We also agreed to meet the following evening when both caretakers overlapped in the building and when I could brief Tony and give him his money.

That meeting went smoothly, thankfully. Tony was much younger than Mac, was fairly new to the job, usually worked the early "unsocial shift" and was nowhere near as worldly wise. He listened attentively as I repeated my story about the Uffizi collection—and seemed excited by the time I had finished. Fifty pounds was obviously a lot of money for him and would, I thought, secure his acceptance. I only hoped the Italian wouldn't offer him more.

We were all set. By now I was very keyed up and ready to go.

Nothing happened. A week passed and Manzu hadn't shown up. Then another. I began to wonder if I should have rented the apartment for three months instead of two—or not at all. I also began to get some odd looks from Mac. Other matters occupied our attention. In America at this time the presidential campaign between Jimmy Carter and Ronald Reagan was in full swing, the hostages were still in Tehran and the Ayatollah was preparing for war with Iraq. In Europe, Stanisław Kania had just replaced Edward Gierek in Poland and the name Lech Walesa had been known to most people for less than a month. In Britain the actor Peter O'Toole was at the Old Vic playing *Macbeth* in the most laughable production anyone could remember.

Then Manzu called. He telephoned my ex-girl friend's flat, of course, and again wouldn't leave a number but said he would call back in two hours. That gave me just enough time to nip round to Shepherd's Bush, where she lived, ready for his second call. He wanted to meet, he said, as soon as possible. He suggested later that same day.

Would six o'clock be convenient? I replied. He accepted—and I breathed a sigh of relief. I had anticipated that, besides meeting to talk, Manzu might want to see A. John Blake in action, so to speak, at work and socially—at the theater maybe, or at an auction. Six o'clock was the perfect time to meet to foil all this: galleries and auction houses would be closed and, provided our meeting went on for a good hour or more, it would then be too late to get to a theater. I judged that restaurants, the theater and the opera were the places I was most likely to bump into friends.

I gave Manzu the address and asked him which direction he would be coming from. I pretended I wanted to give him directions but really, of course, I wanted to find out where he was staying. He dodged this neatly, saying he was moving around that afternoon and didn't know where he would be. Before leaving my ex-girl friend's flat I managed to remember something I had forgotten till then: the slip of circular paper on her phone with the number on it. I unclipped it and took it with me to South Kensington.

I arrived at the flat at about four o'clock. Just in case Manzu was already watching, I was carrying a painting wrapped in paper as if I was returning to my office after a buying expedition. I saw Mac in the lobby and said, "Tonight, I think, at six."

He whistled. "About time, I was beginning to wonder what was going on. I'll be here. . . . I want to take a look at him."

In the flat, I changed the bits of paper on the phone and left once again with a different picture frame wrapped in brown paper under my arm. If Manzu *was* watching I wanted him to see a moderately busy art dealer. I took a taxi to my own house, where my wife rewrapped the same frame in different colored paper. At about five-thirty we both returned to the flat, again by taxi. She was carrying the "picture," as she was to act the part of my secretary.

Manzu was about twenty minutes late. I suppose I should have been nervous but for some reason I was not. My wife took her time unbolting the three locks on the front door: we wanted to give the impression of security-consciousness. She showed him into the sitting room, where I was "busy" going through a set of figures behind the desk.

For an Italian, Manzu was surprisingly tall, a thickset man, black-haired but balding a bit. He had brown eyes, wore a brown suit with a yellow nylon shirt. He didn't look at all like a Mafioso but had a rather pleasant, open face, round with a wide nose. We introduced ourselves and shook hands; most important, I then introduced my secretary, "Mrs. Worcester."

It was essential that this name—Worcester—register. One of our worries was that if Manzu had the inclination—and the means—to check back with the Royal Borough of Kensington and Chelsea tax authority, or the electricity company or the phone company or the gas company, he could have found the name of the tenant who had paid the bills for my flat over the previous months. For a long time I had seen no way around this problem, but then it had occurred to me to assume the same name as the previous tenant. I couldn't do it, of course—I was Blake. But my "secretary" could. The South Kensington flat had formerly been lived in by a Mrs. M. R. Worcester, so my wife assumed that name—"Mollie" for short while Manzu was around. At some point in our transaction I intended to let slip the information that the flat was in her name but that I paid all the bills as part of an arrangement between us.

I had given some thought to how often Manzu would wish to meet. There was no way of being sure but my guess was at least twice and possibly a third time, away from the flat—just to get the "feel" of me. Presumably, he would do whatever checking he thought necessary between the first and second meetings. If he wasn't satisfied there would be no others.

Manzu and I sat on the sofas facing each other and I asked "Mollie" to get us a drink. Manzu said he would have scotch and I drank California wine.

"Your first visit to London, Signore Manzu?"

"No, I have been here three, four times—but not since three years." His voice was fairly high-pitched and the accent quite thick. But his English seemed good. That was presumably why he had been sent, that and because he didn't look like a Mafioso.

"You speak English well?" I asked.

He made a face. "Not so good, I think—but I was in America one year. In Chicago." He pronounced it "Chee-Kargo."

I raised my glass: "Here's to business."

A mistake. There followed what P. G. Wodehouse would have called a slightly *frappé* silence. Manzu half nodded his head but very definitely did not raise his glass. He shot a glance in the direction of the kitchen, where Mollie was getting some ice from the refrigerator. As if to say "Not in front of her."

I felt a fool. And now I *did* begin to get nervous: I started chewing on the inside of my cheek again. And I gulped down my wine in embarrassment. Fortunately the phone rang.

Mollie answered it but, since the instrument was directly behind my head, Manzu and I made no attempt to talk over her conversation.

"Hello? . . . Oh hello, Dick. . . . No, it's fine—yes, he's here, though he has someone with him. What? Okay. . . . It's your dime, talk away."

She picked up a pen and sat on the desk scribbling on a sheet of "A. John Blake" notepaper. "A Rembrandt portrait . . . yes. Petronella Buys. 1635. How much? 650 thou . . . dollars or pounds? Dollars. . . . *Peasants Eating and Drinking*, by Brueghel—yes. Which one? . . . Younger. 140 to 180 thou. . . . One-fifty . . . sure. Ruysdael . . . Holland. October the twentieth . . . *Watermill* . . . 300,000 guilders . . . $120,000." She carried on writing and then turned to me, holding the phone so the person on the other end could hear what she was saying.

"You heard that? Dick has some things for you—a Rembrandt and a Brueghel in New York, a Ruysdael in Holland. Nothing urgent. Reckons he needs nine-twenty and are you in for 350 thou?"

This whole transaction was of course a charade. I had arranged to be called at this time—from New York, where it was lunchtime. The caller was my agent, Robert Ducas, but he was pretending to be Richard Feigen, the real New York old master dealer who had helped in an earlier stage of the project and whose name we were now taking in vain. We had checked that all the pictures mentioned were to be sold in the next few weeks at Sotheby's in New York or in Holland (to add a really international touch).

I didn't take the phone: we had decided in advance that this was more impressive, but said to Mollie to tell Dick I would call him back later. Manzu wouldn't really expect me to talk money with New York in front of him.

After Dick had rung off, and Mollie had asked if she could go, I refilled our glasses so Manzu and I could begin to talk. The exchange that evening was as important an encounter as had been the visit to the professor in Cremona and the drive to Naples. John Blake had to give a plausible account of himself.

"How did you become an art dealer, Mr. Blake?" Manzu had asked. No preamble, no lead in, no subtlety.

I then talked for nearly half an hour. We both knew I was, as it were, on trial. Even if I had been a real dealer I would have been on trial. I told him that my career in adult life had started in the army, in the engineers. As a less fashionable specialty and more dispersed, there was little chance he would know anyone who might conceivably have served with me. I said I had been stationed in Northern Ireland and Berlin. (I had worked on stories involving the army in both places, so could cover there.) And then that I had worked my way into intelligence where I had acted as a British observer in Portugal at the time of the revolution, and had once been stationed for a year in America. (Once again, I had worked on a book for the London *Sunday Times* about the Portuguese revolution, and had spent several weeks on the base at Fort Bragg, home of the U.S. Special Forces.)

"Yes," he said, "but how did you get into art?"

I said I had been awarded a university scholarship on leaving the Army, but that before I could take it up I had met one Malcolm Henderson, whom I had known in the intelligence branch of the Army, and he had asked me to work for him in America. He then owned a gallery in Washington and wanted someone to act as his West Coast agent. So I had spent a little over two years living in San Francisco selling prints, and eventually got out on my own, moving back to Britain and buying a house in the country. I also bought this flat ("we are sitting in") but, for a number of reasons, had put it in the name of my secretary, Mrs. Worcester (there, it was done). Since then, I concluded, things had not gone at all badly. I stood, and offered to refill Manzu's glass.

He asked how I had injured my leg. I told him, as I had told Renzullo and the others before, I had first injured it in a fire in Naples in 1962 and then again playing cricket in 1977. All of this was true—except that, though my leg was weak, I didn't need to limp.

He fell silent. By now it was nearing eight o'clock. Thankfully, it was too late for any social engagement other than a restaurant.

Should I mention McGill? Should I say it was the Irishman who had put me on to Baratti in Naples? I thought not. I would leave that to him. But I should press him on the Caravaggio, surely. It would be unnatural not to do so.

"Enough about me. . . . Shall we talk about—the picture?"

"Not yet," he said quickly. "Not yet. I have other business here first; here and in Manchester. Let us meet in—three days?"

I nodded agreement. "At the same time—six o'clock?" I was anxious to keep things as safe as possible.

"No," he said. "I return to Italy that night. Here—at *mezzogiorno*, noon."

Not the best of arrangements, but what could I do? It was

pretty obvious that he was checking me out: I knew it and he knew I knew it. I didn't believe his story about a visit to Manchester for a minute. But we both knew that was the way it had to be.

"All right," I said. "But I hope there will be enough time on Friday to discuss business."

He smiled slightly and got to his feet. He showed no inclination to look around the flat. If he was coming back in three days, and then really flying out, it looked as though we would have only two meetings. I gave him his coat, undid the three locks, shook hands and watched him into the lift. Then I gave myself a large scotch.

THE INTERVENING DAYS were crucial. If A. John Blake was being watched continuously, which was likely, his behavior during that time could ruin the whole thing. So for that week I lived *entirely* as Blake. I never went near the *Sunday Times*, but instead spent my days at Christie's, Sotheby's, Van Haeften's and Valls' and at the Royal Academy, where there was an exhibition of Van Goghs, Renoirs and Picassos. Or I stayed in the flat, popping out occasionally with wrapped paintings. I never knew definitely whether I was being followed, but I assumed the worst because of one incident.

The day before Manzu and I were scheduled to meet again, there was a morning sale of old master drawings at Christie's. I went, as a matter of course, going through the motions of looking at the pictures in as professional a manner as I knew how. I suppose I shouldn't have been surprised to see Manzu there—but I was. It suddenly made everything seem more than a game—and of course that was his intention. He was deliberately letting me know, I think, that I was being watched and that our meetings were not a charade. He sat in the main body of the Christie's hall (it wasn't busy that morning) too far away to talk—though he nodded when I looked across.

My problem was that I had come unprepared to bid. In fact, I had very little idea of the artists in the sale. (I had overheard somebody going on about "the wrong Tiepolo," by which I assumed they meant Domenico rather than Giambattista, but that was all I knew.) I now understood a little bit about how to conduct myself, so, while the sale was in progress, I occasionally looked across the room to a particular group of people standing at the back. I was trying to give the impression that I was using an agent to bid for me rather than show myself as interested in any particular work. And, about twenty-five lots before the end, I got out of my chair and limped to the back of the hall to stand among this group. After one of them had made a successful bid I leaned forward and asked quietly whether she would be interested in selling again straightaway. She said she was buying, as I had thought, on behalf of someone else and couldn't answer that question immediately. I asked whether taking her out to dinner in Paris that night would change her mind. She smiled at this, as I had intended her to, but she said softly, "Alas, no." I hoped that if Manzu saw this exchange from a distance, or collared the woman after, he would be fooled. Either we looked like two people on friendly terms, close enough for her to be my buying agent, or, if Manzu talked to her, I was a perfectly normal dealer trying to buy from her straight after a sale.

Anyway, I then prowled around one or two other rooms while the sale was finishing, looking at forthcoming works. I was back in the main hall just in time to catch Manzu, say a brief hello, confirm our date on the morrow and check that he hadn't chatted with the woman, who appeared to have left.

Before Manzu's second appearance, my wife and I took further precautions with the flat. We packaged up a few pictures in wrapping paper and leaned them against the walls of the sitting room. I wanted to create the impression of paintings coming in and out every day. With great relief, my wife took off early for the weekend and drove down to our country house in Gloucestershire.

That Friday Manzu arrived on the dot. He was a different man this time: crisp, businesslike and, in fact, rather more likable. I sensed he had made up his mind to do business but had a few checks still to make, to set his mind at rest.

He sat down, looked at my project and asked pointedly what it was.

I raised my eyebrows, as if to imply it was really none of his business, and I delayed a little before answering. "It serves two functions. The photographs ensure I always know an important face when I see one; and second, it helps me absorb who is interested in what." I explained a little about missing paintings and, before he could elaborate, waved toward my own pictures on the walls. "These are what I am really interested in."

He looked around—and then back at me, puzzled. I told him they were my own works, my versions of favorite missing pictures. He stood up now, clearly more interested.

"They are very nice," he said. I noticed he didn't say "good," which would have been the word an English-speaking dealer would have used had he liked something. So I didn't know what Manzu really felt. However, I plunged on:

"Would you like one? Choose one, if you would like to."

Now I could see that he was stumped. The offer had put him momentarily at a disadvantage and he didn't like it. But in the end he decided to accept my offer and chose the "Bronzino." This gave me the opportunity to wrap that picture in the same way as the others already leaning against the wall. To rub in the presence of these other paintings, I laid his next to them when I had finished wrapping it.

While I was doing this, however, he got up again and started prowling around the flat. He stood before my project, taking it in.

"These are paintings and collectors or dealers I would like to bring together. All the pictures are missing." I deliberately did not add "or stolen." He could make that deduction himself. He flipped through the catalogs on the shelves, wandered into the kitchen, came out again. Then he went into the hall.

"What's in here?" he shouted back, tapping on the glass door of the bedroom.

Taking a deep breath, I stood and slowly limped after him. This was the moment I feared.

"My paintings," I said.

"Can I look?"

"Yes, you may," I said, correcting his grammar and making a show of looking for the key to the lock. I felt my pockets: nothing. I went back to the sitting room and searched the desk: they were not there. I looked in the kitchen, along the mantelpiece, dipped into my overcoat hanging in the hall. Still no key. Trying to look puzzled, and a little alarmed, I stumbled over to the phone and called my home in London. There was no reply, as I knew there would be none. Muttering more angrily to myself now, I waved Manzu to take a seat again on the sofa. Then I called our cottage in the country, in Gloucestershire. While I was dialing I grumbled out loud:

"I travel all the time, and am hardly ever here to pay the bills, so the flat is in Mollie's name for convenience—but sometimes she acts like she owns it. . . ." I'd gotten that in once more for Manzu's benefit.

My wife answered the phone. "Mollie? . . . You *are* there. I thought you must have gone away early for the weekend. Tell me, do you have the keys to the picture storeroom? I want to show Signore Manzu the Crespi and the Crivelli." (Both these were minor painters: Crespi was a Mannerist using mainly lemons, grays and pinks; Crivelli was a Venetian imprisoned for adultery in 1457, though he was knighted later, a rare distinction for an artist. He painted fruit a lot.)

My wife, who was of course expecting this call, made a show of looking for the key. She walked around our cottage and then came back to the phone to "admit" that, yes, she did have it.

"Damn," I blurted out, trying to be really annoyed. "And where are the spares? . . . What? No! What are they doing there? . . . For safety's sake—yes, don't tell me. And I suppose your flat is locked? . . . Yes, yes." A few more reproaches and then I said, "Now you won't do this again, will you, Mollie? I must have those keys if you are going to be out of town." We hung up.

Would Manzu buy it? It was our plan to prevent him from seeing my "Portobello Road masterpieces." This tactic was my first move. Had he expressed the desire to see the paintings on his previous visit to the flat, we would have gone through a similar rigmarole then (only pretending the keys had been left down in Gloucestershire). Had he wanted to come back a second time to inspect them, then I would have gone begging to Raf and Johnny for some pictures to borrow. At least by then I would have needed them for only one night—or even a few hours. I could still do it if Manzu insisted on returning to the flat. But, I dared to hope, it wouldn't come to that.

Sitting down, I didn't say anything straightaway but just shrugged. "She's taken the keys with her to the country, a hundred miles away, and the spares are in her London flat—which is locked. Bloody woman. Are you still going back tonight? I can show you on Monday."

To my relief, Manzu shook his head. "I must leave for Italy to-night." Manzu stood and went to examine my copy of Titian's *Ariosto.* "What was it Michelangelo said to Benvenuto Cellini about Titian?"

"That he was wonderful with color but hadn't studied drawing enough." Manzu turned back to me but I went on. "Only he didn't say it to Cellini; he said it to Vasari—in 1546."

Was I being tested? I had the distinct impression I was. Now I *did* begin to feel nervous. I had been lucky once—the anecdote Manzu had chosen came out of Vasari's *Lives of the Artists,* one of the few books I had studied.

Now he stood in front of my Mantegna copy. I decided I couldn't wait for a test but must show off the only anecdote I remembered of this artist.

"Mantegna—the man without patience."

Manzu looked puzzled.

"When Andrea was painting for Pope Innocent VIII, he was paid infrequently. He complained and the Pope got to hear of it. Later, when the Pope was viewing some pictures of the Virtues, which Mantegna had painted, the Pope said gently, 'I see you have left out Patience.'" I grinned at Manzu, who smiled back.

He seemed content enough, and said, "Why don't we have lunch now?"

Relief—for a moment. "Where would you like to eat?" I asked. The arrangements I had worked out were not very important but worth the effort, I thought. In my experience, Italians, like the French, are not terribly interested in the cuisine of other nation-alities and, when in London, for instance, like to eat their own food. To be on the safe side I had made reservations in three res-taurants earlier that day, one Italian and one French, just in case he didn't behave as planned and an English restaurant in case he went completely mad. "Do you want Italian, French, English, Chinese . . . American?"

"I think I'd like to try Italian in London," he said, behaving ex-actly as I had hoped he would.

I leafed through my notebook and picked up the phone. Manzu didn't know it, but my first call was to a friend, standing by.

"Bertorelli? . . . Can you take two in half an hour please?" This was code for "the Italian restaurant": I had reserved a table not at Bertorelli in Charlotte Street, but at San Frediano in Fulham Road. My friend then pretended to be the manager at Bertorelli and said they were full, we would have to look elsewhere. Had I said, "Mon plaisir" that would have signaled to him that we were going to the French restaurant I had chosen, Daphne's, in Draycott Avenue.

I then leafed through my book some more looking for another restaurant. Then I called my own home: Manzu wouldn't know what I was doing, of course. There was no reply, but I pretended there was: "Hello, this is John Blake; could you take two for lunch in about fifteen minutes? . . . You can—good. See you soon."

Both Blake and a friend of mine, Glen McAllister, had booked into San Frediano at separate tables for 1:00 to 1:30 P.M. I judged that this covered any time of arrival between 12:45 and 1:45. I also hoped that since I had allowed Manzu to choose the food, and because we had not been accepted at the first restaurant I had tried, there could be no chance that he would think he was being "set up."

We arrived at San Fred's just after one o'clock. I had chosen it because I was not known there. On the other hand, I had been there two or three times so I knew it. Since I didn't want to run the risk of being recognized as Peter Watson, I had chosen a place as far away from the West End as I dared. Manzu must have no grounds for suspecting that the whole thing was rigged.

Manzu ordered with more gusto than anything I had seen him do previously. He chose *bresaola* with avocado to start with, followed by a chicken in a white wine. I chose *bresaola* too (I always do) followed by liver in the Venetian style. Once the wine—a light Chianti—had arrived I decided to start the ball rolling.

"What do you think of the Chagall theft?" I asked. No fewer than sixty-four modern prints had been stolen that month, en route from Chicago to New York: thirty-four Chagalls, twenty-four Joan Mirós and six Picassos. Rich pickings for someone. Eventually I took a deep breath and introduced the subject of Caravaggio.

"Signore Manzu," I said, filling his glass again. "Are we going to discuss any business?"

"Why do you want the picture?" he growled suddenly.

"I have a buyer," I replied, smiling openly.

"Where?"

"In America."

"Why this one? Why you want this one so much?"

"I don't, not especially." I had thought this out. "There are about a dozen around the world I am keeping an eye on. There's a Zurbarán in Switzerland I'm trying for at the moment, and a Tintoretto, which I believe is in Germany."

Just then I felt a tap on my shoulder. It was Glen, who had of course been eating in the same restaurant. He had a deep plummy voice that boomed through the room.

"Mr. Blake? . . . Thought it was. Look, I've heard from my insurance company. Read this . . . see what they say."

I excused myself to Manzu and read the proffered piece of paper. We had decided that Glen and I should not be friends meeting up in the restaurant—that might be a bit much. So instead we pretended we had been in a slight car crash together in Trafalgar Square about a month before. I thought this was a clever move to further allay Manzu's suspicions. I gave him the phony story while looking over the letter.

"It seems all right by me," I said, "provided my people agree. I should be hearing any day now. I'll write to you."

"Good," he said, smiling. "Enjoy your meal." And he was gone.

The *bresaola* arrived. We ate for a moment, then I said, "Where were we?"

His mouth full of meat, he mumbled across at me, "How much will you pay?"

I had not anticipated talking money at the lunch (I'm not sure *what* I had anticipated, but not that). I was thrown. I tried to recall what Siviero had said all those long months ago. Seven percent, wasn't it, for stolen art? But what was the Caravaggio's real value anyway? A seven-figure picture was all I could remember. Seven percent of a million pounds was £70,000. I virtually halved it. "£40,000," I said. "About $80,000."

He shook his head immediately, took out a pen and card and wrote a figure on it that seemed to contain endless noughts. He turned it around; it was in lire but translated into sterling it came out as £400,000 ($700,000).

Manzu looked at me directly, no doubt trying to gauge my reaction. The waiter took away our plates and brought the main courses. That gave me time to recall some of Siviero's stories. He had started as far apart as this, in his negotiations, and yet somehow had closed the gap. Would I be able to do the same?

I pursed my lips. I didn't want to seem too eager. "I could perhaps go up a little—though nowhere near your figure." I ate some liver.

"How high?"

I finished chewing before saying, "£50,000."

He scribbled away, converting pounds to lire. He shook his head again. "No."

We took some more Chianti and munched on. Then I asked, "Is it in good condition?"

He raised his right hand above the table, flat with the palm down. He swiveled it about his wrist. "So—so."

"Then I'd have to spend money on having it cleaned and restor . . ."

"How high you go? Go higher. No good now." When he got a little excited his English slipped.

I decided I was making progress but still heeded Siviero's words—go slowly. Now it was my turn to do some figures and I took my time, muttering to myself. At length: "If—*if* I don't have to spend too much on restoration and cleaning, I could go to £60,000; but only if, as I say, cleaning and restoration don't cost a fortune."

I realized, of course, that we were both bargaining in a vacuum. I had no money to spend, in the first place, and he, on his side, since he and his cronies had not actually bought the picture, had no investment to recoup. I saw this as marginally in my favor: if they really wanted to sell, and had been unsuccessful in the past, they would force me up to where I stopped—and then accept.

"I return to Italy tonight," said Manzu. "Unless you offer more, that is it. No deal."

Was he bluffing? Did he have some figure in his head which he felt he had to achieve before he could go back to his friends with his honor intact? That gave me an idea. I went back to my scribbling. With roughly 2,000 lire to the pound, as there were then, I was offering him 120 million lire, a funny sum I supposed to an Italian. So I tried it the other way around: 125 million lire— a round sum—worked out as £62,500. So I made my next offer in lire. "125 million . . . I can't do better than that," I said.

He wrote it down, seeming happier with the talk in lire. "Can you do a *little* better? Maybe 150 million. I think they not like 125 in Italy."

At least we were talking again; but now was the time to be firm. "That's it . . . at least until I see what condition it's in."

He stared at the card he had written the figures on, tapping it gently on the tablecloth. I began to feel, not exactly sorry for him, but on his side against the others, unseen in Italy. Had he done well enough?

The coffee arrived. "Brandy?" I asked. "Italian brandy?"—to show that I knew there was such a thing. He shook his head, still preoccupied with his private thoughts.

He tried again. "140 million lire."

$140,000 was quite a long way down from $700,000. Now I thought I could concede a little—but not right away. I shook my head and sipped my coffee. "Tell me about the Caravaggio's condition."

He shot me another reproachful look for mentioning the painter's name in a public place. "It is dirty and had to be rolled . . . there was a little—er, cracking."

Did he mean cracking, which was serious, or *craquelure*, which was less so? I didn't think it worth pursuing, feeling that his English wouldn't be up to it. Instead I said, "All right, 130 million. But only because you are so persistent."

He gave up then, though he remained a little morose for the rest of our time together. I paid the bill and asked him if he would like to come back to the flat to wash. He shook his head and we stood for a while talking on the pavement outside the restaurant. Glen came out, as we had arranged, waved and shouted, "'Bye, Blake." He got into his car, which had been grazed all along one side. This was what had given me the idea about the car crash. I pointed out the damage to Manzu as the car went past.

"What now?" I then said, turning to him. "What happens next?"

He shrugged. "Maybe you come to Italy, maybe not. I don't know. The price is not good."

I had hoped the encounter would end on a more positive note —but I had yet another negative point to make. "Signore Manzu, if I am to buy the Cara—, the picture, I must of course see it first. But I won't bring the money to Naples . . ."

He looked at me sharply, and I raised my voice to stop him interrupting. ". . . the risk of kidnapping is too great. Switzerland, yes. Germany, England, New York—all yes. But not Naples and not the South of France; you must understand."

This had been Don Langton's idea long ago. It was entirely plausible, we felt, that a foreign businessman would be very wary, at that time, of going alone to Italy, especially southern Italy, with a briefcase full of cash. This was the time in Italy when kidnapping was increasing alarmingly. In fact the risk of kidnap was then so great that even going to Naples simply as a businessman was not without danger. The proportion of foreign visitors to the city had slumped from 50 percent of hotel business to less than 10 percent. Furthermore, a report had shown that murders by the Mafia at that time accounted for 29 percent of all killings, as opposed to 13 percent a decade before. Judges and prosecutors in Rome had gone so far as to stage a strike that summer, demanding better protection against terrorists. And three industrialists, the daughter of a wholesale meat merchant, an automobile showroom owner, a Swiss banker and an eighty-five-year-old landowner had all been kidnapped, or attempts had been made to kidnap them, in the preceding weeks. The threat of kidnapping was real—but it also served our purpose—to transfer the transaction to Britain or America, where we could enlist the aid of the police.

Manzu looked really glum now, but it seemed to me that Blake was only acting prudently and I hoped that his bosses in Italy would understand.

A vacant taxi appeared and Manzu hailed it. He turned and shook hands: "Mr. Blake."

"*Arrivederci*," I said, making it a joke.

He had the grace to smile, but said, "130 million is only so-so." Then he got into the cab, said something to the driver that I couldn't catch and was gone.

It took a while for another free taxi to appear, but I still went back to the apartment—just in case there was another man watching. In the lobby I found Mac waiting for me jubilantly.

"Last night . . . he tried it last night. On my way home. Probably didn't want to talk to me in the building in case you came by. But he caught me just as I was going to my car; he must have watched me before. Around seven, it was."

"Was it him, or someone else?"

"Oh no, it was him."

So Manzu probably had come alone to London. "What did he say?"

"Very cunning, the bastard," said Mac, smirking. "Said he was thinking of buying a flat and wanted to know why you were leaving. He gave me twenty-five."

I assumed Mac meant pounds. "And?"

"I was a bit swift, too. I said I was confused. That six-F was on the market—but not yours. Then I asked him how he knew. He said some real estate agents had told him, but I told him that was news to me. He then said the real estate agents had told him you weren't happy with the flat because you hadn't been here long and he wanted to know what was wrong with it. Clever—eh? I just said I didn't know you very well, that you were always coming and going—abroad, I thought—but that you had been here since before me, so his information from the real estate agents wasn't very reliable."

"Did you take the £25?"

"Of course. Wouldn't have been natural not to."

He was right. "What happened then?"

"Nothing. Nothing much anyway. He asked which real agents were handling six-F—had to appear interested, I suppose. He thanked me and got into his car and drove off."

"A car?"

"Yes, blue job. Ford, I think. Rented, I should say. Anyway, it was here again this morning."

"What?"

"Yes, parked in a different spot, but I noticed it. About nine."

"Go on."

"Nothing to tell. You left—what? Nine-thirty? Came back, left again. He drove off around eleven forty-five."

So that's why he had been so prompt that morning. He had obviously just driven around the corner, out of sight, and walked back. It was a good thing I'd lived totally as Blake these last few days; but it looked as though Manzu was alone in London. Mac had earned his second £100, which I gave him later that day.

Had I convinced Manzu? Had the flat been realistic enough,

Mac convincing and, most of all, my "secretary's" weekend away with the keys up to scratch? Siviero had led me to believe that the "search" would be far more thorough than it appeared to have been. But that was not to say it had been cursory. If I was ever called from Italy, my deception had worked. If not: failure.

There was, however, one other thing that happened that day which was encouraging. I hadn't told my wife, and I certainly hadn't told Mac, but I had reenlisted the aid of Don Langton. I had thought it too risky (and too expensive) to have Manzu followed from our first meeting, but Don had tailed us since we had left the flat together that morning to have lunch. And he had picked up Manzu again afterward when he got into his taxi.

Don came around for a drink later that day, having phoned me from the airport. From the restaurant, Manzu had gone back to the President Hotel in Russell Square and then on to Heathrow, where he had caught the last plane to Rome. Don had gone back to the President, where for £25 and an explanation that he was a private investigator who had once been at the Yard, he was allowed to look at the cashier's list.

What was interesting was that no Signore Manzu appeared on the list. On the other hand, a Signore Giovanni Puccinelli, from Naples, who had arrived four days before, had checked out that afternoon. Puccinelli was one of the names on the original list Siviero had given me right at the beginning. He was a member of the gang suspected of stealing the Caravaggio.

12

Naples in November

SOME OF THE PHOTOGRAPHS which had lain about on John Blake's desk in the South Kensington flat, while he had been visited by Signore Manzu/Puccinelli, were of the French Impressionist paintings belonging to Professor Sarrolli. If Manzu had noticed them, and recognized them as stolen, that could do Blake no harm. But I was, in any case, researching the pictures to find out if indeed they were real and stolen or whether they were fakes, like the Tintoretto/Titian and the Bassano/Tintoretto. I was conscious that, gradually, I was spending most of my energies in trying to recover the Caravaggio to the exclusion of almost everything else. This was putting my eggs all in one basket, so, after Manzu left, I turned my attentions full-time to the professor's collection.

I had no luck with the two Van Goghs. They weren't in De la Faille, the official catalog of the artist. They were in the style, and showed the landscapes, of Van Gogh's St. Rémy period, when he was in a mental hospital in that small Provençal town. During this time, so I read, the artist was closely supervised and it was very unlikely that any pictures really by him would have slipped through this protective net and been allowed, so to speak, to escape. I was inclined, therefore, to think that the professor's Van Goghs were fake.

Next, I turned to the Renoir. Convincing as Sarrolli's portrait was, I could not find it in the official records of this warm, marvelously tender painter. Furthermore, and disappointingly, it was neither the Renoir stolen from Niarchos (so bang went any hope of a reward) nor that reported stolen from Buenos Aires.

Then I turned to the Utrillo. Maurice Utrillo showed a superficial similarity to Caravaggio. The son of Susan Valadon, who had posed as a model for Renoir, Toulouse-Lautrec and Degas, Utrillo apparently took up painting at his mother's instigation and as a form of psychiatric therapy. Together with Modigliani, Soutine and Chagall, he completed the *peintres maudits* group. The group's label was partly a pun on Modigliani's name, but also they all knew each other, shared a similar kind of personality defect and had a virulent love of the bottle and/or drugs.

Utrillo, when he wasn't in and out of mental hospitals, was in and out of police custody (which is where the comparison with Caravaggio comes in). In fact, Utrillo's mind became so addled that it was said, in the 1940s, when a case was brought against *several* artists who had forged his work, that one of them was actually better than Utrillo by this time.

It was getting dark when I turned to the green boxes in the Witt which were devoted to Utrillo. I had been in the library all day, in the basement, where the French Impressionists and Post-impressionists are kept. Down there it was murky at the best of times, and now it was fifteen minutes before closing on a wet autumn Friday. The assistants were beginning to pack up and go off for the weekend and I was alone, seated at a large table surrounded by boxes.

Utrillo, though endlessly interesting as a man, is not my favorite painter. His townscapes and views of white, shuttered houses are too unvarying, in my opinion, to be called great art. So I was leafing through the Witt's reproductions hurriedly, not paying much attention, and not really expecting to find anything. Which is why I nearly missed it.

The professor's Utrillo. Or, rather, a painting so similar to the professor's that, unless you put them side by side, you would probably never notice the difference.

According to the records in the Witt, *Paysage à Bessine* was painted by Utrillo in 1922 and last sold at Parke-Bernet on 28 October 1970, lot number 41. It shows a view of a suburban street, lined with trees, people walking in a cobbled roadway and a church at the far end. On the right is a white house with gables and on the left runs a long wall.

The professor's picture was essentially the same view with a number of minor modifications. In addition to the church, there was a factory in the distance with a large chimney and the figures in the roadway were in different positions. What is most obvious, however, from a direct comparison of the pictures, is the difference in their quality. The professor's picture is much cruder. The outlines of the buildings are fuzzy, the trees—which give life to the real Utrillo—are stylized and awkward. Some of the brickwork is amateurish.

Sarrolli's picture was a fake. That much, I was now certain of and it probably meant the others were too.

When I started to examine the Toulouse-Lautrec I made another discovery. I didn't find the real version in the official records, nor did I expect to. But now that I was certain as could be that the professor's "Argentinian" masterpieces were all fakes I looked on them with a new, hypercritical eye. And I noticed something familiar about the Toulouse-Lautrec.

At first I couldn't place it—but then it came to me and I could have kicked myself. The face on the Toulouse-Lautrec had the same eyes, the same nose and the same lips *as the face in the professor's Renoir*. The expression was the same—only the outlines, so to speak, were different. These two fakes had probably been done by the same hand, possibly using the same model. Perhaps this forger had also turned out the Modiglianis, the Van Goghs and all the others as well. If so, he was a talented man.

I flew to New York especially to see Renzullo and gave him a detailed explanation as to why the professor's paintings had to be fakes. I said that in my view the pictures were off their stretchers, not because they had been smuggled, but because the professor and the forger wanted to create as much confusion as possible to prevent thorough examination. I said I had also checked with a colleague in Buenos Aires (which was true). According to this man, the Wildenstein gallery in Buenos Aires said there were only four Van Goghs in Argentina at the time. They had checked with all the owners—and every picture was where it should have been.

Renzullo was impressed, I think. Also, since we had now done some actual business, with money changing hands, our relationship was different and I could start to throw my weight around. On that visit I pushed harder, giving him a list of pictures I *was* interested in. It was the same list as had comprised the research project on the walls of Blake's London *pied-à-terre*. I also pointed out that the paintings I had been offered so far all had vague histories. I emphasized that we would all make more money if I could be shown pictures with known provenances. And, I said, I didn't care whether that history was a legitimate history or an illegal one. As long as I knew where a picture had come from, it didn't matter to me if it had been stolen.

Renzullo promised to put the word out in Italy and he also confided that he had a source "opening up in Rome," a group of men who were very cagey about what they had and would allow no photographs—I would have to go there. I made the usual enthusiastic sounds and returned to London.

Other things were depressing me at this stage. Continued industrial troubles at Times Newspapers in London had forced the International Thomson Organisation to put up the group for sale: a mood of uncertainty prevailed in the office and nobody, myself included, had much enthusiasm for anything. As time went by, and I still heard nothing from Italy, I resigned myself to the fact that our elaborate plot had failed, that the bait had gone unbitten. I also discovered that Manzu was the name of a well-known modern Italian sculptor who had worked on the great bronze doors of St. Peter's in Rome. Had that been deliberate on their part—another test? Should I, as a dealer, have known about Manzu? Had that been a major blunder?

THE CALL came on 29 October. As before, my ex-girl friend answered the phone and the Italian voice at the other end said he would call back in two days—at ten in the morning. I made sure I was there.

"Mr. Blake? . . . How are you?"

"Very well. Is that Signore Manzu?"

"Yes. Can you come to Italy?"

I caught my breath. It looked as though the deal was on. But careful now: I didn't want to sound too eager so I pretended I had to go to New York, and then to Switzerland. I could travel on from Geneva, I said.

"When is that?"

I gave a date three weekends away.

"Where you stay in Naples?"

"The Excelsior, usually."

"Okay. A moment." A pause, conversation with others in the background. Then: "The price is 150 million lire, 150,000 American dollars. No bargaining. You say now—yes or no."

Clever. Very clever. It was a good compromise price, on the high side, but that was only to be expected from their point of view. But it was near enough to my previous offer for them to know that, if I really meant business, I had to agree. They had wrong-footed me nicely and, grumbling but not having much choice, I agreed. "But only if it is in good condition."

Manzu ignored that and said, "Okay. Reserve two—no, three— nights at the Excelsior for the . . . twenty-second, twenty-third and twenty-fourth November. I meet you at the reservation area—"

"You mean in the lobby?"

"*Si*, at six-thirty on the twenty-second. Okay? I will not call again. Okay?"

"Okay, okay," I said, repeating his intonation. "Six-thirty on the evening of November twenty-second."

"I won't call again. *Va bene?* . . . Okay."

"Okay. Don't worry. I'll be there. See you then."

He hung up.

At last! One part of me was elated. Finally, I was getting close. All those dealers, restorers and policemen who had helped would at last be repaid for their efforts. The recovery, I hoped, would cause a sensation.

On the other hand, the dangerous side of the affair suddenly came much closer. Should I consult Siviero? Of course I should have—but I didn't. One of the reasons I didn't was probably vanity: I wanted to recover the picture all by myself. But another powerful reason was that, as things now stood, any help he might offer could add to the danger. Blake had always acted alone, and if I was suddenly to turn up in Naples with what would, in effect, be a bodyguard, it might be seen as a sudden, and suspicious, change of style. And for a man or men to tail me seemed, now that the situation had arrived, altogether too dangerous. If Siviero's men were spotted (and I had no idea where the Italians would take Blake) then the chances were that I would be kidnapped. Possibly worse.

Frankly, I now began to get cold feet. Perhaps I could have taken along Don Langton as a bodyguard—he would have agreed enthusiastically; but he didn't know Italy, couldn't speak Italian, and couldn't be armed, which was the whole point of the exercise anyway. At least I had two weeks to make up my mind. I needed the time.

I flattered myself that so far I had been canny enough to devise dodges which had helped me around most of the difficulties. This time, however, the dodge was a long time in coming. A large part of me felt I was being foolish and that I should stop trying to show off, stop trying to play cops and robbers and beat them both at their own game. I was, no doubt about it, frightened.

Eventually, however, a fall-back plan began to form in my mind. As usual, it was far from foolproof, yet it did provide a cushion of sorts if things went wrong. I suppose I was looking for a reason to go to Naples, alone, and this sufficed. I booked three nights at the Excelsior.

THIS TIME I really did think I might be followed from the airport so I was scrupulous in my behavior, limping perfectly and not too fast and armed with plenty of ready cash to be able to tip outrageously.

I arrived at the Excelsior toward the end of lunchtime, having flown to Naples via Rome. (I was, after all, supposed to be coming from Switzerland, which would have meant changing in Rome.) I checked in, bathed and then visited the Palazzo Capodimonte, which I had not seen before. Just in case I was being followed, I spent some time admiring the gallery's sixteenth- and seventeenth-century paintings. This would fit with my "interest" in Caravaggisti painters and Naples has good examples of the work of Lorenzo Lotto, Luca Giordano and Ribera.

I had by this time also checked out my Neapolitan history, especially art history, and had discovered to my alarm that there was such a thing as the Posillipo school. This underlined, if it needed underlining, how lucky I had been at times during the project. Baratti, who actually *lived* on Posillipo, had never mentioned it, thank god. Having found that out, I took no chances and made sure I was familiar with all the main developments in Neapolitan art such as tenebrism (from the Italian *tenebroso*, meaning murky, as are the backgrounds in tenebrist paintings); such as Luca Giordano, who was known as "*Luca fa presto* [Luke, paint quickly]" because his father was always urging him to speed up his technique; and such as Francesco Solimena, a Baroque painter of the eighteenth century, who may be obscure now but in 1733 was described as "by universal consent the greatest painter in the world."

If anyone was following me that afternoon I never noticed it. I spent three quarters of an hour at the Capodimonte and then sat drinking coffee at a pavement café, conspicuously reading a book on Jusepe Ribera, one of the more intriguing Neapolitan painters. (Ribera, a Spaniard, settled in Naples in 1616. His style owed something to Caravaggio, making much use of chiaroscuro, and in his own day he was considered to be a follower. There are stories, not always believed, that Ribera led the violent opposition of Neapolitan painters to outsiders from Rome, like Guido Reni and Domenichino, which at times caused these painters to flee for their lives, and even led to the murder of one of Reni's assistants.) If anyone *was* watching, I hoped I was behaving exactly as anticipated and as a real art dealer might have.

At about four I returned to the hotel. At the reception desk I asked the porter for the name of the hotel manager: this was the first move in my anti-kidnapping plan. Up in my room, I sat at the table and wrote a letter to the manager, placed it in an envelope and addressed it to *Domestica e Sr. Sandro Pace, direzione.* But I didn't seal it, not yet.

Then I stripped the bed and scattered the sheets, blankets and pillowcases all over the room, except for just near the door. I wanted to be sure that the next morning, when the *domestica*, the cleaning lady, poked her head into the room, the incredible untidiness would draw her in.

Then I spruced myself up, brushed my hair flatter, made sure my magnifying glass was on the writing desk. At ten minutes past six I left the room, first placing the envelope with the letter on the floor inside the door in a position where a cleaning lady could not fail to spot it. The letter, complete with my poor Italian, was still unsealed. I let myself out and locked the door.

The letter I had left read as follows:

To Sandro Pace,   Sabato,
Hotel Excelsior,   22 November 1980
Naples   ora 18:00

Messaggio urgente
Dal occupante camera 220

Signor,

If, on the morning of 23 November, you find Room 220 empty and in disarray, this will mean that I have been kidnapped [*rapire una persona*]. This is not a hoax [*non e inganno*]. I have been staying in the hotel under the name of A. John Blake, but in fact my real name is Peter Watson and I am a journalist working for the *Sunday Times* of London, England. I have been posing as Mr. Blake, an art dealer, in order to try to recover a very famous stolen painting by the Italian artist Caravaggio. Tonight at 6:30 I had a meeting with the men whom I believe to have stolen the picture. One of the men calls himself Signore Manzu, but I believe his real name to be Puccinelli. I shall of course not know where they are taking me during this meeting, but if I can I shall return to my room after the initial meeting in the lobby of your hotel and write in the space here the color, make, model and license number of the car I have been driven off in. This may be of use in tracing the whereabouts of my abductors and me. The car is:

In case you should doubt the truth of this story, let me say that I have thrown the room into disarray to attract the attention of your hotel maid, and that you should contact the following people: [There then followed the names, addresses and phone numbers of Siviero, my wife, the editor of the *Sunday Times* and its Rome correspondent, Tana de Zulueta, with whom I was most closely in touch.]

The letter continued:

But please act quickly. I am writing this on the assumption that if the police can trace these people (my abductors) before they are ready with their ransom demands, there will be the most chance of catching them and of freeing me unharmed. You may find that a useful avenue of approach is through Signore Vittorio Baratti, Villa Roccamoro 33, Posillipo. I have reason to believe he is acquainted with these men. The British Consul in Naples should also be informed.

I repeat: this letter is not a hoax. Please act quickly.

Yours sincerely,

PETER WATSON [signed]

The letter, I should say, was written on *Sunday Times* notepaper and included with it were my two passports, in the names of Watson and Blake. I hoped that the police would see the likeness between the pictures, despite the straight hair and the bow tie.

I went downstairs and sat as unobtrusively as I could but in a position where I could see the road at the front of the hotel. The Excelsior has a large *belle époque*-type lounge which affords a view of the Via Partenope and the Castel dell'Ovo [Egg Castle]. I wanted a view of their car, and its number, as early as possible.

They were late. Six-thirty came and went. A quarter to seven approached and it was already quite dark. If they were much later I would not have a chance of spotting either the color of their car or its number from within the hotel before I met them. Seven o'clock came. And went. I stood near the front door of the hotel for a while—but still no sign of them. It seemed too absurd to have got this far, to have come all the way to Naples, and then to be stood up. There was, of course, no way I could contact them. I suddenly remembered the date: 22 November. Seventeen years ago on this day, President Kennedy had been assassinated in Dallas.

Seven-nineteen—and suddenly a dark, four-door Alfa Romeo cruised to a stop on the far side of the street near a fountain. The car and its occupants just sat there for a minute or so. If this was Manzu and his friends it was very unfair of them to stop where they had: I couldn't see either license plate. I couldn't even tell whether the car was dark blue, brown or green from where I was standing. It might have been black. Two of the three men in the car got out and crossed the street to the hotel—Manzu was one of them. Behind him, as he approached, the sea and the sky were gloomy and empty.

I had considered letting it slip that I knew Manzu's real name. That might show I was a shade sharper than they thought I was, but on balance I ruled it out as too dangerous. At present they appeared to accept that I was who I said I was. Why rock the boat?

"I was beginning to worry," I said, extending my hand to Manzu as he came up the steps inside the door. He shrugged. "We come a long way and the traffic, it was bad. But we would have been late anyway," he added, smiling suddenly. "In Italy, in the south, everyone is always late."

I smiled back and he maneuvered his companion forward. "Meestaire Blake, this Signore Vitanza." So far, so good. That name was on Siviero's list as well. Vitanza was even taller than Manzu, and thinner, with a bony face and a slightly protruding lower lip. He wasn't so much bald as receding fast, with what was left of his black shiny hair swept straight back. He had the type of ears in which the top edges do not curl over, as they do on most people, but look instead like a waxy leaf, shiny and veiny.

As I was ushered out, I took the opportunity to use Manzu's comment about how far they had come. "Will it take long to get back to where we're going? I've only ever been to Pompeii and Herculaneum around here."

"About one hundred kilometers, in the hills—back near Avellino."

This information was invaluable, but more than that, it was also a relief. It sounded as though they weren't planning to kidnap me.

Outside, it was darker than I had anticipated. The license numbers on Italian cars are smaller than in Britain, and that afternoon, as I had limped around Naples on my way to and from the museum, I had worked out just how far away I could be from a car and still decipher its number. But that, of course, had been in daylight: now I was not so sure. I couldn't put on my spectacles—that might be seen as suspicious and, worse, we were approaching the car from the side: I couldn't see the numbers anyway.

"One second," I said, and suddenly slipped away from the car, to the right. I walked toward some steps leading down to the sea from the road. I peered over at the murky water. This had taken me about twenty yards beyond and behind the car, which I now approached from the rear. The license plates on Italian cars are larger there than at the front. I would get only one chance to glimpse the number and Manzu was already looking at me in a puzzled way, lighting cigarettes for himself and Vitanza.

It was a Salerno license plate. There were the letters "SA," in bright orange, followed by six digits: 441665. Fortunately, I am fairly numerate and, having once been a psychologist and become familiar with intelligence tests in which people are asked to remember strings of numbers, I was aware that mnemonics can help the memory in this context: "44"—the year after I was born; "16"—my collar size; "65"—Glen Miller (as in "Pennsylvania six-five thousand"). This I converted into "Birth × Collar = Miller"—nonsense but helpful as a way to remember the digits.

Manzu was still looking puzzled by my behavior at the parapet. "In England," I said, "all the seas have strong tides—there is often a huge difference between high tide and low tide. Here, it is nothing like in England. I wanted to see what change there had been since the afternoon." I had no idea how convincing that sounded, but it was the best I could do. Manzu seemed to accept it and beckoned me into the front seat of the car.

The driver, who was introduced simply as Enrico, was also tall —his head touched the top of the car's roof lining. Unlike the others, he was not wearing a suit or tie but had on a leather jacket with woolen cuffs. In age, he looked to be anywhere from thirty to forty, neither fat nor thin, with rather a pleasant round face. He wore a bracelet on his left wrist.

I was itching to act, but to ensure that what I intended to do was as credible as possible, I had to wait. Enrico engaged the gears and pulled out into the road. I was now leaning forward, fiddling in my pockets and, as he began to accelerate into second gear, I turned to him suddenly and shouted, "Stop! Stop!" I waved at him and turned around to Manzu. "Make him stop, will you?"

Manzu spoke quickly and the Alfa Romeo slid to a halt. We had gone not two hundred yards.

"I've forgotten my magnifying glass," I said, patting my pockets. "I must go back for it."

Manzu looked hard at me, drawing on his cigarette. Then there was a burst of Italian as he explained to the others what I had said. It was Enrico's turn to shrug now, but we were in a one-way street and it was easy enough to reverse.

When we were back in front of the Excelsior I got out and limped into the hotel, where I made a show of collecting my key. Up in my room I first picked up my magnifying glass and hung it around my neck. Then I filled in the blank space in my letter, though I now realized I still didn't know the model of the Alfa Romeo or its exact color. The street lighting had not been good and I had been slightly thrown in having to maneuver to where I could see the license plate. So I simply wrote, "Alfa Romeo, 4-door, dark (blue, green, maybe black), license number SA 441665." And I added at the bottom, "I understand I am being taken near Avellino. P.W., 19:37."

When I returned to the lobby Manzu was lighting another cigarette. I waved the magnifying glass at him and smiled. He kept the cigarette in his mouth and simply said, between clenched teeth, "*Andiamo* [Let's go]."

WE DIDN'T GO TO AVELLINO but to a much smaller town called Laviano on the top of a hill nearby. It was a shabby place, quiet and, except for the main piazza, very dark. It was 9:45 before we arrived. Once in the town I don't say I was deliberately disoriented; I wasn't blindfolded or anything like that, but I did get the feeling that Enrico drove around more than was necessary to get to where we were going, presumably in an attempt to prevent me ever finding my way there again, unaided. Or perhaps we were early and just killing time. Anyway, I didn't worry; I have a good sense of direction and Laviano was so small that however much they tried to confuse me, I felt sure, should I ever need to, I would be able to find where we were going without too much difficulty.

Eventually we stopped outside a bar—if you could call it that. It was a collection of tables, a refrigerator, with a lurid print on one wall of Raphael's *Sistine Madonna*, the whole arrangement bathed in the watery light of a single neon strip. Two women and two men, all fairly old, sat at the tables sipping wine and whispering. They fell silent as the four of us entered. The bar, I think, was called Niccastri's.

Vitanza called out in surprisingly guttural Italian, and a very rotund figure in a white apron appeared at the back of the bar. He beckoned us through into the rear. Here was the kind of Italian room I had come to know so well. An ornate sideboard, a heavy wooden carved table, exactly in the middle of the room, somewhat sickly religious paintings covering the walls. In contrast a bright, cheap, velour sofa along one wall, where I was invited to sit.

The bar owner, if that's who he was, never smiled and wasn't introduced. He said something to Manzu, who turned to me and said, "What will you drink?" Though my Italian was very shaky, I was well aware that this was not a translation of what the barman had said. Curiously, I did not yet feel nervous, so I asked for red wine. I figured it would be less filthy than the local white.

The barman went back to his bar to get the drinks, and Manzu, Vitanza and I sat down. Enrico had disappeared. I asked, "Where's our driver?" I didn't want to antagonize anybody by letting on that I was studying their names.

"He has gone to fetch the man you wish to meet," said Manzu. "We wait, maybe ten minutes."

The wine, when it came, was rather as I had expected. Very thin, though probably not watered in the strict sense of the word. The others gulped down their glasses straightaway and refilled them from the jug. I did the same. Vitanza whistled under his breath, while Manzu, of course, smoked. On the walls sad madonnas and sickly St. Sebastians, stuck through with arrows yet still smiling, seemed to mock the earthly awfulness of the room.

AT FIRST, he reminded me of a bank manager. He arrived with hardly any warning. There was no commotion outside; he just called through the beading that separated the back room from the front one, "Manzu?"

It was a soft, but clear voice, not half as authoritative as I had expected. He was the smallest of the men in the room, grayer with bushy hair and had on an old suit, almost as gray and shiny as his hair. He wore a white shirt with collar points that were barely cut away at all. There was hair protruding from his ears. He brought with him a large, mean-looking dog, with pointed ears and lots of teeth.

He nodded to me and waved me down as I began to get up. There then followed one of those long, animated Italian conversations between this new man, Manzu and Vitanza. Suddenly the new man broke off and shouted through to the bar. I thought he was asking someone to act as a lookout, but no, he wanted a glass so he could join us in the wine.

At last we got down to business. The others seated themselves at the table, while I leaned forward from the sofa. The new man —it was clear I would never know *his* name—had a briefcase with him and he placed it on the lace tablecloth. He unclasped the clip and spoke to Manzu.

"Do you have any money?" Manzu said, turning to me.

"Mr. Manzu, you know I haven't. I'm here to look at the picture. If I'm satisfied you have it, and that it is in good condition, we have already agreed on a price. We would just have to settle when and where to pay."

A pause while he translated. Then: "My friend asks why you not bring the money with you now, if you want the picture?"

I sighed and, acting a bit stagily I must admit, drank some wine to create delay and an effect. "You know well why not, Mr. Manzu. If I had the money you could just take it from me. You will be paid in New York or London, maybe Rome if we can work it out. But not here." I didn't say any more. Both Siviero and Don Langton had advised me to be as brief as possible. "That way you are bound to make fewer mistakes," said Don.

While I had been talking the new man had been pouring himself some wine. Now while Manzu translated he began closing the briefcase and looking doubtful.

Damn. I was so close I wanted to say that I had the money back in Naples, just so they would show me whatever was in the briefcase. But I had to pinch myself and remember what I would do, how I would behave, if I really did have some of my own money riding on this deal. I kept quiet.

Manzu and the new man, who was scowling, were now deep in conversation, each appealing to Vitanza from time to time for support. He would invariably nod when spoken to but otherwise took little part in the negotiations.

At length Manzu turned back to me and said, "Let us agree how you pay."

I was experienced enough by now to know how to counter this —quickly. "No," I said. "I have come all the way here, at great expense and some inconvenience. Before we go any further I want some evidence that you have the Caravaggio." I rubbed in my point. "You must think I have the money, Mr. Manzu, otherwise we wouldn't be here. You know I have had dealings in Italy for some time. Either you trust me by now or you don't. Show me the painting—or at least give me some proof that you have it."

Nothing like a bit of bluster at the right time. It may have lost something in the translation, but since I had done my best to gesticulate during my "speech," the new man was well aware what I was talking about before he heard it from Manzu. And sure enough, while Manzu was translating he began unclasping the briefcase again. He was still scowling though. I thought of Strindberg's comment that he loathed people who kept dogs because they lacked the guts to bite people themselves. Wrong. The bushy-haired man could bite all right, if he needed to.

He reached into the briefcase. All it was was a photograph. Two photographs in fact. But of the picture. . . . It was the real thing.

At last.

It looked terrible. It was very dark, darker than I had imagined it could look. Bits appeared to have flaked off near the heads of the onlookers on the right of the painting and there was a patch, of damp or oil or whatever, in the right foreground covering the ankle and hand of St. Lawrence. Worst of all there was a ragged crack, about a third of the way up, bisecting the Virgin's hands and penetrating St. Lawrence's shoulder. That seemed consonant with the canvas having been rolled for some time, possibly immediately after it had been stolen.

I made a face. At the bottom left of the photograph was a recent newspaper—the classic terrorist approach, then so popular among the Red Brigades—to show that a kidnap victim was still alive: the paper was dated a few days earlier, Wednesday, 19 November.

The second photograph, with the same newspaper also shown, was a close-up of the Virgin and child. They had presumably done this in an attempt to show that the brushwork was the master's and not some copyist's. I was not enough of an expert to tell, but what the photograph did do was give me a better view of that crack. I drew my finger along it and winced again, shaking my head.

"This is bad," I said.

Manzu shrugged.

I went on gazing at the photos, back and forth from one to the other, looking glum.

At length Manzu broke the silence. "You can get it repaired—"

But I snapped at him. "Of course, I can't!" I shouted. "We are talking about a stolen painting. Any restorer worth his salt will recognize the picture, and very probably report me to the police." Another pause, then I looked up and spoke directly to the new man. "I want to see the painting itself, with the crack. Then you will have to have it repaired for me. Or there's no sale."

This was not quite such an enormous piece of stupidity as it might appear. After all, the project needed only to recover the canvas. Siviero would be jubilant about that, whatever its condition. Yet I had to keep reminding myself to act like a real dealer would, not like a journalist masquerading as a dealer and desperate to bring his story to a conclusion. And a real dealer would very definitely have been put off by that crack. A further thought was that these duplicitous characters were perfectly capable of drawing a crack on the painting and then photographing it to see my reaction. The more I thought about it, the more I was sure I had to drive a hard bargain.

I had plenty of time to think since Manzu and the new man were back in one of their long-winded conversations, Manzu stabbing the air with his cigarette and periodically tapping the photograph.

Another worrying thought struck me. "Signore Manzu. You let me go back for my magnifying glass, knowing full well that we weren't going to see the actual painting tonight. . . . Why?"

He lit another cigarette and didn't meet my eye. Eventually, breathing out the smoke, he did look at me and smiled sardonically. "Maybe you wouldn't have come. Maybe you think we do not have the painting." A pause. "But you see we have." There seemed to be a competition as to who could speak in the shortest sentences.

I sighed and shook my head. "This isn't the way to do business." But I remembered how Manzu had paused in the car when I had said I wanted to go back for my glass. He must have been wondering how much to tell me.

Manzu and the new man resumed their previous conversation. Now Vitanza was drawn in, so I finished off the wine. That made four glasses and I told myself to be careful.

Eventually, Manzu turned to me. "This man"—he gestured to the bushy-haired figure—"would like you to see the painting. Right now it is in Sicily, but we can have it here the night after tomorrow. Unfortunately, the crack is bad, but my friend, he say that if we repair it, it should not affect the price." And he was off speaking Italian again before I could express a view. This time I heard words I recognized, words like Milano, Cremona and *restauro*.

Then Manzu was talking again. "My friend knows someone, a man in Cremona who is very talented at repairing pictures. He works in churches. He can maybe cover the crack. Cremona is near Milan—you can pay there, he says, when the painting is finished."

"How long will that take?" I said, sounding and feeling exasperated.

Another burst of Italian. Once again words I could distinguish: *settimana, tela, fessura, vernice, lire*. They were talking about how many weeks it would take to repair the crack and revarnish the painting, and how many lire it would cost.

"A week, maybe two. If you come back here in two days, we can show you the painting. My friend here will have spoken to the man he knows in Cremona and he will say then how long it takes. Then you can return to London and come back to Milan in a few days—the painting will be ready. You say you feel safer in the north. You can pay in Milano."

This was good news and bad news. I would get to the Caravaggio in two days' time. But I didn't relish the idea of having to come back to this tiny town. It felt alien, creepy, frightening I suppose. Nor did I like the delay of days or weeks before the deal was done: too much could happen in the interim. It was a real dilemma. If I brought in Siviero now he *might* advise waiting until the picture got to Cremona or Milano. But he might want to conclude the raid two nights from now, here in Laviano.

There were two other things I didn't like about this latter

course of events, neither of which I would admit to Siviero. One was that I didn't think Laviano a very suitable place to end the story. It was a dump of a town. Second, I would be very frightened if anything happened here. The nature of corruption and violence in southern Italy meant that even Siviero would have a job keeping any operation here secret; he probably wouldn't know the area—so anything could happen. Now that the project had reached this far, I realized I wasn't made of sterner stuff. I chickened out and resolved not to tell Siviero what had gone on until the painting had made the journey north.

I got to my feet and the man with the bushy hair put the photographs back in his briefcase. Could I ask for one? I thought not. The man's fingerprints would be all over them and the newspaper gimmick proved he was a link in the chain, involved with identifiable stolen property.

The bushy-haired man and I shook hands and he said, "A lunedi [Till Monday]."

As is often the case, the return journey to Naples didn't seem to take as long as the journey out to Laviano, partly I expect because I slept some of the way. We arrived at the Excelsior at about 1:15 A.M. I thought I might ask them in for a drink, but then remembered there was just a risk my letter had been already discovered, so I didn't. We arranged to meet outside the hotel on the Monday just as we had done that night.

My room was in the mess I had left it, with the letter intact and unread. I tidied up and fell into bed excited and exhausted.

The next day, Sunday, was cold but for most of the time clear. For an Englishman in a double-breasted suit it was the perfect weather for sight-seeing and for a bracing walk (or limp). I decided to get away from Naples for the day and so at about eleven that morning I took a taxi to the Capri ferry. As far as I could tell as I clambered on board the boat, I wasn't being followed.

I spent a pleasant day on the island, had a long lunch with plenty of wine, ate ice cream and watched the boats. I bought no souvenirs and did not see the Blue Grotto. I had a couple of slender books with me, John Steer's *Concise History of Venetian Painting* and Graham Greene's *The Confidential Agent*, and I read through both of them with ease.

I sailed back to the mainland at about seven o'clock and, since it was still clear, and I had nothing better to do, I decided to walk to my hotel. That decision may just have saved my life.

AT 7:36 THAT EVENING an earthquake measuring 6.5 on the Richter scale struck southern Italy. Its epicenter, I later learned, was near Balvano, a hundred miles southeast of Naples. I remember limping past one of those tiny cafés that line Naples Bay and noticing a group of boys watching a football match on television. Later I found out there was a big game that night, Inter-Milan against Juventus. Next I recall a large flock of sea gulls suddenly rise screaming into the air. Then I heard a rushing sound, followed immediately by a loud ringing crack—and the earth shifted. Upward a bit to begin with, then juddering from side to side.

I had read about those Chinese claims that animals spot earthquakes before humans do, so I had a good idea early on what was happening. I also realized I was lucky. I was walking along the edge of the bay, on the side of the street away from the buildings. Some flats and offices appeared to shudder—or it may have been me. One just settled quickly, dropping a few inches perhaps in one dumpy, sudden movement, then remained quite still. Only the sound of crashing stone inside, as staircases collapsed, betrayed what was happening.

Immediately after that the first people came screaming out of the various buildings. I caught the word "*terremoto*." My own first reaction, however, was to look out to sea. Would there be a tidal wave [*maremoto*], as I heard Neapolitans with similar ideas to my own call it? My geology wasn't up to it. (A quote I couldn't place flashed into my mind: "We all learn geology the morning after the earthquake.") The bay looked choppy, very choppy, but as far as I could make out, not threatening.

This is not the place to give a full history of the Naples earthquake. The world already knows what devastation it caused and what a scandal were the rescue arrangements. What I should confess here is that, to my shame, I was at the time more concerned about the effects of the earthquake on the project than on the number of lives lost and the families left homeless. Like many people, I had from time to time wondered what it would be like to be in an earthquake and how I would behave. The answer to the first question is that earthquakes are terrifying. After it was all over I read avidly everything I could about the earthquake (and geology) and in one report it was said that the first shudder lasted ninety seconds. At the time it seemed to me as though the shaking would never stop, but I now realize that where I was it couldn't have gone on for more than, say, fifty to sixty seconds. People in the street were naturally concerned that there would be other tremors, but the next one didn't come for about an hour.

Nor was I in the part of Naples most affected. Poggioreale, a suburb of the city about five miles away, was much more badly hit than the bay area. It was in Poggioreale that a nine-story apartment building collapsed, killing thirty-six.

How did I behave in the earthquake? Well, like all situations that are similar—being in an accident, for example—I found time to think to myself, "Is this it? Is this the way people die, unceremoniously, unglamorously, unwarned?" I had once had quite a strong electric shock from a toaster that had been incorrectly wired. First, I didn't realize what was happening, then two things happened at the same time—I thought I was probably going to die, and I pulled my hand away. Finally, shock set in and I started shaking. Much the same happened with the earthquake except that, for me, the earthquake reaction was not nearly as bad as being electrocuted.

I realized that during the rumbling (the shaking of the ground was more or less similar to the shaking of one's body when one gets an electric shock) I had heard sounds that I presumed to be falling masonry, but from where I was I couldn't see any. I saw no one injured.

The road lining the bay was now filling with people, shouting and looking back up at the buildings. But there was still electricity, or appeared to be. A lot of traffic had stopped and people had hurried out of their cars; but by no means in every case. If this was the "panic" which the newspapers described later on, it was fairly dull panic.

The point is, of course, that at that moment I had no idea how serious the earthquake was in the Naples hinterland. I had no family and loved ones in the area. Many of the people still moving in their cars were presumably on their way home—quickly— to see what was what. I just continued on my way back to the hotel. And, though it seems silly to say it now, I limped.

Outside the hotel a group of people were standing talking, as there were outside every other building. The hotel itself seemed hardly to have suffered at all. Inside, a crowd of people sat in front of a television set, but I didn't know then whether they were looking out for news or watching the football. I didn't go to my room straightaway but had a drink at the bar. No one knew any more than I did at that stage.

There being little else to do, I started to reread *The Confidential Agent,* and in this way, with several whiskeys and water at my elbow, I spent a rather tedious three hours.

Not until the next afternoon did the full impact of what had happened come home. For instance, I read later that there had been another major quake, measuring 4.9 on the Richter scale, at 8:39 that same evening. This was recorded at the Trieste observatory, but it didn't so much as spill my whiskey. When I talked to the reception desk the concierge simply said that they didn't know what was happening.

However, no one showed any inclination to go to bed that night and around twelve, Sandro Pace, the manager, threw a spaghetti party to help take his guests' minds off events. People where I was seemed more concerned about fresh tremors than those which had already occurred. Possibly this was because they were mostly businessmen from out of town who knew that their relatives would be safe.

Afterward, when I thought about bed, I was told at the desk that many Neapolitans would be sleeping in the open air that night. I understood well what the hotel management was trying to say, but what could I do? I knew no one in the city, in whose garden I could sleep, save for Baratti. I didn't favor that. It was November and you don't sleep outside in November without good reason. For many people the threat of an earthquake *is* good reason, but I was inexperienced and, perhaps due to that, not as afraid as I should have been. I had no car, which would have been a good place to spend the night, so I went to my room at about two, tucked myself up in bed with the windows open (so I could escape) and said a prayer (a thing I had not done in years). I slept like a log.

Next day I was slow to grasp what had happened since, not speaking Italian well enough, I did not tune into the news. The first sign was that the taps ran dirty, but in Italy who reads anything into that? The streets were jammed with traffic; I heard the honking very early. But it was a Monday morning after all, and that might have been normal for a weekday, for all I knew. Then, when I went down for breakfast the receptionist asked me when I was leaving. I told him the following day and he asked if there was any likelihood I would be staying on. I said no and asked why he was so concerned.

"The earthquake is very bad in the mountains. Many dead. The government may want to fill hotels with the homeless people. We have to say how many rooms we have free."

Many dead. I didn't know then that the death toll would eventually rise to 3,000 and the homeless be put at somewhere between 200,000 and 300,000. As it turned out, the Excelsior wasn't called upon to provide beds, but a couple of "poorer" hotels were.

Monday was cold and foggy. I didn't go far. *Il Mattino*, a Naples paper that I did see, was headlined, I think, "One Minute of Terror, Hundreds Dead." I flipped through it but the earthquake had happened too late in the day for it to devote more than three pages to the tragedy. It was already clear, however, that there were a hundred dead in Balvano, seventy killed in Avellino and that there had been a revolt in one of Naples' jails— Europe's most crowded—where frightened prisoners had overpowered their guards.

Only gradually throughout the day did the dimensions of the catastrophe dawn on me. Many businesses appeared closed that morning, but again businesses in Naples and in Italy generally have idiosyncratic opening hours to an Englishman, often being closed around midday for an indeterminate period; and many restaurants close on Mondays anyway. Traffic remained heavy throughout the morning, though it died away later; and it was obvious even to me that many people were leaving the city with sleeping bags, blankets and food. I saw a few people walking around in dressing gowns and pajamas. Small pieces of plaster and stucco littered several streets, shaken loose by the shuddering. I read later that cars had been buried by the rubble, but that day I didn't see any. Next to the cars in some of the wider streets there were signs of fires, lit during the night to keep warm those who had spent the night in the piazzas.

Some shops did open and queues formed outside grocers and a

couple of fruit stalls. There were plenty of school-aged children around, but there always *are* hordes of children in Naples.

Without too much trouble I found a restaurant that was open, indeed crowded, and treated myself to a long, vinous lunch. I was now reading, and enjoying, Harold Schonberg's *Lives of the Great Composers,* and did not leave the lunch table until past three. By then the only sign of commercial life was a chemist's which was still open. Normally, it would have been closed for the afternoon.

When I got back to the hotel, there was a message from my wife, who was naturally very worried. I telephoned her in London—the lines seemed fine—and reassured her that I was quite safe. But that was how I really learned a lot of the Italian news that day, from my wife in Britain. *She* told me that the Rome-Naples rail link had been cut off; *she* told me that buildings in Naples had crumbled completely, killing scores of people; *she* told me that a car outside the city had plunged into a deep crack that suddenly opened up in the road; and *she* told me that a church had collapsed in Balvano, killing many of the children inside, who were singing hymns at the time.

I suppose it was during that conversation with my wife, which took place in the early evening, that I first thought Manzu and Vitanza might not rendezvous as planned. I knew that Laviano was just inside the earthquake zone, but had found no mention of it in that day's *Il Mattino.*

Still, I prepared to meet the two men, as I had done the previous Saturday. At 6:30 I was seated in the hotel lobby, ready to go back to the mountains. The traffic had died down somewhat, no tremors had been felt all day and life in Naples at least was returning to normal.

I was more optimistic than I should have been, and even by 7:00 P.M., when they hadn't appeared, I still felt someone might come. At 7:30 I started to accept that—well, maybe they had other, more important things on their minds. At 8:00 I went into the bar for a beer but kept my eye on the door. At 8:30 I went into dinner, leaving a message at the reception desk that Mr. Blake was in the dining room should he have any visitors. By 9:00 I told myself that even if they came now we wouldn't get to Laviano until after 11:00 and so couldn't get back to the hotel before the small hours.

By that time, too, I had reached Chapter Fourteen of Schonberg's *Lives*, about Donizetti and his great opera *Lucia di Lammermoor*. Donizetti had a tempestuous relationship with Naples, just as I was now having. *Poliuto*, one of his operas, had been banned by the Neapolitan censor in 1839, but *Lucia* was first produced in the city and was so well received that Donizetti had to retire to bed for several days "with nervous fever."

Manzu and Vitanza didn't come. Of course they didn't come. I learned later that almost every house in Laviano had collapsed, killing 1,500 people out of the 2,500 who lived in the town.

THAT NIGHT I had to make up my mind what to do. Should I stay on, in the hope that they would still contact me? What would they expect me to do? Would they think about me at all? If they had gone to Sicily to get the painting, did that mean they and it were safe? Presumably some of their group or gang lived full-time in Laviano, like the bushy-haired man? Or maybe they were really based in Salerno since the car had a Salerno license plate? Salerno had also been affected by the earthquake, as far as I knew. So many questions, but no answers.

I am not good at sitting still. Besides, as a newspaperman, I was itching to get to the center of the action. Half of me wanted to break cover, call the office and tell them that, for once, they had someone in the right place at the right time. But my other half told me that was foolish, that to return to Peter Watson would risk destroying what was left of the project. In any case the paper would soon send someone from Rome or London. So I compromised: I stuck with my limp and cane but resolved to hire a car next morning and see Laviano for myself.

I had slept in the hotel again, though many were still spending the nights in the piazzas. Tuesday's *Il Mattino* was headed "Thousands Dead; 100,000 Homeless." It also gave the news that the Pope was to visit the stricken areas that day and it had many pictures by now of "canceled" villages, as the Italian idiom has it. One stark photograph showed long rows of dead covered in makeshift *veli*, or shrouds, made from tarpaulins.

Hiring a car was a bit of a problem to begin with, since so many had already been taken by relatives worried by the news and who had rushed back to their native villages. But as ever in a

situation like this, there were profiteers, men who knew that journalists, with more money than the peasants, would soon be on the
scene and spending cash that was not their own. It took me three
attempts and a bribe, but by a quarter past ten I had a car. I
checked out of the Excelsior and started for Laviano.

It was a mistake. Everyone knows now that aid was a long
time in coming. It was a scandal throughout Italy. On that Tuesday, relief workers and supplies were just beginning to flow
through to some areas. Many more people—relatives—had decided to return to their villages, now that it looked as if the worst
tremors were over. I later learned that Alitalia and some foreign
airlines like British Airways were flying in relatives free of charge
and they were arriving on that Tuesday as well. So the *autostrade*
south of Naples was very busy.

I got to the edge of the city without too many problems, but
from there it got progressively worse. Near Vesuvius, black out-
crops of volcanic rock edged the roadway, grim, dour reminders
of an earlier tragedy on a similar scale. The first signs of major
damage appeared beyond Salerno, driving past evocative place
names, like Angri. Eboli, Battipaglia and Scafati all showed scars
—crumbled buildings, fire engines, white staring faces. Ironically,
in making a move I had missed another tremor that morning,
around Naples.

It took me four hours instead of the previous two. Beyond
Salerno, beyond Eboli, I left the *autostrade* and made for Contursi. The valley of the river Sele, where Laviano is located, is
beautiful—in summer. Near Contursi, a spa town, the smell of
sulphur from the baths can be very strong. As I picked my way
carefully up the valley the police got more numerous until they
were on guard at almost every crossroads.

Mud slides were everywhere. One could see whole chunks
of hillsides that had simply dropped away—fresh, black/brown
stains of still-moist earth. Houses, which had in any case been
built on impossible spurs, had disappeared. In places the road
was deformed into congealed, frozen waves of tar. At Quaglietta,
a weird town with a ruin on a rock outside, half a bridge had
disappeared, and that took some negotiating.

Helicopters, more often heard than seen, went racing by overhead. What I didn't know then, but found out soon enough, was
that Italy's President, Sandro Pertini, was in the area and was in

fact visiting Laviano that very day. Animals ran wild. Poles supporting vines sloped at every crazy angle.

I turned off the valley road, onto the S 381, at a big house, a Casa Cantoniera, and from there things got worse very quickly. As I drove, the *Sunday Times* editorial meeting would have been in progress in London, where no doubt the decision to send a reporter and a photographer to the area might already have been taken. I was several hours ahead so there was no danger of my bumping into Manzu or the bushy-haired man and a newspaper colleague at the same time.

The hills grew stonier, bonier and closer together. Just as the road started to rise steeply I came to a bridge. The stonework was intact—amazingly—but the stream which was supposed to run *under* the bridge had changed course—and now ran alongside it, over the road. Besides the water that drenched the roadway, stones and grit were strewn across the tarmac, making it slippery and treacherous.

The first sight I had of Laviano in daylight reminded me of those curious villages in the Yemen, high up on inaccessible pinnacles. I saw the wall of a house—just that, with an arch in it— balanced precariously two hundred to three hundred feet above me: stark, slender, devoid of meaning or life and thrown into contrast against the hostile skies. It looked as if it might give up and fall at any minute.

I passed a road sign indicating, I think, wild dogs, and a caravan with a cattle skull hanging outside, just like a Hollywood version of the wild West.

Into the town and the road deteriorated still further. Girders, waste pipes and wine vats were now exposed. I could go no farther by car. "All places are distant from heaven alike," wrote Robert Burton in his *Anatomy of Melancholy*. Wrong. On its beautiful pinnacle, Laviano should have been closer than most, but now it looked abandoned by God as much as by the rescue services.

For a hundred yards or more, as the ruins of the town came into view, cars lined the road, abandoned hurriedly by relatives anxious to reach their loved ones. I had to do the same and, ridiculously, limp the last part of my journey with my cane.

As I have said, I later learned that 1,500 of Laviano's 2,500 inhabitants were killed that Sunday night. To many people these bald statistics would not be enough to convey the devastation, the human misery and the chaos caused by the earthquake. But for me the figures were eloquent. Cruel as it may seem, the number of people actually killed in a disaster is usually much less than could occur. Not this time: 1,500 out of 2,500 was, for me, awesome. I didn't believe it then and I still find it hard to comprehend now.

The town, or village, wasn't there. It was as simple as that. There was just rubble—of stones and plaster, of wood and glass, of mangled metal and cracked plastic. Many areas seemed to have been sprayed with powdered bottle glass—a deep, shiny green. To a generation raised on a cultural diet dominated by television and movies, the temptation in any crisis is to look for the small visual detail a camera would record, or which the newscaster would seize upon, that could be made to seem symbolic of the wider tragedy. What mattered in Laviano wasn't that one could find a whole, semicircular window, unshattered by the disaster, or a child's broken doll, a cracked bottle of medicine or a straggle of winter flowers thrown out of their vase but not yet withered. What mattered in Laviano was the scale of the devastation—what had happened happened to everybody. Nothing could be symbolic of *that*.

Grimly, I remembered my boast to myself, only two nights before: that, if need be, I could easily find the bar where I had met the bushy-haired man. Not now I couldn't. Whole streets had ceased to exist. It was not just that buildings had collapsed: the patches of ground on which they had been built appeared in many cases to have moved closer together, or farther apart.

Amid all this mess there moved three kinds of people. There were the survivors, aimlessly picking away at the stones or the splinters of furniture, older people not simply shocked or grieving but also confused at not being able to find their way about, surprised that they did not recognize what should have been so familiar. Second, the early volunteer relief workers. Not many of them just yet, but more purposeful in their stride and bearing—respectful of the survivors, yes, but—one can say this at a distance—just a little full of themselves now that they had a very obvious job to do. Here was a new order and they were at the top. Later, when government help failed to arrive, the villagers would turn against most volunteers. But not yet.

Third, the relatives, from the north, Switzerland and Germany. People who had traveled all night and whose fear and anxiety often gave way—in loud exchanges—to anger. There was also the local priest, Father Giuseppe Zarra, a man not given to plain speaking, but who now voiced the villagers' dismay and resentment at their neglect by the authorities. President Pertini had come and gone by the time I arrived, and though he is well loved throughout Italy as a man "above politics," even he had been jostled and called a "thief." Four young boys had been heard groaning beneath the rubble but there had been insufficient equipment to rescue them. The priest had heard the boys' cries and then witnessed the silence that followed. "What are you going to do about *that*?" Pertini had been asked.

A dormitory of tents had been set up in the football field. Villagers stood by in woolens, smoking and talking quietly, as if they had been there all their lives. Pertini's visit had not been helped when the wind set up by the rotor blades of one of the helicopters in his party flattened one of the tents. As the survivors pointed out bitterly, the government could arrange for helicopters to bring the President and his entourage but not material help.

A few children stared back at me from the camp. Dogs scrimmaged in and out of tents, smelling the newly unrolled canvas (or whatever modern synthetic it was). A fire at one end crackled away, almost the only sound.

I didn't stay long in Laviano. I didn't find the bar—I didn't even find the street it was—had been—in. I saw no faces I recognized. I could have gone among the tents on the football field but, to be honest, I wasn't sure of my reception. A well-dressed, well-fed foreigner, in an expensive coat and a silly bow tie, was scarcely to be welcomed. And if I *had* found someone, and we had been able to communicate, what impression would I have made? I might have been seen as prying. Possibly it could have done more harm than good.

I did visit the small war memorial in the main square. Strangely, it was untouched save for one of the First World War bomb shells, used as adornment, which had fallen over. I noticed how the Coppola family, the Lupo, the Fusella and the Ceriello families, had been decimated. Their names formed a sad link with that huge cemetery in Birmingham, all those months before, when the project was getting going.

But of course the earthquake was a much bigger disaster for Laviano than both world wars put together. There were bodies now in the square. The coffins hadn't arrived—that was another scandal—and the corpses were wrapped with whatever material was at hand, just as I had seen in that morning's newspaper. The smell of *putrefazione* was already seeping into the air. Father Zarra moved between the square and the football field to celebrate mass for each new body that was found.

During my brief visit that day I began to pick up the wrong kind of Italian: *sciagura* [disaster], *grigioverde* [the gray-green khaki worn by the soldiers], *gemiti* [groans], *urlati* [shrieks], *corpi straziati* [mangled bodies], *feriti* [wounded], *topi* [rats], *sepolti vivi* [living graves], *senza tetto* [homeless], *bari* [coffins], *repescaggi* [miracle], *straziato* [heartbroken].

So I retreated. More relatives had arrived since I had, and parked behind my car. But there was not, as far as I could tell, any more relief. Some young children, standing on the road and too young to help their parents (if they now had parents), watched me go.

As I went I did pass a truckload of blankets, but the comfort they offered must have been offset by the deterioration in the weather. On the way back to Naples, the gray mist turned into icy rain, and what with that, the roads and the trucks, the vans and the police cars, it was almost 8:30 before I passed the Neapolitan conglomeration of lights and indifferently graceful black hills, sliding into the bay. I was headed north on the *autostrade*. I had decided to give in. There was no point in hanging around and I was very thankful when, a few miles out from Naples, one of those huge Pavesi service areas, ablaze with welcoming civilization, suddenly appeared. I stopped, ate soup, pasta, roast chicken, salad, bread, chocolate and drank half a liter of wine (probably more than was good for me since I still had a long way to drive before I reached Rome). Then I had some more pasta. It was not lost on me that the desolation of Laviano was barely a hundred miles from where I was eating so greedily.

I arrived in Rome some time after midnight and made my way to the Excelsior. Next day I flew back to London. I told no one what had happened—not Siviero, not Andrew Purches, not Renzullo. I was ashamed to have been so near the earthquake and to have done nothing, not even report it. And I was depressed with myself for failing to recover the painting. As far as I was now concerned, John Blake and the damn Caravaggio conspiracy were dead.

Part II

The Del Sarto Swindle

13

The Second St. John

THE EARTHQUAKE and its aftermath dominated the news for some time. Christmas came and went. Hope has as many lives as a cat, said Longfellow. But not in my case. I was thoroughly dejected. As if to rub salt in my wounds, a major theft occurred over Christmas in, of all places, Buenos Aires. Twenty-three works were taken from the Santa Marina collection at the Museum of Fine Arts, including paintings and drawings by Cézanne, Degas, Daumier, three Renoirs, a Matisse and a Rodin. Van Gogh's *Paysage de St. Rémy* and Picasso's watercolor *Au café* had been taken from a collection in Paris; Rubens' *Triumph of Constantine* had disappeared from Queenstown, Maryland, and Cranach's *Three Graces* and Correggio's *Adoration of the Shepherds* had gone from Venice.

With so much activity I was gloomier than ever about my failure. From time to time people like Don Langton or Andrew Purches would get in touch and ask how things were going. Usually I just blustered and pretended it was all going to come right soon. But what could I do, even if I had the inclination? My only route to Manzu was via Baratti again. But Manzu, if he was still alive, knew that, and knew how to contact me directly if the Caravaggio still existed and he still wanted to sell. So I made no attempt to get in touch with Baratti. And no call came from Manzu.

AT THIS POINT—February, 1981—I changed jobs. Harold Evans, my boss at the *Sunday Times,* was asked to edit the (daily) *Times,* and before he changed papers he mentioned to me the possibility that I could follow him, to write a daily column, known as "The Diary," which he wanted to revamp and enlarge. By now I could admit to myself that the art-theft project was dead, a failure; I wanted to forget all about it. I set about making preparations for the launch of my new column.

In any event, "The Diary" did not start until May, but in the interim I was busy, as almost every journalist in Britain was busy, with another project: the royal wedding. In the last week of February it was announced that Prince Charles would marry Lady Diana Spencer on 29 July that year and Harold Evans decided that for one of his first projects at the *Times* the paper would produce a color magazine to celebrate the marriage. I was given the job of getting the magazine off the ground, thinking through the format such a magazine might have and commissioning articles. I was less than enthusiastic about the project, and was really more anxious to get on with "The Diary," but March and April had to be spent getting the wedding magazine rolling. I did pay one visit to New York, where I saw Renzullo fleetingly. He said that he hoped soon to have a Caravaggio for me, a *St. John the Baptist.* Given Renzullo's record, I didn't pay much attention.

The spring passed and in May my column began. To do my new job properly I had to read each of London's ten daily papers closely and so couldn't help noticing that a Rembrandt, *Battle Scene,* had disappeared from Ordan-la-Roque in France, or that four Dürer woodcuts had been stolen from Palermo in Sicily. Three more Renoirs had gone, two from Paris and a third from Palm Beach. A Van Ruysdael, *Forest Scene,* had disappeared from Bad Fuessing in West Germany, and a Canaletto from Lisbon. Four De Chirico's had been stolen in Galliano, Italy, and a Brueghel and a Picasso oil from Barcelona. A Renoir stolen from the Musée de l'Opéra in Paris months before had been recovered in the United States. I tried to put all this out of my mind, but could not. On "The Diary" I had a staff of three, but even so it was quite a hectic life, producing 1,500 words a day, five days a week. There was very little time for anything else.

However, in my general reading I had begun to take notice of the movement of famous paintings around Europe and to America. I had become particularly interested in the sales of paintings at various points in history, when huge collections were broken up. There was the Commonwealth sale, when Charles I's pictures had been sold off by Oliver Cromwell after the monarch's execution. There was the sale of the Orléans collection after the French Revolution, when many of the paintings were being smuggled to London for an auction at the Lyceum. Most intriguing of all, for me, was a much earlier sale, which helped make up Charles I's fantastic collection of 1,387 paintings. This was the sale of the Mantuan paintings owned by the Gonzaga family. It outraged all Italy at the time.

Though they were Dukes of Mantua for more than two hundred years, the Gonzagas are not as well known to us as the Medicis in Florence or the Sforzas in Milan. But they were in some ways more typical of the Renaissance. They were not a great warring family and their city-state of Mantua was fairly small. Yet they had a fabulous court: it was situated on an artificial peninsula, a masterpiece of twelfth-century engineering; its painters included Giulio Romano, Andrea Mantegna, Rubens, Veronese, Pisanello, Tintoretto and Titian. Monteverdi was court musician (his orchestra played every Friday night), the stable contained 650 horses and Leon Battista Alberti was at one time court architect. The Gonzagas were first-rate.

Toward the end of May 1981, London's Victoria and Albert Museum announced that, the following November, they would stage an exhibition entitled "The Splendors of the Gonzaga." Though I was not the *Times*'s art critic, still less its historian, I asked that I be allowed to visit Mantua, which I had never done, and write a curtain raiser to the exhibition, to be published just before it opened. The request was granted and I made arrangements to visit Mantua in September.

Before that I visited America for the July the Fourth weekend (making use of cheap stand-by fares). This was the only time I could get away from "The Diary," but it meant that John Blake could pay Renzullo another fleeting visit—I couldn't quite let go of the contact. Renzullo naturally assumed I traveled everywhere first-class, and was impressed that I could afford to "blow" $2,400 just in airline tickets for a weekend away (I had, of course, checked the first-class air fares). He said on that weekend that he had yet another new source opening up with "some very interesting paintings." I mentioned I was probably going to be in Italy in September and he replied that he would try to be there as well.

So the summer passed without a holiday. The royal wedding came and went (the magazine was a sellout, with railway porters stealing many copies and selling them at black-market prices). By the time September came around I was very much looking forward to Mantua. I planned three nights in Venice, a night in Padua, three in Mantua, two in Verona, one each in Vicenza and Bassano, since I was also to write an article for the *Sunday Times* about Venetian art.

I was due to leave for Italy on 17 September, a Thursday. A week before, the phone rang near midnight. A soft whooshing sound came down the line—it was an international call.

"Hello . . . Mr. Blake . . ."

"Hello, Renzullo."

"I hope the hour is not too late?"

"No, no. It's fine. What's your news?"

"Are you going to Italy? You said you were going to Italy."

"Yes—yes, I am. I am leaving on the seventeenth. Why?"

"Where are you going, to the north?"

"To Venice to start with. Vicenza, maybe Verona." I didn't want to tell him everything. "Why? Why?"

"Perfect." He seemed to be only half-listening to what I was saying. He spoke in Italian to someone in the background; I heard the name Vincenzo so I took it to be his partner, Del Peschio.

"Vincenzo will be there then, Mr. Blake, in Milano and Parma. We have a new source of paintings for you, Mr. Blake, in Cremona. We have a Van Gogh—a very beautiful Van Gogh—and a Del Sarto, a *St. John*. And maybe a Stradivarius. You want a violin, Mr. Blake?" He sounded very pleased with himself.

"That depends, Renzullo."

This was a curious development, for it brought to the fore a nagging worry that had been running around in my head for some time, which I had never quite resolved or raised with Renzullo. The first time he had mentioned Cremona, when he had wanted me to meet the professor with the modern paintings, we had in fact gone to a village called Voghera. I had assumed at the time that Voghera was on the outskirts of Cremona. But when I returned home and looked at a map, I found that in fact Voghera was nowhere near Cremona. Why should Renzullo have misled me on that occasion? Why did he not say Voghera was a long way from Cremona when, during the journey, I started to show off my knowledge of the city's artistic history? I couldn't explain it, but one possibility was that they *had* intended to show me some paintings in Cremona but had then changed their minds at the last minute. And in order not to appear suspicious they had not told me about their change of plan. If I was right, then Cremona was a significant site in their operations, a place I wasn't allowed to see earlier on. If they had now decided to take me to Cremona, it might mean that at last I was getting near the center of their network. Provided, of course, that we did actually go to Cremona this time.

"Where is the violin from?"

"It's from a man in Turin, Mr. Blake. He says it's from a museum. But he wants a lot of money, Mr. Blake. You understand?"

"Of course. Do you mean it's stolen?"

"Yes, of course, of course. It's stolen, it's stolen. He can get more, he says. But you must pay good money, Mr. Blake. The man is at risk."

"I understand, Renzullo. So what do you want to do?"

More talk with Del Peschio in the background. I, too, was thinking. I had to do my research for the Gonzaga article, which meant I had to have a few days to myself (and *as* myself). Did I really want to get involved, all over again, in disguises, expensive flights to Italy and New York, late-night transatlantic phone calls and all the other deceptions? I should have said no. But at that time a major recovery had just been reported in America: ten Impressionist and modern works stolen from the Heller collection in Miami, including a Renoir, a Pissarro, a Sisley and a Vlaminck, had been found undamaged by a private investigator. If he could do it, I could do it. My failure with the Caravaggio didn't smart so much after all those months, and I was again tempted by Renzullo's offer. Van Gogh, Del Sarto and Stradivari were names just as big as Caravaggio. After a little dithering I decided to give it one more go. I would probably regret it; it would be a waste of time, a waste of a vacation and expensive to boot.

SEPTEMBER 22—A TUESDAY—was foggy. I was due in Parma at noon, as A. John Blake. Yet I had traveled to Italy, for the paper, as Peter Watson. So I had to leave all my credit cards and my own passport at the hotel in Verona where I had spent the previous night. It was a bit risky, but I slicked down my hair, picked up my walking stick and limped past the hotel receptionist, hoping she wouldn't notice my strange behavior. The fog meant the drive from Verona to Parma was difficult, and I was late arriving.

I met Concerto Battiato and another of their group, a journalist called Gianni Zanichelli, and off we went for our usual long lunch. Once again we went to the restaurant in Sorbolo, where Giancarlo Viappiani joined us. I was a bit perturbed by this time, however, for it appeared that Del Peschio's father had died and Vincenzo was still in New York. That left only Concerto, who spoke some English but not much. Over the next few days, my Italian had to improve quite dramatically.

The next few days were not to lack drama. After our lunch (two hours, acres of Parma ham, white wine, red wine, Italian brandy, two types of pasta and some elaborately cooked lamb), we drove back into Parma. There I was shown a "Tiepolo" in the home of a doctor. It was a weak-looking head, and while it could have been a Tiepolo, it could also have been any number of things. I said no, I wasn't interested, though of course I took away a photograph, just in case.

It must have been after four by the time we set out from Parma. The sky was black by the time we reached Cremona, but at least this time it *was* Cremona, I wondered to myself, as we passed the sign at the city limit, whether the project would end here.

The city struck me as a fairly untidy, scruffy town, possibly because the alleyway where we ended up consisted on one side of studios, garages and small workshops (some of them empty) and, down the other side, a high wall, dark, dirty and damaged, buckled in places with bricks strewn around in a rubble. The alleyway was cobbled and had a sharp left-hand turn part of the way along. We rounded the corner and stopped outside a garage-cum-workshop, more prosperous-looking than most.

We were met by a small, round, pleasant-faced man with a beaming smile. He was introduced as Giordano Garuti. We entered the garage-workshop, which was unlit, cold, and full of workbenches, long strips of wood and many picture frames in various stages of construction or restoration. After a brief look around we climbed to the third floor. Since the steps were made of slippery marble, and there were plenty of them, I made the others go ahead; with my limp such a staircase required careful negotiation.

The stairs were lined with paintings, all of them modern, usually abstractions and, for the most part, hideous. The steps rose past an apartment and gave out, on the top floor, into a studio. It was just like Rodolfo's garret in *La Bohème*. The ceiling was slanted, as the roof of the building closed in over us; there was a door leading to a tiny, railed balcony with, as I was to learn, a wonderful view across the terra-cotta roofs of old Cremona. In the center of the room was an easel, with a huge lamp alongside it (curiously, for a studio there was not much in the way of windows). To one side there was a sofa and some easy chairs and in front of them a low coffee table in the shape of an artist's palette. Pictures lined the walls; again most of them were modern lurid things and all, I was told, Garuti's own work. To me they were as bad as the efforts up the staircase, but even worse were a number of almost black wooden sculptures from Africa. These stood about the room with long narrow faces and short, dumpy bodies. Paintings and empty frames also stood stacked against one of the walls, and a workbench, at hip height, occupied another. There was a shower and lavatory in one corner.

I was invited to sit in an armchair that was loosely covered in some sort of animal skin, and we were all offered Italian sparkling wine in individual bottles.

Once we had our drinks, Garuti disappeared downstairs and returned a few minutes later with a package under his arm. He unwrapped it and handed me a painting, a photograph and a document, a photocopy. The picture was a view of a house and a garden, the house with gables and the garden with lush bushes. The work was done in short, bold strokes, with thick pigment mostly in primary colors. The brushwork and style were unmistakable: Van Gogh.

I tried to look impressed. The photograph was a black and white rendition of the painting, but the photocopy was of a page in the official De la Faille Van Gogh *catalogue raisonné*. This, too, showed a photograph—of a painting identical with the one I was holding. The caption to the photograph in the catalog showed that the painting, called *Houses with Sunflowers,* formed part of a private collection in Frankfurt, Germany—but no more than that.

I examined the photocopy and made a show of comparing it with the painting. They looked one and the same to me. My mind was racing as I racked my brain to remember what I had read about Van Gogh thefts and fakes. Since this picture was in the catalog it stood a chance of being genuine. The problem, of course, was that the *catalogue raisonné* was published in 1928. I was pretty sure this Van Gogh had not been reported stolen in the lists I had so my only means of checking it would be by tracing the person who owned it in 1928, then working forward. I didn't look forward to *that.*

"Where did you get hold of this?" I asked.

"*Come?*" said Battiato. He hadn't understood. "How's that again?"

"How did the painting get to Cremona?" I also translated, crudely, as best I could, "*Il quadro, come arrivato a Cremona?*" Brilliant.

Smiles all around, and not just at my Italian. "Knowing grins" might be a better description.

"Well?" I said, since no one else spoke.

Garuti spoke to Battiato, who turned to me. "The picture . . . is owned by a family . . . in Milano. Garuti—he get it through a friend of family." Actually, what he said was closer to "He got . . . with . . . friend of . . . family"—I have just polished the syntax. But whether this meant the painting had been bought, borrowed—or stolen—I didn't know. Gently, I pressed the point.

"Who is this friend—a relative? How long has Mr. Garuti had the painting?"

Came the reply: "Just a man . . . no . . . relative. He has picture . . . many months."

Hmmmm. What now? "How do I know it's not a copy?" A

long exchange between Garuti and Battiato followed, with a lot of shrugging. It ended with Battiato turning to me and shrugging again.

"Why . . . Garuti . . . he copy? It . . . is . . . painting . . . you expert, Mr. Blake."

I had walked into that so I spoke quickly to cover my gaffe. "Not with modern pictures, Mr. Battiato—only old paintings." And on again quickly: "How much does he say he wants?"

Another burst of Italian. By now Giancarlo Viappiani had hold of the Van Gogh and was telling me, in very rudimentary English, "Very good picture . . . *molto* beautiful." Quite.

Battiato turned back to me. "You like . . . this picture?"

I made a face. To appear too enthusiastic would push the price up. Real dealers wouldn't do that. Battiato spoke to Garuti and then turned back to me again.

"One hundred million lire."

I kept a straight face and wrote the figure in my pocket notebook: $100,000 seemed rather cheap unless it was really stolen, so I didn't haggle there and then.

"I hope it's better than the professor's Van Goghs," I said, turning to Giancarlo.

After Battiato had translated he smiled and said, "*Si,* is in catalog."

"It may take some researching," I said to Battiato and Garuti together. "You must give me time."

I then looked around the studio, got up out of my easy chair, limped across to the stacks of modern paintings against the wall and began leafing through them. Most of them, to me, were just as hideous as everything else in the room.

"Does Mr. Garuti have anything else I might like?" I looked over to Battiato.

After he had translated, Garuti reached into one of the stacks of pictures leaning against a wall. He took from it a canvas which must have been about three feet six inches high and three feet wide. It was yet another of Garuti's monstrosities, two young mangled heads. There followed quite a long speech from Garuti, accompanied by yet more knowing grins and gestures. Long before he had finished, I began to get the idea. The painting he was holding was not all it appeared. He mentioned the word *tedesco*

[German] several times, as well as the name of a wonderful six-teenth-century Florentine painter, Andrea del Sarto.

Battiato took up the story. "The . . . canvas . . . here . . . by Garuti . . . but under . . . is picture by Andrea del Sarto, *St. John*. It go to Germany . . . like this . . . covered with canvas on top . . ." He smiled. "If . . . the Germans . . . not buy . . . you can have."

"May I see?"

"No, is . . . ready . . . to go . . . with cover. Sorry."

Terrific. A Van Gogh which it might take years to follow up and a Del Sarto I couldn't even see. It looked like another wasted trip. I was very depressed on the drive back.

During the journey I had also arranged to meet Giancarlo and Zanichelli in Rome the following Friday: Giancarlo said they had another "*molto* beautiful" painting to show me, a Rubens, owned by a "professor." I didn't know how we would get on without a translator (Battiato had to get back to Sicily) but I agreed to the meeting since I didn't see what I had to lose. Giancarlo dropped me at the main crossroads in Sorbolo, where I had left my car. It was just after eight o'clock. They were under the impression I was driving to Mantua that night, since I wanted to keep them deceived, just in case.

Before I left them I asked Battiato to ask Viappiani to check into the man in Turin about the Stradivarius. Viappiani said he had called this man several times in the past few days, but could get no reply. He would continue to try and would let me know on Friday. We arranged to meet in the lobby of the Excelsior on the Via Veneto at 11:30—Viappiani, Zanichelli and I.

A Van Gogh, a Del Sarto, a Stradivarius, a Rubens. If any one were real *and* stolen, that would do nicely. But I didn't hold out much hope.

I SPENT the next couple of days in Verona, driving down to Rome on Thursday for an appointment with Siviero. We met, as usual, in his office in the Via Degli Astalli. He seemed a good deal older than I remembered, less witty, less energetic and less ambitious, both for himself and for me in the project. I later learned that he had been ill. I showed Siviero the photograph of the Van Gogh and he said he would check it (though without much enthusiasm

—I suspect because the picture was neither Italian nor an old master).

I mentioned that I was supposed to see a Rubens the next day, and he said there were two of this master's works missing. There was a *Baccanale*, stolen from a private collection in Rome in October 1976, and a painting entitled *Virtue,* showing three feminine figures and three *putti.* This picture had been looted by the Nazis in World War Two from another private collector in Rome. Siviero's manner clearly doubted that I was on to either of these, but he promised to look for photographs of the missing works so I could compare them with what I would be shown.

TANA DE ZULUETA had booked me into the Hotel Gregoriana, a delightful small hotel, on the Via Gregoriana near the Spanish Steps. It was a narrow street, filled with smart clothes shops and other boutiques, always blocked with traffic. On Friday I awoke to find my rented car had been towed away by the police. I had parked illegally. None of my possessions were in it, but Blake's cane was. Yet another stick, therefore, had to come out of the (already considerably overspent) budget.

The Gregoriana was not too far from the Via Veneto, however, so despite this setback I was able to rendezvous with Viappiani and Zanichelli at the Excelsior only a few minutes after 11:30. As usual, and despite the early hour, our first move was lunch. Zanichelli—I have to hand it to him—knew a marvelous restaurant just off the Via Veneto. So delicious was the food there that we each ate *two* antipastos, including deep-fried fresh anchovies, the only time I've had anything other than the canned type, *two* pastas, a main course (a wonderful bass in a white wine sauce), *two* desserts and, of course, *two* types of wine, red and white. And, since John Blake, the wealthy dealer, offered to pay, we all drank *two* brandies.

About 2:30 we took a taxi *"a la casa del professore,"* as Zanichelli put it. We were conversing that day only in Italian so, as may be imagined, we weren't saying a lot. The professor's apartment was near the Piazza Navona, in the old part of Rome, and like Garuti's stairwell, it was lined with pictures. Many of these were garish modern efforts, but he did have some mellower older paintings as well. I remember there was a gate at the top of the stairs leading to the apartment; this was to keep a large dog from straying down into the street. No one seemed to notice that my cane that day was brown, not black, as it had been two days before.

The professor, if that's what he really was, was a small man with high cheekbones and graying hair swept straight back. He had very small eyes, almost black, and a sly way of moving them that made him seem suspicious of everything and everyone. He moved his jaw with a circular movement, which usually indicates the wearing of dentures. He wore a gray suit and a shirt with a collar that was too big for his neck.

When we arrived he and two colleagues were admiring a large portrait, rich in reds, creams and browns. It was certainly Vermeer-esque, but I doubted it was actually by the master, as they tried to claim. After the introductions were made, I was largely ignored as Viappiani and the professor talked away between themselves for several minutes. I passed the time looking over the professor's paintings. Most of them, as I recall, were very neatly framed, and some of the older ones, landscapes and one or two pictures of Venice, seemed quite good. This room was very tall, as is sometimes the Italian style, and the paintings went high up the wood paneling. The sheer number of pictures gave the room a warm, studio or study "feel."

Eventually the long conversation between the professor and Viappiani finished and, from what Viappiani then tried to tell me, it appeared that the professor was not sure of me, and had needed some persuasion before I could be shown the Rubens. But he had now agreed and we were off to see it. We made our way back down the stairs to Zanichelli's car, the professor and two of his colleagues, plus a woman who had appeared from somewhere else in the apartment, traveling in another one. There followed quite a long drive out into the suburbs of Rome, and during it something very curious occurred. As usual, I was sitting in the front; Zanichelli was driving, with Viappiani leaning forward from the back seat so as to talk to him. They had been rattling away for some time, far too quickly for me to understand, when suddenly I caught the words "Hotel Gregoriana."

My tongue went dry. What on earth were they talking about? Why were they talking about my hotel? Did they know I was staying there? Were they planning to stay there? Were they on to

THE SECOND "ST. JOHN"

me? Was my ludicrous deception in fact transparent—had it been
transparent all along? The white wine, followed by the red and
the brandy, precluded any effective action or much thought. All I
could decipher (though I couldn't be certain) was that one or
another of them had stayed there. Whether this meant they were
thinking of moving over—well, it didn't bear thinking about. The
thought that they might have shared the same hotel with me the
night before brought a smile to my lips—a smile of fear.

By this time we had arrived at a huge office building in the
middle of a shopping center somewhere very definitely not in the
heart of Rome. I hadn't been watching closely where we were
going, but we were by now thirty-five minutes from the Piazza
Navona. We turned off the main artery and descended a service
road which sloped under a block of offices. There were two elec-
tronically operated grid gates to be negotiated and we found ourselves in the bowels of the building, surrounded by security men.
There was space for about ten cars inside the second grid and in
one corner was a counter. We were in a kind of drive-in safe-
deposit bank—I could see all sorts of packages and parcels on the
shelves beyond the counter.

It now turned out that the painting was not the professor's
after all. One of his colleagues, a fatter man with light brown hair
and his own walking cane, went forward to the counter and produced some identification. A package was brought out, and then
just three of us, the fat man with the cane, the woman, who
turned out to be his secretary, and I, went to the viewing room.

To get there we had to go through two more security doors.
We couldn't get out without phoning the guards: there was no
handle on the inside.

The fat man, whose name I never learned, opened up the package, taking his time about it.

It was, without doubt, the best picture they had shown me. It
was on copper, not very large, and showed six women in two
groups of three, all scantily clad in white diaphanous dresses,
frolicking and playing in a wooded scene. Their skin was an exquisite white-pink, the expressions on their faces suitably innocent
and playful-looking, and the trees and leaves were a perfect blend
of fine detail and vague, evocative touches. As far as I was concerned, it could easily have been a Rubens. What's more, it could
have fitted the title *Baccanale* and even, given the grouping of

the women into threes, might just have fitted the description of the three graces in Rubens' *Virtue,* stolen by the Nazis. I scribbled furiously in my notebook, describing the painting to myself, just in case they wouldn't give me a photograph.

Then we discussed price. The fat man wanted $700,000. It was the first time they had not named a figure in lire. Was that significant? I said I thought that was far too much and asked him how he had come by it. He said promptly that it had been in his family since before the war. Was there anything suspicious in *that* sentence? He had said *before* the war and I wondered whether he was trying to deflect me from looking at the movement of Rubens' paintings during it. For now, I couldn't be sure.

He asked me how much I thought the painting was worth —encouraging, for that question usually means someone is willing to haggle. I said I wasn't certain, but I did know that an early Rubens, *Samson and Delilah,* had sold for £2,300,000 at Christie's in July 1980. As a rough rule of thumb, I therefore offered Siviero's 10 percent for stolen works: £230,000 or $400,000. The wrong tactic, for the fat man took quite an offense at this and shouted, "*Molto piu, molto piu* [Much more, much more]"—and ordered the girl to start wrapping the picture again. Had I made another error? I attempted to calm things down by using the knowledge I had picked up at the Jan Brueghel exhibition at the Brod Gallery months before.

"I will be honest with you," I said to the fat man. "Rubens collaborated quite a lot with Jan Brueghel. There are said to be three thousand misattributions. This could be one of them."

He shook his head. "Brueghel, no; is Rubens, yes." I shrugged; there was nothing to gain from doing anything else, not until I could be certain the "Rubens" was stolen. But a photograph would be helpful.

I waited while the woman finished wrapping the picture and until the fat man had called for the guard to let us out. Just as he arrived I asked, "*Ha lei fotografia?*" To my relief, the fat man nodded to the woman, who reached into her briefcase and took out not one but two photographs, one in black and white and the other in color.

We rejoined Giancarlo and the rest, still waiting by the cars, and the fat man and the professor went off to talk by the grid gate. I indicated to Viappiani that the Rubens was "*il più bello dipinto* [the most beautiful picture]" I had seen *"con lei* [with them]" and that I had a photograph to take back to London *"per ricerca* [for research]." But, I added, it was very expensive, and rubbed my thumb and forefinger together. Viappiani's eyes lit up when I said it was a very beautiful picture and he agreed enthusiastically.

It was naturally assumed that I would go back to London, check out the painting and let them know. I was also given a set of documents designed to prove that it was a real Rubens. They were all in Italian and I read them later. The professor and the fat man had now finished their conversation and we shook hands. I said *arrivederci* to the fat man, the professor and the woman. Zanichelli and Viappiani asked me where I wanted to be dropped off, and this posed a problem. I really wanted to get back to my hotel as soon as possible, since it was now four-thirty and I had plans to catch the seven o'clock flight to London. If I could avoid paying an extra night at the hotel, it would help the budget. I couldn't have them drop me at the hotel itself, however, since they had been talking about the Gregoriana and I still didn't know why. And there was another reason to avoid the hotel: since I had flown to Venice on this trip as Peter Watson, and had changed my return ticket from Venice-London to Rome-London, the ticket was still in my real name. For this reason, I very definitely wanted to avoid any possibility that they would offer to take me on from my hotel to Leonardo da Vinci airport.

I therefore made up a story about wanting to buy some shoes on the Via Condotti, Rome's most expensive street (where Gucci, Bulgari, Giorgio Armani and other smart names have their shops). It was in keeping with John Blake's flash image, but it was another mistake. The road leading into the Via Condotti is reserved for taxis and buses only, and when Zanichelli tried to bluster his way past the traffic policemen he failed. That meant we had to turn around, wasting more time (it was now getting very close, from my point of view), and drive the back way to the top of the Spanish Steps, from where I could descend to the Via Condotti. The only problem with this was that from the top of the Spanish Steps you could see the entrance to the Hotel Gregoriana—the very thing I wanted to avoid.

It was ten minutes past five when we finally approached the top of the steps. Imagine my feelings when, just as we arrived

there, Zanichelli contrived to hit another car coming in the opposite direction. It wasn't a major crash in the sense of there being
danger to life or limb, but the scraping of metal on metal made a
loud noise as we shuddered to a halt. Immediately a crowd
formed and Zanichelli, Viappiani and the other driver were ges-
turing madly, presumably each blaming the other. It was now
five-twenty and I had a seven o'clock plane to catch. A farce.

I shouted to Viappiani that I didn't have much time and would
be in touch. He broke through the crowd and came to shake my
hand, saying "*Arrivederci,* Meestaire Blake." I limped off as fast
as I decently could.

I pretended to descend the Spanish Steps, but then casually
doubled back, hoping no one was watching. The crowd still
milled around the crash, with several people knowingly inspecting the damage and, no doubt, guessing what it would cost to
repair. I ambled down the Via Gregoriana, looking briefly into
the shops, as though I intended to buy. Level with the hotel, but
on the other side of the street, I looked back. There was a throng
of people at the top, but I couldn't be sure if Viappiani or Zanichelli were among them and looking my way. Just then a large
van came trundling down the street, partially blocking the view.
I leaped across the narrow set of cobbles and up the steps into
the hotel. I had already packed in the morning, so all that remained was to pick up my bag, pay my bill and call a taxi. I just
hoped that the others wouldn't come by while I was in the hotel
lobby: the cashier's desk was easily visible from passing cars.

I called a taxi, which, thankfully, was less than ten minutes in
arriving. It gave me just time to go to the bathroom and flatten
my hair down some more. Now came the next worry. The street
was so narrow that, when the taxi stopped to pick me up, the
traffic behind was not able to overtake and had to stop too. What
if Viappiani and Zanichelli were immediately behind the taxi?
They would see me.

I had no choice but to wait for the driver of the taxi to get out,
come into the hotel and collect my luggage, and then open the
car door for me to get in. I stepped out of the hotel quickly, looking down.

There was no cry of recognition, no blaring of the horn, no
shouted offer to take me to the airport. When the taxi got down

the Via Gregoriana, to the messy crossroads leading to the Piazza Barberini, I saw Zanichelli's now-mangled Renault. It was two cars in front. They must have gone by the hotel just as I was coming out of the bathroom.

THE PRINCE OF STOLEN PICTURES

14

The Woman with the Collar

THAT ALL HAPPENED at the end of September 1981. In the first weeks of October it was announced that an office was to be opened in Florence which would eventually house complete records of all stolen art. Pietro Annigoni, the Queen's portrait painter, was associated with the project, but the real guiding light was Siviero. It had been his idea and it had taken him ten years to get the thing off the ground. I sent him a card, wishing him luck, but I wondered then (as I still do) whether this new set of records would ever be as complete and up-to-date as Siviero would like. (It has since been moved to Greece.)

I also began trying to trace first the Van Gogh, then the other works I had been offered. From my records I knew of at least one Van Gogh missing at this time, but *Paysage de St. Rémy,* taken in Paris, was nothing like the picture I had been offered. Siviero, when I heard from him, could tell me nothing I didn't already know; and a friend on the *Corriere della Serra,* the Milan newspaper, went back through the file copies for two years without finding any reference to a stolen Van Gogh in the area. This didn't mean the painting wasn't stolen, of course, merely that it probably hadn't been taken in or near Milan. I had only Garuti's word that it came from a collection in that city, and of course he had a vested interest in misleading me. With a heavy heart I realized there was nothing for it but to write to the person who had owned the painting in 1928 in Frankfurt, when De la Faille had originally assembled his catalog. God knows where that trail would lead, but I had no choice.

After sending off that letter, I turned to the Rubens. Here again I had no luck. There was no trace of the Rome painting in any of the catalogs I had access to, and, moreover, when Siviero finally sent photographs of the two missing Rubens, they turned out to be very different from "mine." The *Baccanale* showed an evil-looking man with horns, a leopard and a tree trunk; the *Three Graces,* or *Virtue,* picture, the one looted by the Nazis, certainly showed three women, but it also had three *putti* and a dove.

I have to confess that I didn't research the Del Sarto or the Stradivarius violin in great detail. Having not seen the painting, there was no way I could recognize it if I saw it in my records. There was, in any case, only one Del Sarto recorded as missing at the time and that was the *Portrait of a Shepherd Boy,* which had disappeared in Santa Ana, California. A *Shepherd Boy* could be retitled as a *St. John the Baptist as a Young Man,* but it seemed unlikely.

YET AGAIN, THEREFORE, I resigned myself to the fact that the project had failed. In fact, so depressed was I that I couldn't bring myself to speak to Renzullo.

He kept on at me, however, and in November he remembered something I had forgotten long ago—that the first fake news clipping which I had arranged for him to receive, via Steffanotti, reported that A. John Blake had spent $200,000 on a Del Sarto at Sotheby's in London. Renzullo phoned to say that he had persuaded Garuti to offer the Del Sarto *to me.* The Germans were being lackadaisical in coming up with the money, I clearly knew something about Del Sarto (he said) and I also gave plenty of evidence of having ready cash. The painting was mine if I wanted it.

I asked what the provenance of the painting was and Renzullo volunteered to find out. He called me again the very next day and this time he was more excited than ever. It turned out, he said, that the painting was exactly the type I wanted: it had come from a collection near Vicenza, from a private family. Garuti had exact details of who the former owner was.

I wasn't sure what was meant by this. They had never given me a proper provenance—legal or otherwise—of any painting they had offered. I pressed Renzullo as to what he really meant and he shouted into the phone:

"Yes, it's stolen, Mr. Blake, but you don't say these things over the phone. Please, be careful—but have no worries at all. I assure you, everything is as you wish it to be."

This was new, the first time they had actually admitted they were dealing in stolen paintings. My instinct about Cremona being the center of operations may have been right after all. I made the usual very enthusiastic sounds, but asked Renzullo to find out from Garuti more details so that, for my own purposes, I could verify where the Del Sarto had actually come from. He said he would do what he could.

Before our conversation was over, Renzullo threw in two more snippets. Garuti had another painting for me to see, he said, a very beautiful Bronzino portrait, and there was an important new figure in New York whom he wished me to meet. This new man wasn't a source of paintings but was a diplomat. He could be very useful, Renzullo said, in helping "bring paintings from Italy to New York." It was a tantalizing snippet, but to tell the truth I didn't pay as much attention as I should have.

By now it was getting into December and the pre-Christmas rush. I was very busy with my day-to-day journalism, but I did get time to spend a morning in the Witt Library and confirmed for myself that there were no Del Sartos in any private collections in the northern part of Italy—in the Veneto—as Garuti was claiming. As Christmas approached, therefore, I switched off mentally from the project once more and concentrated on the festivities. The day before Christmas Eve, Renzullo called again.

"Mr. Blake, I have some good news."

"Oh yes?"

"Garuti, he has a newspaper report—of the painting."

"What do you mean?"

"A report of the Del Sarto, Mr. Blake, near Vicenza. Is that good enough for you?"

"That depends on what it says."

"It says, Mr. Blake, that the painting is a Del Sarto, worth eighty million lire, and that it comes from near Vicenza. There is the name of the owner, a marchese."

"Yes, but does it say it was stolen?"

"Yes, Mr. Blake, yes, it says it was stolen. But not on the phone, eh?"

"Have you got the newspaper?"

"No . . ."

"Has Garuti?"

"No, not yet . . . but in a few days, Mr. Blake, a few days."

I was determined not to go back to Italy unless I was absolutely certain I would be looking at stolen material. So I said:

"Mr. Renzullo, you have worked hard; but I am not leaving London until either you or Garuti has found the clipping." Then I had what turned out to be a brainwave. I added, "But if you do come up with the clipping, Mr. Renzullo, I will also pay for you to come to Italy. I need a proper translator, unlike last time, and I know I can trust you."

I could almost hear him grinning down the phone; his smile was all over his voice.

"You will pay for me, Mr. Blake?"

"Yes, but only if you have the clipping." This was working out rather well, even though I had thought it up on the spur of the moment. If Garuti could indeed find the clipping it would be worth it to me to pay for Renzullo to travel to Italy, because Del Sarto was as important as Caravaggio and it might make a splendid ending to the project.

He hung up as though he would be calling back in a matter of hours so confident did he appear. But I wasn't surprised when I didn't hear for some weeks. It was well into January before he phoned again, but, as on the previous occasion, he was very excited.

"Mr. Blake, I think we can do some business now."

"You have the clipping?"

"No, not yet. But soon."

I was disappointed, and not a little exasperated. "Not good enough, Mr. Renzullo; you know my conditions."

"Mr. Blake, I will make a deal, eh? I think Garuti—he tells the truth. There is a cutting, but he cannot find it yet. I feel so strongly he is telling the truth, Mr. Blake, that I will come to Italy myself. We will see the Del Sarto. If there is no clipping you do not buy and I will pay for my ticket. But if there is a clipping you pay my ticket as well. How do you say, Mr. Blake . . . is that not fair?"

Interesting. Renzullo certainly seemed to have faith in the man; if he was willing to risk $1,000 on the trip that suggested there might indeed be a clipping somewhere. It also reinforced my growing conviction that Cremona was the center of the network. I agreed to another visit. It would, I told myself, be my last.

THURSDAY, 28 JANUARY, was a cold but brilliantly sunny day and both of Milan's airports were fog-free. I arrived at the Hilton, about twenty minutes late, to find Renzullo already there and badly in need of a shave. He was also angry.

"There is no one here to meet us, Mr. Blake; Giancarlo—he didn't give the message to Garuti."

Now it was my turn to be mad. "You mean Garuti doesn't know we are here? Renzullo, this is too much. If we don't see him or the pictures, *you* are going to have to pay *my* fare, from London."

"Do not worry, Mr. Blake. We will just be a little late, that's all."

He made some telephone calls and then we did what we always did on such occasions: we had lunch. I led Renzullo to a trattoria I knew near Milan's central railway station and we took our time. It appeared that Giancarlo was coming from Parma and would be an hour and a half at least.

Over lunch, Renzullo reminded me of something he had said before that I had forgotten: that he had a friend, a diplomat, who could help bring paintings into the United States in the diplomatic pouch. He now said this man had ambitious plans for helping the third world. Renzullo thought that I, being a wealthy man, might like to get involved in the third-world project as a financier. I let him ramble on, but of course cocked my ears at the plan to have the diplomat smuggle paintings.

Around three we made our way back to the Hilton, to find

Giancarlo already there. He was the same as ever: covered in cigarette ash, the broken veins in his angular face very visible. After
Renzullo had spent a few minutes berating him for his tardiness,
we left.

We reached Cremona just before dark. Garuti's beaming face
welcomed us and showed us straight upstairs. As before, I did my
careful production number on the cold, slippery staircase. The
pictures on the walls hadn't improved. By the time I got up to the
studio, Garuti had brought out the small bottles of fizzy, pink
wine that we had drunk before. We toasted each other and
Garuti disappeared back down the stairs.

When he returned he had with him a package measuring, I
would say, three-feet-six high by two-feet-six wide and wrapped
in brown paper. He placed the package on his workbench and
tore at the paper. Underneath was a picture I recognized: two
garish, angular, distorted heads, the ugly mark of Garuti's own
work. Immediately, however, he turned over the painting and
began picking at the staples which fixed the canvas to the
wooden stretchers at the back. One by one he pulled them all
away.

Under the two heads was—well, a very beautiful painting. It
was of St. John the Baptist. But that does nothing to convey the
emotional impact of the picture. The man was young, with long
brown hair, and was holding a slender cross made of cane. The
saint's right arm reached across the canvas from left to right,
about halfway up. This gesture, allied with a wonderfully tender, trance-like expression on the young man's face, gave the picture a most moving, soft and gentle quality: this was no fiery
baptist but more a young man who knows life before experienc-
ing it and who already has a premonition of the suffering to come
and who accepts it, if not willingly, with grace.

Andrea del Sarto was born in 1486. In his biography, Vasari
makes it clear how much he loathed Del Sarto's wife Lucrezia
and, indeed, he didn't have too high an opinion of Andrea's character either. In 1518, Del Sarto had accepted an invitation from
Francis I to go to Fontainebleu, but he didn't stay long and only
a handful of pictures can be attributed to his time in France.
Vasari says that when Del Sarto returned to Florence the painter
embezzled a large sum of money given to him by the French king
for the purchase of paintings, and examination of bank records

does show that Andrea made a large deposit immediately on his return and afterward built himself a house and studio. Vasari completes his vitriolic account with an attack on Lucrezia. Not only did she ruin Andrea, Vasari says, but she abandoned the painter on his deathbed.

Despite this, one of the hallmarks of Del Sarto's pictures is that they usually include "an unmistakable type of face with dark smudgy eyes, short nose and wide slightly open mouth— Lucrezia's famous face." So great were Del Sarto's gifts that he was acclaimed as the perfect artist, the painter who never made mistakes. In the nineteenth century, Robert Browning, who spent much time in Italy, composed a poem on Del Sarto, which he subtitled "The Faultless Painter." Browning tries to explain why Del Sarto failed to live up to his early promise and his verse includes the lines:

> Come in from the window, love—come in, at last,
> Inside the melancholy little house
> We built to be so gay with. God is just.
> King Francis may forgive me . . .

and

> Let us but love each other. Must you go?
> That cousin here again? he waits outside?
> Must see you—you, and not with me? Those loans?
> More gaming debts to pay? you smiled for that?
> Well, let smiles buy me! have you more to spend?

I was effusive in my praise of the picture, but nevertheless spent some time examining the canvas and its stretchers. The canvas had been cut back at the edges so that it did not wrap around the wooden stretchers—no doubt to confuse the prying eyes and fingers of any customs official who might examine Garuti's modern heads more closely than they deserved. The painting had been relined, the canvas at the back was quite new (but that is not unusual for a Renaissance picture). The stretchers were new, too. I made these points and Garuti just nodded without elaborating: the relining and the new stretchers might have been done by a legitimate owner, or Garuti might have done it as part of some elaborate disguising procedure.

However, the painting did not look cut down so I assumed it had not been severely tampered with.

Garuti next offered to put it under the ultraviolet light. I had not seen this done before but knew that it would show where the painting had been retouched. It was an encouraging sign and, sure enough, there were not many shadows on the picture, and those that there were were few and far between and relatively small.

After this, when Garuti had put the lights on, we sat down, opened more fizzy wine and discussed a price. It took a surprisingly small amount of time. Garuti started at 80 million lire, or $80,000, the price the painting had been valued at, allegedly, in the newspaper clipping. I offered 20 million lire, 10 percent of the value of the "Del Sarto" I had "bought" at Sotheby's. Garuti and Renzullo then chatted away in Italian, until Renzullo turned to me with his usual grin.

"Mr. Blake, you improve your offer—eh? Garuti, he would like to please you—he will come down, I think; he would like to please you, because there are other things—eh?—in the future. But he would like you to go higher."

"Twenty-four million."

More talk, mainly centering around the words "ottanta milioni," "ventiquattro" and "ventotto."

"Twenty-eight million, Mr. Blake. Garuti would like you to offer 28 million lire. What do you say? That's a good price, is it not?"

I'd been in this sort of situation before: in Laviano. Garuti had lowered his sights very quickly and there were two ways of looking at it. It might mean that the picture really was stolen, and he wanted to off-load it to me quickly. On the other hand, it could have been a test to see how keen I was to get my hands on the Del Sarto. From my point of view, therefore, it was important that I drive a hard bargain.

"No," I said. "If the painting is stolen, as you say, 24 million is already too much. Be satisfied with that."

Renzullo smiled. "Mr. Blake, please . . ."

"Tell him what I said."

He did so. As Renzullo spoke, Garuti's ever-present smile faded and he launched into what I took to be a long tirade against me: it involved a lot of shrugging and waving—and then the name

Bronzino started to occur. Renzullo had mentioned a Bronzino in January, but had given no details.

Before he started to translate, Renzullo let out a long breath. "Mr. Blake, now Garuti—he is angry. He says, why can't you meet him on the price? What is four million lire to you—you are a rich man, eh, a millionaire? He says you must give him 28 million —or he will not show you the Bronzino."

And if I didn't play ball? Did that mean I would still get the Del Sarto? I judged that I would, that there was an element of bluff about Garuti—but what about the Bronzino? Was it worth a look? Bronzino was a very different artist from either Del Sarto or Caravaggio, but in many respects on a par with both of them. I had to weigh how it might appear to the others if I now allowed myself to be "bid up." It didn't *feel* as though they were testing me—indeed it occurred to me that Garuti was possibly as anxious to get rid of the Del Sarto as I was to recover it. It therefore seemed safe, after all this haggling, to increase my offer for the *St. John*—but I did so reluctantly.

"Twenty-eight million—if you can give me a good frame."

Renzullo sighed out loud in an amused way. "You drive a hard bargain, Mr. Blake. You are a tough man." But he translated and before he was finished Garuti was nodding again and pouting his agreement: I had a frame and we had a deal. We shook hands and drank to it.

Garuti then brought out the Bronzino—it was stacked amid the pictures propped against one of the walls. While Garuti was doing this Renzullo went to the small balcony at the other end of the studio and beckoned me to come and look at the view. It was certainly remarkable and reminded me even more forcibly how much Garuti's garret resembled Rodolfo's in *La Bohème*. The sky, darkening now, was a rather forbidding blue, but it also had yellow in it, and this reflected on the many terra-cotta roofs that stretched as far as we could see. Being several hundred years old, the tiles on the roofs were in fact of many different shades even though, for the most part, they were the same color. The colors, the strange light, and the layout reminded me of Giorgio de Chirico's surreal landscapes.

When Renzullo and I turned back into the garret studio, it was to find a new picture on the easel. I blinked hard. It was the

Bronzino and, if anything, even more beautiful than the Del Sarto.

It was on a piece of board about two feet high and eighteen inches wide and showed a woman at bust length who was wearing a red-brown brocade dress, with a large stand-up lace collar. She had a cold face that might, according to taste, be seen as beautiful, but was without doubt very stern. Her dress had a deep V neck and she wore a pearl necklace and pear-shaped drop earrings. Her hair was chestnut brown, piled high, and the whole ensemble certainly *looked* like a Bronzino.

Angelo di Cosimo di Mariano, born in Monticelli, near Florence in 1503, had worked predominantly at the court of Cosimo de' Medici in Florence. Vasari, who was a contemporary of Bronzino's, described his art as the epitome of all that had been achieved earlier by Michelangelo, Raphael and Leonardo. Few would now go as far as that, and in fact, since Vasari's time, Bronzino's approach to portraits—stylized and cold to the point where the personality of the sitter is suppressed for the sake of some inner ideal in Bronzino's mind—has been roundly criticized as lacking in meaning. For my part, I can see what Vasari meant. Bronzino's portraits, especially, have a luminous quality, and his sheer brilliance in painting clothes, skin or hair is so subtle that one is drawn back to his pictures despite the lack of emotion shown in the sitter's face. One scholar has written that this iciness in Bronzino's work portrays better than any other artist the "inherent cruelty" of the Italian mid-sixteenth-century and that, as much as anything, makes Bronzino unique.

Garuti's portrait had all these qualities. The woman *was* icy; her clothes were beautifully rendered in exquisite detail, and the background was dark yet luminescent, a clear but mysterious green, typical of the master.

"How did you come by this?" I asked, taking out my note pad again.

"It was taken from near Piacenza," Renzullo confided, translating. "Two or three years ago. Garuti—he can tell you no more because the man who stole it was killed in a car crash last year." How very convenient.

"Who is she supposed to be?" I asked.

Renzullo translated again and Garuti beckoned me closer. He pointed to some very faintly visible lettering at the top of the picture, just above the woman's head. There, in capital lettering made from gold leaf, but on a scarlet ground, I could just make out the words GLORIA FARNESE. I didn't know then whether this was the name of the woman in the portrait or whether it was meant to be a tribute to the entire Farnese family.

The Farnese had ruled the duchies of Parma and Piacenza from 1545 to 1731. Since Bronzino was, more or less, court painter to the Medici in Florence from about 1539, it seems likely the picture was done before this date. The Farnese family was established politically in 1534, when Alessandro Farnese was elected Pope Paul III. The years after saw Pierluigi Farnese ascend to the duchy: he had been a ruthless *condottiere* but was an efficient ruler. Two of his sons married powerful women: Orazio wed Diane, legitimatized natural daughter of Henry II of France; and Ottavio married Margaret of Austria, natural daughter of Charles V. It seemed possible, then, that the portrait had been commissioned to honor one of these marriages.

Garuti next led me around to the back of the painting. There in black writing—whether it was ink or oil or charcoal, I couldn't tell —was another woman's name: Isabella D'Este. I knew she was wife, and then widow, to Federigo Gonzaga. But whether this meant that the picture once belonged to Isabella or was a portrait of her, I didn't know, nor did Garuti.

It was undoubtedly a beautiful painting, possibly, I thought, worth more than the Del Sarto. Its condition, however, was a little worrisome: there were quite a lot of woodworm marks on the board and it had a nasty fissure down it, slightly to the right of center. These blemishes did not affect its beauty, still less my enthusiasm for recovering it, were it to be truly stolen. But I had to tell myself that such marks as these would affect the price a genuine dealer would be willing to pay. So I sat in front of the portrait and pointed to the fissure.

"Pity about that."

"It is a fault in the board, Mr. Blake. It is not Mr. Garuti's fault."

"I know, but it affects the price."

"Come, Mr. Blake. You always want something for nothing. It is an old painting; the board is cracked; you must expect such things." He translated for Garuti's benefit.

"Then there are the wormholes, Renzullo. Not good."

"A hard bargain, Mr. Blake. You want blood, eh?" He smiled his sickly grin.

"How much?" I asked suddenly, hoping to make it seem I was trying to catch them off guard. I said directly to Garuti, *"Quanto?"*

This time I knew well in advance what they were going to say. *Quarante* means forty.

"Forty million lire, Mr. Blake."

"Twenty."

"Come, Mr. Blake, meet us halfway. Garuti wants to help you with more pictures—but the price must be good. Say 30."

"Twenty-six."

"No, Mr. Blake. Thirty is not expensive." He translated for Garuti's benefit. "Garuti agrees—30 it should be."

I had of course absolutely no idea what the Bronzino was really worth. (I had only their word that the newspaper clipping said the Del Sarto was worth 80 million lire, but at least they knew they had to produce the clipping before there would be any deal.) Then I remembered that the painting attributed to the studio of Bronzino, which Johnny and Raf had bid for at Christie's so many months before, had gone for £18,000. I also recalled the comment by various art dealers that the difference between a studio work and one by the master himself is tenfold. So this picture was worth something between £18,000 and £180,000. I was fairly relaxed and said, not too grudgingly, "Okay, $30,000 —but I shall be tougher next time."

Renzullo grinned and translated. Garuti came across and shook my hand. However, our negotiations were not over yet. Garuti now produced a quite beautiful Italian primitive painting, with that delicious gold background I am so fond of. The subject was the Deposition, with the dead Christ slumped in an awkward pose at the foot of the picture and three or four heavily cloaked figures looking on.

It is quite possible that this picture was the most valuable painting I was shown that evening. It is also possible that it was stolen and that it was by an even more famous hand than Bronzino or Del Sarto (or Caravaggio, come to that) and that its rightful owner, reading this, will recognize the description. Nevertheless, I had to remain conscious that I was really supposed to be interested in sixteenth- and seventeenth-century paintings and that this primitive might also be a test (though I doubted it). Renzullo particularly knew that I was not supposed to be an expert on fourteenth- or fifteenth-century pictures (which I knew this was) and it might have looked odd for me to buy it not knowing how good it was or even whether it was real. I looked it over, scraped my pin across it and looked at the back, where there were checkered stretchers. I asked the price—60 million lire. Garuti said it had been written about by both Berenson and Zeri, also a famous art historian, and that it had also been stolen from near Piacenza. I dismissed the possibility of a sale by saying I didn't know enough about this type of painting to feel safe—and that therefore I would leave it. That may have been another mistake.

But they didn't mind, seeming pleased that we had got far enough to agree on two pictures, and I gathered from what was said that a celebration dinner was proposed. We went around the corner from Garuti's studio to a small square where there was a café with a packed bar. The restaurant section was closed, but was soon opened up for our benefit.

We then ate another marvelous meal—soup, pasta and veal, with an indifferent red wine, but a remarkably good local white. The wine came in very large bottles. Whatever the project's outcome in art, the rewards in pasta were prodigious.

While we sat eating, the fog silently descended around us, making Cremona appear more mysterious and shabbier than ever. In the circumstances I assumed that our drive back to Milan would be slow and tedious, but, as it turned out, Giancarlo had to get back to Parma and Garuti offered to drive Renzullo and me. Whether it was the wine, or the prospect of concluding a successful deal worth 58 million lire, or whether it was Garuti's car, which was old and rickety, the drive was another nightmare journey in Italy and very nearly fatal. Garuti didn't take the motorway, saying he knew the back roads better. That made no difference to his speed. Although visibility was running at sixty to seventy yards, he bowled along cheerfully at sixty miles per hour. He certainly knew the roads—and there was no shortage of traffic circles, fierce curves and narrow bridges. How we missed some of the oncoming trucks I will never know. It seemed a miracle when, all in one piece, we reached the lights of Milan.

THAT NIGHT, AFTER GARUTI had left us, Renzullo made a proposition. He had decided, he said, that I had more money than Giancarlo, Concerto, and the others put together, and he wanted to
work for me. I was surprised by this, but agreed. It might, in
some unpredictable way, help the project go forward. Renzullo
said he was seriously thinking of leaving Italcraft and going into
business with the diplomat he had mentioned. We agreed that he,
Renzullo, would receive a commission on all paintings he found
for me, plus a bonus if I got them exceptionally cheaply. From my
point of view it was a purely academic exercise, but it was supposed to reflect our "developing relationship," as he put it. Meanwhile, he thought I should take the opportunity of getting to
know Garuti better. There would be more paintings in the future.

The next morning—a Saturday—was very sunny. Garuti picked
us up in Milan early, and drove us back to Cremona. He was to
take me sightseeing, not to say window-shopping. He had mentioned on Thursday that he had worked in various churches in the
north of Italy and knew where some very valuable paintings were
to be found. He had told me that, for a price, he could copy these
paintings, replace the originals with the copies, and let me have
the former. We were to go off that Saturday morning and look at
a couple he had in mind for me. I was now 90 percent sure he was
the top man in this network. Ironically, I had read in the previous
day's English newspaper that twelve modern masters, including
pictures by Modigliani and Rouault, had been taken in a theft in
Sussex. It made an appropriate topic of conversation on our way
back to Cremona.

Garuti spent some time outlining his plan. He had worked in
many churches, he said, as a restorer and, besides knowing where
some of the best pictures were, he had also become good friends
with the priests, the organists, the caretakers and all the other
souls who help in the life of a church. Many of these people were
poor, he pointed out, and the churches badly lit. These two factors, he emphasized, could always be made to work together to
his—to our—advantage. People, even priests, could be bribed to
turn a blind eye where necessary, and the bad lighting meant
that months, even years, could go by without anyone noticing
that a particular painting was a copy. After such a delay it was
easy for church staff to claim ignorance of a swap.

To make copies, he said, he first needed to take a color slide of a painting. Then he would blow it up to its actual size in his studio. This would give him the lines and shapes of the composition. Color was not as important as it might seem, so long as he maintained an internal consistency throughout his work. Most book reproductions of paintings, he said with a smile, are nothing like the originals, so that even scholars could be fooled if they had not seen a picture before. He added that it took him two or three weeks to make a copy, though it sometimes took a lot longer to soften up a priest or a church caretaker. Before sending paintings to England or America, he would paint over the old masters with something of his own, probably in acrylic. Acrylic, he said, responded to different solvents than oil and so it was easy and safe to clean off once customs had been safely negotiated.

By this time we were in Cremona and making our way to the old part of the town. Like all Italian Renaissance cities, the center of Cremona was a maze of small squares, cobbled, crooked streets and secret courtyards, often lush in the sunlight with deep green leaves. Garuti's main object that morning was a visit to the church of St. Augustine. Just as we arrived a man came by on a motorized bicycle wearing one of those black astrakhan hats so popular with Rusian leaders and TV spies. It was the local priest.

He braked hurriedly, and leaped off his bicycle to talk to Garuti. They chattered away amiably enough, though at one point the priest looked across the street to where I was standing, waved, and then said something rather sternly to Garuti. After he had gone they both broke into sheepish laughter, and when I asked why, Renzullo, still grinning at Garuti, said, "The man says he hopes we haven't come to steal any of his beautiful paintings."

I wondered about this remark as we now trooped inside the church. Was it a genuine black coincidence? Or did it mean that Garuti already had *this* priest tied up, so to speak? I reminded myself not to underestimate the round-faced restorer.

St. Augustine's was a large church with many sizable paintings, but down the right-hand side of the nave, almost as far as you could go and in the darkest corner of the building, was a large canvas that was easily the most beautiful. It was a holy family by Perugino, very similar to his better-known version, in the Uffizi in Florence. There was no doubt about the authenticity of the picture. Painted in 1494, it was in all the books and singled out by Sir Charles Lock Eastlake in *Methods and Materials of the Great*

Schools and Masters as one of Perugino's best works. If Garuti could really steal this painting and replace it with a copy without anyone noticing, I was definitely onto something big (and who knew how many times he had done it before, with equally famous paintings? Italy might already be denuded of half its masterpieces without anyone knowing). Garuti whispered to Renzullo, who asked me not to be too obvious in my attentions to the Perugino, or to spend too long looking at it; so, after a quick look around the rest of the church, and a somewhat ironic offering placed in the appeals box at the back of the nave, we left.

Outside in the sunshine I expressed my admiration for the picture and Garuti seemed pleased. When I asked him, he said he didn't know how long it would take to remove the picture but that after about three more weeks he would be able to give me a date. I assumed that he first had to fix the priest or someone else working at the church.

During this return journey Garuti recounted a long tale about how he used to be an explorer in Central and South America, and how he had once discovered a "lost city" in—I think—Guatemala. Unfortunately, he said, he had been "ripped off" by two English archaeologists who had claimed the discovery as their own and, worse, salted away all the valuable artifacts without giving him his share. I asked for the names of the Englishmen, but he wouldn't say. I muttered something to Renzullo to the effect that there seemed to be a "buccaneering" aspect to Garuti's character. Renzullo nodded and didn't translate.

When we stopped for our regulation long lunch at about one (by now I was as keen as anybody on these meals) Renzullo discovered he had left his wallet-cum-handbag back in Cremona. This may have turned out to be a blessing in disguise for it meant that he had to travel back with Garuti after they had dropped me in Milan, rather than go on directly to Rome as he had planned. It was during this time, I later learned, that Renzullo impressed on Garuti the importance of the newspaper clipping to the success, or otherwise, of our deal.

I made my way back to London and the next day flew to New York where I was to take up a new job as a correspondent for the London *Times*. Before I did so, however, I just had time to consult my records on stolen art. Garuti had said that the Bronzino had been stolen from near Piacenza a year or two before. He had been vague, saying that the man who had stolen it had subsequently been killed in a car crash. But, if he was right, that would have placed the theft sometime in 1979, 1980 or just possibly early 1981.

The glossy red *Bollettini* of stolen art produced by the Italian Carabinieri showed nothing—but then the records I had ended in 1978. *Stolen Art Alert*, the monthly newsletter produced by the International Foundation for Art Research in New York, was more up to date: I had every one of these since it started publication in January 1979 as *Art Theft Archive*. However, compared with the Carabinieri's booklet, *Stolen Art Alert* had relatively few pictures and it was difficult to tell from some of the brief descriptions whether the wording fitted "my" pictures or not. There *were* two paintings recorded as stolen from Piacenza in 1979. Though both were described as portraits of ladies, and might therefore have been "mine," they were cataloged simply as "Venetian," which ruled out the Florentine Bronzino.

I turned to my third and final set of records, the least complete and, usually, the least up to date: Interpol's file of stolen art.

And there it was. File number 2492/121/80 recorded a theft from a private home in Piacenza in August 1979 of a portrait of a lady, attributed to Bronzino. What is more, there was a photograph of the painting, showing a woman with an icy beauty, a deep V neck to her dress, a row of pearls around her throat, pearshaped drop earrings and an elaborate stand-up lace collar. At last.

15

The Man with the Collar

THE SCENE NOW SHIFTED to New York, where, I dared to hope, a successful recovery would take place. It was a stroke of luck that I had just begun to live full time in Manhattan, thanks to my new job as the London *Times* correspondent. It meant I would no longer have to spend a fortune on transatlantic airfares.

Nevertheless, I still faced a dilemma in New York. Should I tell Charles Koscka, my contact in the U.S. Customs, immediately? He and his colleagues would help ensure a successful recovery of the Bronzino, but they might take matters out of my hands completely. Or should I wait, in the hope that the Del Sarto clipping would still turn up? If I did, and the clipping really did show the St. John to be stolen, I stood a chance of recovering *two* great paintings—better than I had ever dared hope. Moreover, from what Renzullo said, the two paintings were from different thefts, in different parts of Italy, and had been carried out more than a year apart. The primitive picture, which I had turned down, may have been from a third theft. That seemed to suggest that Garuti, at least, was a bigger figure in the art-theft underworld than he let on. This was an added, and decisive, incentive for trying to recover both pictures. I decided to wait. It suited me that Renzullo did not arrive back from Italy for several days. I guessed that he was spending some time in Rome, as he had indicated he might. That gave me time to acclimatize myself to Manhattan.

Stolen paintings continued to make news. A Gainsborough belonging to Paul Mellon had been taken from Sotheby's in London, where it was due to be sold. And Pieter Brueghel's wonderful *Christ and the Woman Taken in Adultery* had gone from the Courtauld Institute Galleries, also in London. Valued at £500,000, the picture hadn't been insured because the institute couldn't afford the premiums.

Renzullo didn't return to New York until the middle of February, but immediately called me early one morning.

"Good news, Mr. Blake, good news."

"The clipping has arrived?"

"The clipping has arrived."

"Splendid. What does it say?"

"Not on the phone, Mr. Blake, eh? Not over the phone."

"Very well, we should meet."

"Let's do that, Mr. Blake. Today?"

"Why not?" I had stories to write. It was already lunchtime in London. But I had an instinct, now that the clipping was here at last, to move as quickly as possible.

We agreed to meet at 12:30 that day. However, for the first time we rendezvoused not in Italcraft but at the ground-floor entrance to the Furniture Exchange, the building at 200 Lexington Avenue, where Renzullo's offices were located. It turned out that he did not wish Del Peschio to know about our impending piece of business, so we were to meet downstairs and go around the corner for a drink.

For once I was early (out of character for Blake) but Renzullo was even earlier. When I arrived he was standing in the lobby of the building reading an Italian newspaper with another stuffed untidily in one pocket. He grinned when he saw me approaching, folded the paper he was reading and reached into his pocket for the other one. As I came up to him he stretched out his arm, offering this other paper to me.

"Mr. Blake, this is it."

I took the paper and unfolded it; it was a copy of *Il Gazzet-*

tino, a Vicenza paper dated Wednesday, 15 April 1981. On page four was a small article, in a box, entitled "*Svaligiata una villa vicentina, Asportati mobili per 250 milioni* [Furniture worth 250 million lire stolen from a villa near Vicenza]." But before I could read the rest of the article Renzullo said, "Let's go upstairs."

I raised my eyebrows questioningly. I didn't think this was the plan.

"Don't worry. Del Peschio—he is away today. It's okay."

So we rode the elevator to the thirteenth floor (the Furniture Exchange is one of the few buildings in New York with owners unsuperstitious enough to admit to a thirteenth floor). Once we were in the Italcraft showrooms and settled in the inner office, Renzullo translated the newspaper article for me:

"VICENZA: *Paintings and antique furniture worth 250 million lire, at a first rough estimate, were stolen some time the other night from the villa of Marquis Dr. Giuseppe Roi, 57, in Montegalda.*

"*The thieves broke into the villa after making an opening in a side wall and defusing the alarm, which was connected directly with the* carabinieri *station at Longare.*

"*They took away 15 paintings of the 15th, 16th and 17th centuries (including one of the school of Del Sarto, worth 80 million lire), two 18th-century cabinets, three small 19th-century dressers, a prayer stool and other pieces.*

"*The Marquis, Dr. Roi, who was in Rome at the time, was immediately informed. On the spot, the* carabinieri *of Longare and Vicenza were headed by Captain Scursatone and Lieutenant Bruschetti who found no useful clues to help identify the perpetrators of this substantial theft. The Ministry of Fine Arts has also been informed.*"

I breathed out gently, quietly. The cutting gave no picture of the Del Sarto, nor did it prove that the painting I was being offered was actually the one stolen in the theft. But it was interesting that the furniture stolen was exactly the sort of stuff on sale here at Lexington Avenue. More immediately important, I now had the name and address of the man from whom it had been stolen: that should prove crucial in enlisting customs' aid in making the recovery. But for the moment I tried to seem unimpressed; I had to maintain the fiction that I was a real art dealer to the end.

"Pity there's no picture."

"Mr. Blake, you always want miracles, eh? We can go ahead now? I can tell Garuti?"

I thought it would be unnatural of me to express no enthusiasm at all at this turn of events, so I put on what I hoped was a beaming smile, leaned forward to pat Renzullo on the shoulder and said, "Yes, Renzullo, it looks like it. You have done well."

He beamed back and seemed not to have noticed what I had just noticed myself: that a minute before I had been skeptical and now was all sweetness and light. After all this time as Blake, the sophisticated dealer, I was still making mistakes.

"Another thing, Mr. Blake. I would like you to meet my friend, the diplomat. And he would like to meet you. He knows many people, Mr. Blake, many people, and he has big plans. He can bring in many paintings."

"What nationality is he?"

". . . er . . . Italian, Mr. Blake, but of Yugoslav extraction."

I got the impression that Renzullo had hesitated then. Why? Was he not giving me the whole picture—or had he been genuinely confused before remembering that the diplomat was of Yugoslav extraction?

"All right, Renzullo, I'll meet him if you say so. How about Wednesday?" If we were going to have a diplomat smuggling in our paintings I wanted to be able to tell Charles and his people at customs as soon as possible.

"I don't know, Mr. Blake. I will call him and let you know. He is not there—at his place of work, I mean." There was that hesitation once more. "When can you meet on Wednesday? In the evening?"

"Sure. What time?"

"Late, I think, six-thirty maybe. But we meet downstairs again, eh? Del Peschio does not know about this deal—the Del Sarto, I mean, or the Bronzino. And he does not know about the— diplomat, you understand? We meet at six-thirty downstairs, like today."

Renzullo called me the next day to confirm the Wednesday meeting, but it still did not occur to me to call Charles at customs. I didn't know when Renzullo or Garuti intended to bring the paintings into New York and until I did there seemed little point. I liked Charles, but one never knew how leaky customs was. I didn't know then how the Wednesday rendezvous would change things.

The diplomat was late and Renzullo and I stood in the lobby of the Furniture Exchange talking. Renzullo explained that the diplomat was attached to the United Nations, which meant he traveled a lot and so could be very useful to "us" (his word) in smuggling paintings, using the diplomatic bag.

In a way, I was by now quite intrigued to meet the man Renzullo kept talking about in such glowing terms, but I also began to doubt whether he was coming that night. It was already six fifty-five and, since I had a dinner date later that evening, I suggested to Renzullo that we go across to the pub we always used—Brew's on Thirty-fourth Street, between Lexington and Third avenues. We would have one drink and I would then have to leave. Reluctantly, Renzullo agreed. "We will go—but I will come back after a while and look for him. I think he will still come."

It wasn't necessary. Just as we were crossing Lexington Avenue we heard a car horn and a large, four-door brown sedan swung to a stop near the far curb, parking illegally in front of a fire hydrant. "It's him," said Renzullo, grinning his grin. "He has come."

You have to be very careful crossing the busy uptown-downtown avenues in Manhattan: you get no sympathy from the traffic even if you do have a cane and a limp, and after long practice I had learned to wait until the road was entirely clear. Real limpers cannot scamper the last few yards out of harm's way. On that occasion Renzullo and I had quite a wait. Just as the traffic was clearing and we prepared to cross, Renzullo whispered, "Don't be put off by the man's appearance, eh?"

He wore a slight smile as he said this and that mystified me. What on earth was there about the diplomat that could be both amusing and off-putting? I struggled across the road to where the man was standing. The curb was exceptionally high at this point and, as I was carefully negotiating it, I didn't examine the man closely as I approached him. Only when I was safely on the pavement did I look up and see what Renzullo meant with his cryptic phrase about the diplomat's appearance. I nearly dropped my cane. I *did* drop my jaw.

Underneath his black astrakhan hat and brown raincoat the diplomat wore the small black and white collar of a Roman Catholic priest.

HE WAS INTRODUCED TO ME as Father Lorenzo Zorza, from the staff of the Vatican Mission to the United Nations. He was about five foot ten or eleven, medium build, brown eyes—with a small brown moustache. In a distant way he reminded me of the actor Karl Malden, since he had a slightly bulbous nose and very mobile lips.

A priest, a diplomat—and a smuggler. So that was why Renzullo had hesitated when referring to Zorza? He must have been trying to make up his mind how much to tell me.

For the moment, on the pavement on Lexington Avenue, I tried to avoid showing my astonishment too much. I managed to mutter something about a famous British journalist called Zorza. "Yes, I know," said the priest, *"The Manchester Guardian."* Our conversation was off and going and my continuing astonishment was, I hoped, smothered by the talk. Ironically perhaps, Zorza and I talked about British journalism as we walked around the corner. He was an admirer of British newspapers, he said; and he added that he had particularly enjoyed a book called *The Pope from Poland,* written by three journalists on the *Sunday Times* of London. At this it was again my turn to be astonished—and this time out of anxiety. One of the three *Sunday Times* authors of *The Pope from Poland* was the newspaper's Rome correspondent, Tana de Zulueta. Tana had acted as my researcher, translator and super-link with Siviero ever since this project had started. Was this coincidence or did it mean they were on to me, and just cruelly teasing until some point when things would turn nasty? Or was I simply being paranoid again? Before I could think it all through, we arrived at the bar.

Brew's is a long bar with low yellow lighting and seats toward the back. There is sawdust on the floor and a cigarette machine halfway along the wall on the right. Any time I have been in the bar it has always been very crowded. Being the "wealthy" one, I was expected to pay for the drinks—beer for them and scotch for me. We stood talking by the wall, near the cigarette machine, just where the sawdust was deepest. Unaccountably, after all this time posing as A. John Blake, I was suddenly very apprehensive about being spotted by someone I knew. I stood with my back to the room.

To begin with, Renzullo did most of the talking. He said that Father Zorza did plenty of traveling between Rome and New York and knew many, many people, "including someone in Alitalia at Leonardo da Vinci" (Rome's airport).

"Have you brought in much before?" I asked as offhandedly as I could, mumbling most of it into my whiskey.

Zorza nodded, and sipped his drink. "Small things are better," he said. "Jewelry is good; you have jewelry?"

"You have brought in jewelry?"

He nodded again. "Yes."

"No," I said. "I have no jewelry at the moment, only paintings." Observing Zorza, I wasn't sure if he was nervous or if his behavior that day was normal—for him. But he kept looking from side to side, moving his head in a jerky fashion, like a bird; and his eyes darted about darkly in their sockets. It was Samuel Butler, I think, who said that clergymen should be "human Sundays": there was very little that was Sunday about Zorza.

"Mr. Blake"—Renzullo was speaking again—"the father—he cannot bring paintings from museums—it's too much. Only from private collections and foundations."

I wasn't sure what was meant by this statement. Was it in some way less dishonest to smuggle privately owned, as opposed to publicly owned, pictures? Possibly, I decided, it was more dangerous to smuggle museum paintings since they would tend to be better known, and their thefts more widely reported. But I didn't say anything out loud; I just nodded.

I then broadened the conversation and asked Zorza how long he had belonged to the mission at the UN. He replied that he had been there several years, that his time was coming to an end and that he had ambitious plans for afterward, after he had left the mission, that is. But these plans needed financing.

"That's why we want to talk to you, Mr. Blake." Renzullo again.

It turned out that their "scheme" was for a kind of bank to help the third world. This bank, or fund, would be so arranged, I was told, that companies from the major Western nations who deposited money with the bank would be granted certain tax exemptions. For some reason, which was never fully explained, the bank was to be based in Brazil. They wanted to know whether I would be interested in providing financial advice—and of course some actual cash. I have to confess that I didn't pay as close attention to this idea as I might have done, since I wasn't ever going to have to put up any money. Even so, two things struck me about this scheme. One, if it was all so simple and yet such a good idea, how come no one else had thought about it before? Two, why was Renzullo grinning so conspiratorially while the explanation was going on? It occurred to me that this scheme, too, might be a gigantic hoax. Father Zorza was clearly a complex and mysterious man.

I brought the conversation back to art. I asked Zorza what size the diplomatic bag was, and, holding his glass of beer in his right hand, he sketched a size about two feet six inches square. Suddenly I had a brief flash of my conversation months before with the professor in Voghera. His pictures—the Van Goghs and the so-called Utrillo—had been brought out of Buenos Aires in the diplomatic bag. Was there ever any room for diplomatic papers?, I thought.

"That's about the size of the Bronzino," I said. "Which is on board."

The priest made a face. "It's better if it can fold," he said. "Canvas is better."

"Well, the Del Sarto is much bigger—but that is on canvas. It must be about three feet six by two feet six. You won't fold it, though, will you? You'll roll it?"

"Of course," said Zorza. "There's no problem."

"When do you go to Italy again?" I now asked. Was I being too pushy?

"Soon . . . a few days . . . maybe next week."

"And you will see Garuti?"

"I will try. I don't know if I can go to Cremona. Maybe he will come to Rome."

I looked across to Renzullo, who grinned and said, "No problem, Mr. Blake. Garuti—he can go to Rome to see the father."

So far so good. But I was now extremely nervous. It really did begin to look as though I might at last recover two stolen pictures *and* have them smuggled into New York by a corrupt priest. To be spotted now, and have my cover blown at this critical stage, would be too much. In reality, of course, it was extremely unlikely that anyone who knew Peter Watson would walk into the bar at that precise moment; but that was small comfort.

As well as being nervous, my conscience was uneasy. Was I being a bit cavalier in leading this priest on? If he did smuggle paintings for me, and was caught, that would ruin his career far more comprehensively than any of the others. Was I being fair? I cannot say now that, in the bar that night, I thought through all the pros and cons in a thorough and detailed way. But Zorza had been, to some extent, foisted on me—I had not asked for him to be involved. And it did appear that he had done this sort of thing before, with jewelry at least, and had gone so far as to organize someone in Alitalia at Rome airport to help him. Then another thought occurred to me: we had never actually spotted how Concerto Battiato brought in the first *St. John:* perhaps it wasn't him at all—perhaps Renzullo had just allowed me to think it was but had used Zorza all along. That was the kind of low cunning Renzullo would have relished.

I didn't put that to Renzullo, but I did comfort myself with the thought that these sorts of arguments meant I was probably right to continue the deception and see where it led. The fact was that, however good or bad the paintings were that Renzullo had offered me down the months, none of them—not one— had a proper provenance. All had vague backgrounds which almost certainly indicated that, in one way or another, the pictures were not what they seemed. All, that is, except the Del Sarto and the Bronzino; and these, I was now certain, were stolen.

The bar filled to the point where the crush and the noise made conversation difficult. My nerves were getting worse by the minute. I made my usual excuse, that I had a dinner engagement (which was true), declined the offer of another drink from Renzullo, wished Zorza luck and limped out. I told Renzullo I would call him the next day.

Outside on Thirty-fourth Street I went down to Third Avenue and caught a taxi uptown. Once in the taxi—one of those hideous New York contraptions with scratched, dirty, bulletproof plastic between the driver and passenger—I allowed myself to relax, undid my bow tie and loosened my collar. It was very cold outside but I was sweating. Alone in the darkened cab, I couldn't help grinning: at last it looked as though the years of work might not be wasted.

RENZULLO CALLED early the next morning and suggested a meeting. He said that Zorza had gone to Italy that very morning. There had been a death in the family.

"When will he return?" I asked.

"Next week, maybe Thursday."

"And will he bring the paintings?"

"I hope so, Mr. Blake. This is my idea; but first I must call to Garuti."

It struck me that Zorza was behaving strangely—almost suspiciously. Had there really been a death in the family? Or had he gone especially to get the pictures, in a deliberate attempt to ingratiate himself with me so I would help his Brazilian project? If so, why was he not coming back for a week? More likely, he had been going to Italy today all along, and the previous night's meeting had been held for him to check me out, to see what sort of a man I was and whether I was worth smuggling for. Zorza was obviously a cunning man, more so than Renzullo, I thought. This further allayed my residual worries that he was not really corrupt: all his behavior pointed in the opposite direction.

Again Renzullo and I rendezvoused in the downstairs lobby of the Furniture Exchange, and, again, Del Peschio was away. On the way over to Italcraft I had decided to say to Renzullo that I was leaving for California for the weekend. Partly, this was designed to keep Renzullo from getting in touch with me. If things were about to start moving quickly I would much rather telephone Renzullo than the other way around. It meant I knew his movements, but he wouldn't know mine. I said, too, that I would be going from California directly to London unless Zorza planned to bring the pictures to New York the next week, in which case I would return to Manhattan myself to take possession and to pay for them. This way I was gently forcing Renzullo's hand. I thought he would assume that if I went back to London it would be some time before I returned again to New York—and before he received any cash. He said he wouldn't know for certain when the paintings would arrive until the following Sunday, by which time he would have spoken both to Garuti and to Zorza, who was moving around in Italy until then.

"By the way, Mr. Blake. Zorza, he wants $10,000 to bring in the paintings."

I pursed my lips and responded straightaway, "$5,000."

"No, Mr. Blake. It's too risky. He's a priest, eh? Not good if he gets caught. Improve your offer."

"Okay, $8,000. But only if he brings two paintings—$5,000 for one."

He nodded, accepting. "I will confirm it on Sunday, after I have spoken to the father."

We arranged that I would call Renzullo "from California" at 6:00 P.M. New York time the following Sunday. Renzullo was now getting nervous himself and asked me not to mention the word "paintings" over the phone. Instead, he wanted us to talk in code and he wrote out on a piece of Italcraft notepaper the words "On Sunday I will tell you if the man in Italy is bringing in one or two books." I thought it was somewhat melodramatic and just as suspicious as an open conversation, but if that was what he wanted—well, I had always persuaded him to incriminate himself on the phone before and I hoped I could do it again. At any rate I took the piece of paper with the code on it with me, in case it should prove to be evidence later on. I then wished us both luck and left, ostensibly for California.

I didn't get around to calling Charles Koscka, at customs, until the next day, a Friday. I had to spend the rest of the Thursday working on an article for the London *Times*. The movie, *Absence of Malice,* opened that day in London and I had been asked to file a feature on journalistic reaction to the film, which ironically concerned investigative journalism and how, if handled clumsily, it can do more harm than good. Needless to say, the position of the priest in my own story was never very far from my mind as I put this article together. At customs a woman with a deep voice answered and said, "He's out in the field, sir." It turned out that Charles was at that moment helping make a recovery of $70 million worth of heroin, one of the biggest hauls ever made. Large numbers of arrests followed and that meant he could not return my call until the following Monday. By that time I had spoken again with Renzullo when I called him on Sunday "from California."

I was of course calling from New York, so, in order to make my voice seem as far away as possible, I folded my handkerchief over the mouthpiece and pretended I couldn't hear him very well. "That's odd, Mr. Blake," he said, "you sound as if you are just around the corner." So much for my deception.

He had spoken to Garuti, he said, and to Zorza, and he was very hopeful that the priest would bring in the "books" next Thursday.

"One or two?"

"Two, Mr. Blake, both of them. He wants the $8,000, eh?" So the priest had agreed to the fee.

But Renzullo also said Garuti would go to Rome and might try to bring the books to New York himself, without giving them to Zorza. I was alarmed by this. It was very risky. If Garuti was caught, all our plans for the future would come to a stop.

"I know, Mr. Blake, I know. But what can I do? I do my best but Garuti—he is a buccaneer, eh? Remember South America. And right now these are his pictures."

"Try to stop him, Renzullo, please. It's too risky."

"I will try, Mr. Blake—but I can make no promises. Garuti, he is his own man."

On Monday Charlie called back at last. We had our usual banter: he gave me details about the heroin bust, which I had already read about, in outline, in the newspapers and I asked him what the tally was on the number of his children ("Still eight," he replied). Then I told him the entire story. As usual he immediately became very businesslike and took the names of everybody concerned—he would run the new names through the customs computer to see if any had criminal records. We arranged a meeting later in the day, so I could give him a copy of the newspaper clipping reporting the theft of the Del Sarto. He needed that, he said, because he had to satisfy himself that both paintings were truly stolen.

"Peter, you're sure the clipping is real? Not like the fake you had made up, some time ago?"

I smiled into the phone. "Oh yes, I'm sure. Renzullo gave me the entire newspaper."

Charlie came into the office later on to examine the clipping. "There should be no problem in tracing the marchese," he said.

"Montegalda probably isn't very large, and everyone will know a marchese."

He reminded me, however, that there was one problem I should have considered. It was just possible that the Del Sarto theft was part of an insurance fraud with the marchese himself involved. If this was so, then informing him that one of his pictures had been located might alert the "thieves" and, in turn, Garuti. Even if Dr. Roi himself was not involved, it was still possible that someone in his household was. If they found out about our plans indirectly through the marchese, that would be equally disastrous.

Charles pointed out, however, that the customs people had no choice. They needed "prior cause" before they could act. Under their regulations, information from a "contact" could be acted upon only if that contact's information had proved reliable before. Leaving aside the logical difficulty of how any informant's information became reliable in the first place, it made not the slightest difference to them that I had been on the project for months, that I had known Charles on and off for over a year or that I was a reputable journalist.

As it happened, I got to the marchese before customs did. Their Italian speaker was less than fluent, and although there was no problem locating the marchese's number in Montegalda, he wasn't there. But Tana de Zulueta got the marchese's Rome number from the housekeeper in Montegalda and had no difficulty in reaching Dr. Roi. When she spoke with him, and described the picture, it was soon obvious that the painting was his and he appeared very excited. But then he would contrive to appear very excited, even if he had been involved in the original theft, so that did not necessarily mean we were out of the woods yet. Anyway, I passed the news on to Charles.

The next morning Charles phoned Dr. Roi himself, taping the conversation, which gave him the "prior cause" he needed to begin an investigation. He warned the marchese not to say anything to anyone, especially his household staff. That was all that could be done before I was scheduled to call Renzullo, again "from California," on Wednesday. And for that Charles came with me to our New York office and bugged the phones.

It was exceedingly simple. All he did was fix a small black induction coil by suction cup to the earpiece of the receiver. The coil, so Charles said, cost $1.50 at any electronics store. A wire fed from the coil into a tape recorder, and a few seconds before 6:30 P.M., when I was scheduled to call Renzullo, Charlie switched on the tape and, for the record, dialed the speaking clock: the number—976 1616—was inscribed on the inside of the tape recorder's casing. Then he spoke into the machine himself, describing what we were up to. He gave the date, then said, "This is Agent Koscka. I have just affixed a recording device to informant's telephone, prior to his calling suspect, Achilles Renzullo, on . . ." and he gave the number. The recorder remained on while I dialed; an expert at a later date could have deciphered the number from the order of the touch tones. I put my handkerchief over the mouthpiece and Charlie picked up another extension to listen in.

Renzullo was waiting for the call and picked up his receiver before the second ring.

"Mr. Blake? How are you? Bad news, Mr. Blake."

My heart sank and I made a grimace at Charles. In telling the marchese, had we alerted the whole chain?

"What's wrong, Renzullo? What's happened?"

"Garuti—he tried to roll one of the . . . er . . . books; and it has cracked."

What did that mean? Was he telling the truth? Or was this their way of easing out of the deal? I had no way of knowing and I had no choice, as I saw it, of doing other than accept for the time being that this "excuse" of Renzullo's was genuine.

"Can't we have the crack repaired here in New York, Renzullo? I know a good restorer," I lied.

"This is it, Mr. Blake. This is what I tell Garuti. But he is very distraught, you know, very upset. He is worried it will affect the price. He says he doesn't want the book moved until he has repaired it himself. After all, he is a restorer, and these are his books."

"Where is Zorza?"

"That is another thing. I cannot reach the father anymore. I do not know where he is staying in Rome. I know he has talked with Garuti but I do not know if he has met him yet."

"Renzullo, couldn't Zorza just bring the Bronzino if the Del Sarto is damaged? Garuti could repair the St. John and bring it later."

"Exactly, Mr. Blake, this is what I tell Garuti. But he is a buc-caneer, Mr. Blake. Maybe he wants to bring the . . . er . . . books, himself."

"Look, Renzullo, can't you call him—now, I mean? Say it is very important to have something sent across tomorrow; that I have a client waiting."

"I cannot, Mr. Blake. Garuti is not there. He went to Rome, that I know. But I don't know if he saw Zorza."

I was flummoxed. Was Renzullo deliberately playing difficult—or was it all true? Charlie had begun to scribble instructions to me on scraps of paper; I tried to read them but—well, his writing left something to be desired. One that I could decipher said, "Can we make the priest stay in Italy for a few days—and bring the pictures later?" I put this to Renzullo.

"No, Mr. Blake, that is the problem. Do not think I have not thought about that. Zorza has business in New York on Friday; he must return tomorrow. It is a pity because Zorza—he has a contact in customs, here at the airport. The man will help him, but maybe not Garuti."

Charles raised his eyebrows and I was about to pursue this when the door to the office suddenly burst open. In the doorway stood a large, hairy woman. She looked like someone from the KGB in a James Bond film and I almost expected her to have a poisoned stiletto hidden in the toe of her shoe. But in fact it was now after seven and she was the cleaning lady. She wore pale-blue overalls and was pointing into the room. The fact that there was one man speaking into the telephone through a handker-chief, that the phone receiver was very obviously bugged and that there was another man listening in to the conversation seemed neither to intrigue nor amuse her. Unfortunately, it didn't send her away either: she continued pointing.

Charles guessed what she wanted sooner than I did. He reached over and picked up the wastepaper basket. It was empty and he showed her it was. She gestured her thanks, closed the door and left us to it.

By now Charles and I were finding it very hard not to laugh aloud, but I managed to stammer into the phone, "Renzullo, there must be some way of contacting Zorza in Rome tonight; you *must* have someone who can help."

"I cannot, Mr. Blake. I know a man, yes—but I have already called to him. He cannot help."

Charlie was passing another scribbled note now. Fortunately, I could read it. "Remember, I will not pay your ticket to Milan if this does not work out."

"I know it, Mr. Blake, believe me I know it. It cannot be helped."

"Look, Renzullo, I have decided to come back to New York tomorrow, just in case. This is an important deal and you and I must try hard to make it work."

"Yes, yes, Mr. Blake. Don't tell me . . . but what can I do? No miracles, eh?"

"You can call me tomorrow, Renzullo, in New York, when the priest has arrived."

"Of course, of course, what time?"

I had to work it out quickly. Say a 9:30 A.M. flight from L.A.— that was already 12:30 New York time. A five- to six-hour flight, that meant arrival at Kennedy six-ish.

"Say eight o'clock, Renzullo, nine to be safe."

"Okay, Mr. Blake, I will call you. But I can tell you, I do not think Zorza will bring in any paintings—I mean books—tomorrow."

Charles slapped his thigh in delight. Renzullo had broken the code and in doing so incriminated himself nicely. After we had hung up, Charles tested the tape—it was all there.

16

Undercover at Kennedy

WE DID NOT EXPECT ZORZA to smuggle anything the next day, but—just in case—Charles wanted to stake out the airport. In order to do that, however, I had to be there, to identify the priest; and in order to do *that*, Charles wanted me to see the assistant U.S. attorney the next morning. This was a new move and one that made me apprehensive. Things were gradually slipping from my control. I suppose I had always known at the back of my mind that something like this would have to happen: journalists take the law into their own hands only in fiction. But now that things were escalating, I wasn't sure I liked the way they were going.

The next morning Charles picked me up at my apartment and we drove south on the FDR drive, bound for City Hall, and the U.S. attorneys' offices. The assistant attorney we met was a feisty woman called Minna Shrag. She had curly hair, spectacles that hid rather than enhanced her very nice eyes and a manner which belied Sophocles's dictum that "it is better to be just than clever" —because she was both.

I gave her a quick rundown on the entire project, to place the latest events in context, and described how I had come by my information.

Charles's boss sat in on the meeting. Ben van Inwegen was slightly taller than Charlie, about five feet ten, boyish-looking and with a rather quiet, studious manner. Minna's boss also looked in from time to time; her name was Shirah Neiman. After an hour and a half of questions and answers, Charles was given the all-clear. There was enough "prior cause" for us to stake out the International Arrivals Building at JFK that afternoon, to observe Zorza's arrival.

Charles, Ben and I had lunch in the customs canteen in the World Trade Center, overlooking the Hudson River and the Statue of Liberty. It was a beautiful day, sunny and cold, and we sat in silence for a while, eating apples and enjoying the view and watching several large ships making for the open ocean.

Since Zorza knew me as a smooth dealer, Ben and Charlie fitted me out from the customs "undercover closet" with jeans, a rough bomber jacket and an astrakhan cap. Then it was on to Charlie's office for a pair of binoculars, my eyes being what they are. "Office" was a grand word for the desk area he had, separated from the others in his squad by a five-foot-high partition. You only got an inkling of Charlie's interest in art if you looked up: taped to the dirty white polystyrene panels above our heads was a colored postcard measuring about eighteen inches by six— it depicted Michelangelo's efforts on the ceiling of the Sistine Chapel. An ironic touch.

We drove to the airport in two cars: Charlie's was Alpha 14; in the other, Alpha 12, were two special agents, Eddie Choo, very nice, young, half-Chinese, and Walter Meyer. Choo had recently joined customs from the Bureau of Alcohol, Tobacco Tax and Firearms, which President Reagan had said he intended to disband though I think he never did. It was pointed out to me, as if it were reassuring, that should any shooting be involved, we were "well covered." This was the first time it really came home to me that I was in New York, not London, and that criminals and law enforcement officers in this city regularly had shoot-outs. I tried not to think about it.

Alitalia flight 310 from Rome was due in at 2:40 P.M. We reached the arrivals terminal by 2:30 and stood around talking and enjoying the early spring sunshine. The plan was for Eddie Choo and Meyer to enter the arrivals building from the outside, pose as tourist passengers with cameras, then pass back through customs near Zorza, see who met him, and follow. Charlie and I would enter the customs hall from the "airside" (i.e., from the tarmac). If Zorza did have a contact in U.S. Customs at Kennedy, this would help divert attention from our investigation, since we would be operating as unobtrusively as possible in twos, rather than in fours.

While we were talking, and before we could get our game plan all worked out, I suddenly noticed the green and red tail fin of an Alitalia 747. It was taxiing at speed on the far side of the airfield. I grabbed Charles' arm. "It's here, it's early—look!"

Charles turned to where I was pointing. "Okay," he said, running to his car. "Let's go."

We had no problem getting "airside." The security guard at the slip road was reading her *National Enquirer* avidly, and the security pass Charles waved at her might just as well have been the *Mona Lisa*. It was a good thing there were no terrorists around that afternoon: JFK was wide open.

Once we were on the tarmac, however, it was a different matter. There are "roads" marked on the apron in painted lines, but the Alitalia jet was now three hundred yards away and we had some catching up to do. Charles paid no attention to the roads.

It was a mistake. Our first "near miss" was with an Air Canada 727 just starting to taxi to takeoff. The plane and our car emerged from different sides of the same building both doing about fifty miles an hour. Charles could have braked hard and allowed the plane to pass but he must have judged that was too long a wait: instead he accelerated and, in a wide curve (taken at about seventy miles per hour), we passed in front of the jet and almost under its nose. I looked back to see the flight crew waving crude international gestures in our wake. Before we could straighten up and Charles regain full control of the car, we were almost hit by a 707 of Lan Chile. It was coming straight for us, so Charles steered away to the right, to pass by its port side. As he did so, however, the jet also turned—toward its gate and in the same direction as us: we were now headed on a ninety-degree collision course. Charles brought the car to a sharp stop. As he did so, one of the Boeing's two starboard side engines approached dangerously close to his side of the car and I had visions of our being sucked into that whirling maw. It couldn't have been more than a second, however, before Charles had engaged reverse and we backed away, out of trouble.

Now we had to catch the Alitalia jumbo. Charles put his foot down, and drove in a straight line across the apron to where the red, white and green jet was still taxiing. We were closing on the aircraft from the rear when the narrowest escape of all occurred. Charles's car, a Pontiac, was, like most American cars, rather spongy, in its suspension and steering, and not terribly stable under fierce braking. We must have been about seventy yards behind the jet when it suddenly braked, prior to turning to its gate. Jets, of course, don't have stoplights at the back as cars do. We were more or less behind the plane's starboard wing and, in no time, we were approaching one of the engines far too quickly for comfort. Having just seen the front of a Pratt and Whitney at close quarters, I was now getting a better view than I wanted of the back of one. Charlie's braking foot hit the floor, and at the same time he swung the wheel hard left. The tires screeched, I was thrown against the door and could feel the hot exhaust from the plane's number four engine through the window. We must have missed the back of it by a couple of feet—no more—and the Pontiac, fortunately a low, blue model, finished up at a standstill, under the wing.

"Jesus," said Charles, and you have to remember he is a devout Catholic who rarely swears or curses. "*Jeeesus.*"

Just then, the whine of the Alitalia's engines rose to a pitch, died away, and the aircraft rolled forward and turned its corner. I believe no one on the flight deck could see what had happened. I could only hope that Zorza, if he was aboard, was seated on the far side of the plane.

We parked around another spur of buildings and out of sight of the Alitalia jet, whose captain had just turned off its engines when Charles and I leaped from the Pontiac. It would be some time before the Alitalia passengers deplaned and got through immigration and into the baggage area; but we had to set up our observation point and it could take time to find something suitable.

It was as well we hurried. The customs officers inside the terminal could have been more helpful. As Charles later explained, the boys at Kennedy regarded the arrivals building as "their turf" and viewed the special agents from Investigations with jealousy, as people who had all the fun (which was true) and none of the drudgery (which was less true). Charles's task was more difficult that day because he could not tell them what we were up to in case we inadvertently alerted the priest by briefing his contact. We were taking something of a risk as it was: it was obvious to the customs officers in the building that I was a stranger, there (with my binoculars) to identify an incoming passenger. If the customs man who was a friend or colleague of the priest knew Zorza was coming in that day, bringing something with him illegally, he might just put two and two together.

Eventually, the local officers agreed to open up the observation booth which U.S. Customs has in the arrivals terminal. This had a raised floor, darkened glass and, on that Thursday, a hospital bedside screen, so I could remain well hidden with just my binoculars discreetly showing. After I was ensconced there, Charles walked off with one of the local men. I overheard the latter say, "Who is this guy, Charlie? Is he undercover? Because if he is, you better tell him to look to his shoes. He's wearing a leather jacket, jeans—and Guccis, for Christ sake."

I looked down. It was true. We had all forgotten about my shoes.

By this stage enough time had elapsed for Zorza to have entered the baggage area. It was teeming with people, hundreds if not thousands of individuals, arrivals on Mexicana, SAS, Iberia, El Al, Singapore Air Lines. Charlie did point out, however, that all passengers had to come into the arrivals building through a single entranceway at the far end. Unfortunately, that was a long way away, a hundred yards or more, and I wasn't certain that, even with binoculars, I would recognize Zorza. I began to sweat. What a fool I would feel if the priest was to sneak through without my recognizing him. I pointed the binoculars at the entranceway and twiddled the center knob until the arch came into focus.

That was our first piece of luck that day. I saw him. It was a classic piece of psychology. My hormones recognized Zorza before my brain did. I had a sensation run all the way down my back and it was that, rather than sight, which told me I was looking at the man I had last seen in the Brew's pub on Thirty-fourth Street. He came down the ramp by himself, walking quickly and purposefully, as befitted a man who used the airport so much. He was carrying something, but such was the crush of people, that I could see only his head and shoulders. What I didn't know then, but found out later, was that Zorza was by now a naturalized American—so he didn't need to go through the notoriously slow American immigration system. That was how he had deplaned so quickly.

I alerted Charles, who dashed off to tell Eddie Choo and Walter Meyer. After Eddie and Walter had followed Zorza through customs, Charles was to reclaim the priest's declaration form, or "dec," on which he either would or would not have declared what he had brought into the country. It was also Charles's job to keep a look out for any customs official who looked like an accomplice of Zorza's. Following that, Charles and I would have to make another dash for it across the tarmac to catch up with Eddie and Walter, who by then, if everything went according to plan, should be tailing Zorza. (They had let slip the comment that they didn't want me too close to the tailed car—in case things got nasty and shooting started.)

The next piece of luck was that Alitalia Flight 310 from Rome, the one Zorza had arrived on, was flagged on the baggage carousel right opposite the observation booth where I was hidden. That meant I had a perfect view of the priest as he waited for his luggage. He was wearing the same brown raincoat as he had on the first evening we had met. It was eerie watching him and I was far from sure I liked, or approved of, this prying. I had to keep telling myself he was a criminal, or potential criminal, with a perfect "front." A dishonest priest either deserved special consideration—or quite the opposite. I wasn't sure which view I held.

From his manner I was tempted to think he was nervous: he kept looking from side to side, like a bird, as he had in the pub the week before; and he kept walking about the baggage area, well away from the carousel where his luggage would appear. Charles and I had told Minna Shrag, the assistant attorney, that we didn't expect any paintings to be brought in that day, that this exercise was just so I could identify Zorza to the customs agents. But now, watching the priest's manner in the arrivals building, I began to get a feeling in my bones that he just might have something with him.

Seconds later the crush of people parted at last and my heart leaped as I got a look at the luggage he had been wheeling around on a trolley since shortly after his arrival in the hall. Wedged on the trolley was a black imitation leather portfolio; the portfolio wasn't zipped up, however, because what was inside was slightly too big for it. And what was inside was a package wrapped either in white paper or in newspaper—I couldn't make out which. The package was exactly the size and shape of the Bronzino. I immediately relayed this to Charles. He did not appear to share my excitement but did speak to Eddie Choo. Eddie melted into the crowd of passengers near the carousel and discreetly took some photographs of the package while Charles sidled up to the priest to take a closer look. He could spot nothing definite but I was still excited; it might not be a dry run after all.

There now followed a long wait. Luggage was already coming on to the carousel from the Rome flight, but Zorza's was a while appearing. During this wait he continued to walk about the arrivals building, often out of view from where I was positioned; but the others went with him just in case he had guessed he was being watched and tried to slip out through customs without his luggage. Each time he came back to the carousel, though twice he had another man with him. Was this his contact at the airport, a plainclothes customs officer? It appeared not, for Eddie Choo managed to overhear the two men talking about the flight they both had just been on. He was a fellow passenger, and shortly afterwards his luggage arrived and he went on, alone.

It must have been another twenty minutes before the rest of Zorza's bags arrived. The terminal was still very crowded so all I saw him do was reach over, bend down, turn and place something on his trolley. Then he straightened up and hurried off to a part of the hall where I couldn't see him. I later learned that he did seek out a particular customs official, a uniformed man, who helped him go through the usual formalities without having his bags checked.

I caught sight of his trolley as he trundled it across the building and again I experienced a surge of feeling and I swallowed hard. On the trolley was a roll of something about a foot thick and two feet six or so wide. It was wrapped in brown paper, and to my distant eye it was exactly the shape the Del Sarto would have made had it been rolled.

Now I was hopping with excitement—and frustrated that I had

to keep hidden in my little box. Zorza had brought both pictures, I was convinced—despite all the palaver the night before on the phone with Renzullo. The thought occurred to me that he had been trying to mislead me deliberately. He may have been worried, as he had been that day with the professor in Voghera, that I would contact Zorza directly and leave Renzullo out of the deal. If so he wouldn't want me to know when Zorza was coming in.

Charles was just as unimpressed with my feeling about the Del Sarto as he had been about the Bronzino. However, he did send Eddie off to photograph the roll. Eddie would now stick with Zorza while Charles took charge of the declaration form the priest turned in. I now had quite a wait: U.S. Customs is almost as slow and thorough as U.S. Immigration. Fifteen or twenty minutes later, by which time it was getting very hot in my booth, Charles came back waving the card. "He has declared gifts," he said, "and books."

I smiled. "Books were the code we used for the paintings, Charles. I bet you he's brought in the paintings."

Together we now sprinted across the arrivals terminal and ducked through a door marked no exit, back onto the apron. The drive back to the security gate was a model of safety: all we had to contend with was an Aerolineas Argentinas 707 and we outpaced that easily. On the other hand, getting out of the airside zone was more difficult than getting in. Charles's pass was scrutinized thoroughly, as if making up for the failure on the way in, and he had to explain who I was. All very reassuring but a crucial delay for us, since we were anxious to catch up with Eddie, Walter, Zorza and whoever had met him beyond customs.

We needn't have worried. When we were on the expressway back into Manhattan, Charles switched on his radio and gave the call sign:

"Alpha 14 to Alpha 12, do you read me?" A pause. "Alpha 12, are you there?"

Another pause, suddenly, out of nowhere: "This is Alpha 12, ten-four." Then the shock. "Sorry, Charlie, we lost them."

"What!" screamed Charles. "I mean ten-four, Alpha 12; this is Alpha 14; how in hell did that happen?"

As they were leaving the airport, Eddie said, they had got stuck behind a truck and some buses and the car in which Zorza was traveling "just disappeared." However, Eddie did have the number of the car the priest was traveling in and on his "dec" form Zorza had given an address on Forty-third Street between Lexington and Third avenues. Ironically, this address was less than a block from where the London *Times* offices were then situated in Manhattan: I had probably passed Zorza on the street more than once without knowing it.

As we drove back to the city (more slowly now) the details of the car Zorza had been picked up in were fed into the customs computer. Within minutes the information came back that it was owned by a certain gentleman on Long Island who had no record; and the car hadn't been reported stolen. We couldn't be sure, but this man did not seem to be part of the smuggling operation.

Charles was not too perturbed that we had lost Zorza because he felt pretty sure that, sooner or later, he would make his way back to the mission where he lived and where customs could reach him whenever they wanted. Now we had to wait for nine o'clock that evening when Renzullo was scheduled to call Blake at home with any news. We all went to my apartment for my phone to be bugged. Again this was simply done and Charlie showed me how to switch on the tape. For an incoming call I was to switch it on before picking up the receiver, while the phone was still ringing. This would make it clear to anyone listening to the tape later that there had been no editing, and that all the tape was intact. If the incoming call was a personal one, unconnected with the project, I was to switch off the recorder as quickly as I could. For outgoing calls, I was to follow the same procedure as Charlie had in my office the night before: switch the tape on, dial the speaking clock, then the number I really wanted. Charlie and the others went home after the bugging system had been fixed up and I promised to call him as soon as Renzullo had spoken to me.

He called right on the button: 9:01 P.M. I was supposed to have arrived that evening from L.A., after a long flight, and when I answered the phone I pretended to be only half awake and in the middle of a nap.

"Mr Blake . . ."

"What? . . . Oh . . . Renzullo? . . . Wh- . . . what time is

. . . is it nine o'clock already? Sorry, Renzullo, the flight was rather full and bumpy. I was tired and I've been sleeping. I'll be all right soon." What a ham.

"Mr. Blake . . . I have some news to make you sleep very well tonight."

"Oh yes?" My heart was thumping so loud I thought he might hear it over the phone.

"Yes, Mr. Blake, you will pirouette."

"Zorza brought something?"

"Yes, Mr. Blake, he did."

"One of the books?"

"No, Mr. Blake . . ."

"Two books!"

"Yes, Mr. Blake. I said you would pirouette. Zorza brought both books."

I stared at the tape recorder, daring it not to be recording all this. I had been right. That feeling in my bones was to be trusted after all. What a pity Charles was not a gambling man. I could have made good money out of him. "Well done, Renzullo. You've pulled it off at last. You will make a lot of money from this sale."

"Thank you, Mr. Blake, thank you. I hope so. Mr. Blake, we have things to discuss. Are you busy tonight?"

"I have a dinner engagement"—I looked at my watch: it was 9:05—"in thirty minutes. Where are you?"

He named a bar with a weird name on the Upper East Side: "At the Sign of the Dove." He was clearly elated and I sensed that he wanted company as much as anything, someone to share in his triumph. But the Upper East Side posed problems for me. If there was one place in New York where I ran a risk of being recognized it was there, especially the bars. I couldn't risk that at this late stage. I sensed, too, that Renzullo might get very drunk that night and I wasn't sure I wanted to be around. He might attract too much attention. I didn't want to risk having too many drinks myself.

"No, Renzullo, I don't think I shall be able to make it tonight. But what is there to discuss—and when can I see the paintings?"

"That's it, Mr. Blake; Garuti—he is coming on Saturday. He says we must not unwrap the paintings until he is here."

He had not noticed that he hadn't corrected me when I re-

ferred to "paintings," then he had obliged by referring to "paintings" as well. Splendid.

"Why on earth not?" I asked.

"He wants to repair the crack in the Del Sarto, and put it back
on stretchers. And the Bronzino has something painted over it; he
wants to clean it before you see it."

"I'd rather like to see the Bronzino the way it came in, Renzullo. Just out of curiosity."

"No, Mr. Blake, you cannot. You know Garuti; he says we must
not open the packages."

I didn't push it. Garuti was clearly the boss. "Where are the
paintings now?"

"At the mission with Zorza. That's another thing . . . where
can I put them tonight? The banks are closed, eh?"

Should I meet him? Could I turn such a meeting so that I got
an early look at the paintings? I decided it would be too pushy.
"That's your problem, Renzullo."

"Thank you, Mr. Blake; I like your sense of humor."

"Don't worry, Renzullo, you have done well. You are going to
be a rich man."

"That's a thing, eh?"

"Shall we meet tomorrow?"

"Of course, of course. I meant to say, Mr. Blake, I have a new
source opening up. A Caravaggio and a Giorgione maybe."

I made disbelieving noises.

"Yes, Mr. Blake, it's true; let's meet tomorrow. Where you
want to meet?"

Perhaps he just wanted to keep in contact now, to make sure I
didn't suddenly disappear at this last moment.

"Okay, how about our usual bar, on Thirty-fourth Street? At
seven?"

"That's good, Mr. Blake. At seven."

"I shall pirouette in my sleep, Renzullo. Well done, again."

"Thank you, Mr. Blake. Good night."

I called Charles and relayed the news. He decided that in view
of what had transpired we should meet again the next day with
Minna Shrag. At that point I didn't quite understand why but
agreed cheerfully, hung up and, unlike the previous few nights,
fell asleep easily.

Next day I soon found out why Charles wanted me to meet the

assistant U.S. attorney again. In order to obtain conclusive evidence on this final stage, Ben van Inwegen, Charles's boss, wanted to wire me for sound. Minna had to clear it.

I suppose that being wired for sound is nothing special in these post-Watergate days. Many investigative journalists seem to do little else. Still, I was dealing with real criminals and, should I be found out, the whole project would be ruined. So I was very nervous that night when I went to meet Renzullo. At 6:00 P.M., Eddie Choo had arrived at my apartment with Charles and, with masking tape, fixed a Nagra tape recorder to my abdomen, just above the waist on my right side. A small plastic skin-colored wire with a tiny metal microphone was taped under my breast to a point just below my sternum. With my shirt on and my jacket buttoned, to my own eye I looked a little bulky and suspiciously lopsided around my middle. But both Eddie and Charles said I looked fine. Eddie activated the machine and spoke into it: "This is special agent Choo. I have just affixed the recording device to the informant who is due now to meet with suspect Achilles Renzullo at Brew's pub on Thirty-fourth Street." He then gave the date and time and told me not to deactivate the machine but to leave the tape running until he and Charles met up with me again after the rendezvous with Renzullo. That way it would be clear to any court that might want to hear the tape that there had been no tampering with it. Besides being a very slim recorder, the Nagra also operated silently; there was no whirring movement of the spools, nor any clicks when it switched on and off. Each tape lasted three hours, which should be enough, I thought. The Nagra is quite expensive, costing several thousand dollars, I believe. Customs had only one.

Charles and Eddie dropped me off at the corner of Thirty-third Street and Second Avenue and I limped to the bar. Renzullo was waiting outside, wearing a kind of beret, and he greeted me warmly. We found a table away from the noise and where I hoped his voice would be picked up clearly by the microphone. As I ordered drinks I noticed Charles and Eddie slip into the bar and stand chatting where they could see us talk and watch us leave.

Nothing much happened that night. Renzullo incriminated himself some more, and cursed a lot about the stupidity of his colleagues, especially Del Peschio. Then he sang the praises of

Zorza, but said in future $8,000 would not be enough. The priest was growing greedy already, I thought, but I said nothing that might interrupt Renzullo's flow. Finally, he pulled out yet more photographs—"from a new source," he said. There was a Caravaggio that wasn't, a Bellini (a portrait of Alex de Imola), a Velásquez (a portrait of the Cardinal Gianfranco Arcari), a Raphael drawing in red chalk—the head of a young man or girl, a madonna and child with the infant St. John the Baptist, attributed to Del Sarto, a "Rubens or Luca Giordano" ("*Ecce homo*"), a Guercino and last, but not least, a Van Dyck. I showed interest, of course, took all the photographs offered except the Caravaggio, since it was so obviously not right, and said I would do my "research." I was aware that almost every one of the paintings he was offering had featured in my catalog of fakes, right down to the Raphael red chalk drawing. Moreover, as I later learned, when I compared it, Renzullo's *Portrait of Alex de Imola* by Bellini looked disturbingly similar to a forged Bellini *Portrait of a Lady* in Otto Kurz's book on fakes.

Still, everything seemed to be going well that night, although I remained very nervous about the tape recorder. Renzullo was leaning across the table, speaking right into the microphone, with the tip of his nose only about eighteen inches from my chest. I was apprehensive that he might notice the wire through my shirt. To be on the safe side I had kept on my overcoat as well as my jacket, and so after about half an hour and two drinks, I was sweating copiously. He kept urging me to take my coat off, but I kept saying I had to go.

Renzullo thought it would be a good idea if I went out to JFK airport with him the next afternoon to meet Garuti. It would, he thought, reassure the restorer. It seemed to me yet another opportunity for me to make mistakes, but I could see that keeping Garuti reassured was in my interest too. So I agreed.

The next day Renzullo picked me up, in Zorza's car, at 4:00 P.M. outside Tiffany, where I'd said I would be shopping to keep him from coming to my apartment. This in itself posed a minor problem since Charles was planning to follow us out to Kennedy, and we didn't know from which direction Renzullo would arrive, down Fifth Avenue or along Fifty-seventh Street (Tiffany is on the corner of Fifth and Fifty-seventh). This was important because if we got it wrong it might prove impossible for Charles to turn his car fast enough to keep us in sight. We got over this by having Charles park his car on Fifty-seventh Street and stand where he could see me. I entered the store by the Fifty-seventh Street entrance and crossed to the Fifth Avenue door. When Renzullo appeared, heading down Fifth Avenue, I told him I first had to go and finish some business in the Schlumberger jewelry department, and that it would take me a few minutes.

"Take your time, Mr. Blake," said Renzullo. "No problem."

I disappeared into Tiffany by the Fifth Avenue door, crossed the store back to the Fifty-seventh Street entrance and waved Charles into his car, indicating that Renzullo was on Fifth Avenue. At that point I felt a tap on my shoulder. Renzullo! I had been caught out.

No. It was a Tiffany security guard who had observed me crossing and recrossing the store from one door to the other, then gesticulating—just like a robber might.

"Have you lost someone—or something, sir?"

"No, no," I said. "It's all right; I was looking for my chauffeur." That impressed him, I hoped. It impressed me. But in any case I limped across the store for the third time, stepped out on to Fifth Avenue and got into the car with Renzullo.

Renzullo was one of those people who never really achieve a proper road sense. We had one very close shave indeed with a Buick near the midtown Tunnel and it occurred to me that I had sampled so much bad Italian driving during the project that if I came away from it with a real limp it would be no more than par for the course. For what should have been a quiet Saturday afternoon the tunnel and area around it were chaotic—traffic fanned out in a solid jam for two or three blocks around the entrance. On top of that Renzullo managed to annoy a policeman so that he kept the line we were in from advancing for five more minutes than the others. A typical New York encounter.

Renzullo filled in the time by taking up where he had left off the night before, bad-mouthing Del Peschio and the others, incriminating himself and swearing. It all made for an eventful drive, with the Nagra tape at my side silently soaking up everything.

At Kennedy there was no sign of Garuti. The Alitalia flight from Milan had landed, according to the notice board, but it might be an hour before the restorer got through immigration and customs. But to begin with, Charles kept me amused. He appeared nearby and stood with his Polaroid camera, an unsophisticated tourist, meeting a relative, taking pictures of the inside of an airport! He was of course photographing us. I kept Renzullo preoccupied and made a point of standing under one of the overhead lights so Charles could get as good a snap as possible. Later Charles came and stood right next to us, so I got Renzullo to incriminate himself more and to say what his future plans were. Having Charles overhear the conversation was a different kind of evidence from a tape recording.

After we had been waiting for about an hour, Renzullo began to grow nervous. His fear was that Garuti, the self-confessed "buccaneer," had maybe brought other stolen paintings with him—and been caught. Just my luck to have that happen.

Twenty more minutes passed and still no restorer. Now *I* began to grow worried. Garuti was taking his time, even though I knew the U.S. Immigration people could make snails look like bullets.

"If he doesn't come, you will still buy the paintings—eh, Mr. Blake?"

"Sure, why not?"

Then, to my astonishment and dread: "You know, when we first met, Mr. Blake, Giancarlo and Concerto—they say your limp was false. What do you think of that, Mr. Blake?" I stared at him. He said, "I told them they were not students of human psychology, they do not think, they are not intellectual, eh, Mr. Blake? I know better."

Charles was standing just behind Renzullo at this point, with his back to me but within earshot. I saw his back shaking—he could afford the luxury of a laugh—but I had to compose a sardonic smile for Renzullo's benefit and try to give nothing away. *Handshakes can be faked,* wrote Rex Stout. *But smiles cannot.* Let's hope he was wrong. My eyes met Renzullo's as steadily as I could muster. Was that a chance remark by him? Or was it yet another sign they had been on to me all along and I was walking into some mysterious trap?

I was saved by Garuti. At that moment he emerged through the doors of the arrivals building. Renzullo shot off to embrace him warmly in the Italian style. After these preliminaries, he turned and pointed to me. This was a piece of psychology that

Renzullo *had* got right: Garuti was surprised, but very pleased to see me there. I could see it register inside his head that the deal really was going through.

He was traveling light—just a small bag of clothes and a bag for his tools—so we were soon in the car. After he had told Renzullo about his flight, and the weather in Cremona, and the weather in Milan, I asked when I could see the paintings and when we could conclude the deal. Renzullo was of course still acting as interpreter: "Garuti says he needs a few hours tomorrow to work on the paintings—you can see them at five tomorrow evening. Monday you pay."

"Fine. But I can't see the pictures till seven tomorrow. Is that okay?" There was method in this. Ben van Inwegen thought that we had "control" of the case and that we shouldn't push things too much before the actual transaction. So I was under instructions to keep the Sunday meeting very short. My plan was to turn up around seven, in black tie, and to use the old trick, saying I was due at a formal dinner at seven-thirty. That way I needn't stay with them more than ten minutes; all I needed to do was verify that the paintings were really there and find out what room Garuti was in. (Ben had said this would be a safer way of finding out than asking at the front desk.)

Seven was fine, said Renzullo, and during the rest of the drive into Manhattan, Garuti, now relaxing, grew garrulous and said, through Renzullo, that he had plans for two more thefts: one of a Caravaggio and a Giorgione (who seemed to be very popular targets among this group) from a "Venetian foundation," and the other of seven major old masters from the Prado in Madrid. Either Garuti was romancing at this stage or he really was a big wheel in the art-theft business. Not for the first time, I prayed that the Nagra was recording this conversation clearly.

I tried to look impressed by the thefts Garuti proposed, then introduced the matter of money since I thought that would keep them interested and distracted. I said I proposed to pay in $100 bills (Ben had instructed me in this, too) and that I couldn't get all the money before lunchtime on Monday. Customs had asked for this slight delay since they had problems of their own in clearing their cash for use by a non-customs person. I told Renzullo my money was coming up from the Bahamas and that it would take a couple of hours on the Monday to arrange. Renzullo, I think, would have taken payment in yen or rubles, so delighted was he to be talking cash at last.

By now it was dark and we were heading south on the FDR drive. Renzullo was still having a problem keeping the car straight: it must have been exhausting for him to wrestle with the wheel, as he seemed to have to. Thank god he never had to land a space shuttle.

"Where are you heading, Renzullo?"

"The Sheraton Centre Hotel, on Seventh Avenue. It's in the Fifties, Mr. Blake."

"Can you drop me at Sixty-sixth and Park?" I said. "That's near enough to where I live." This wasn't true, of course, and by the time I had caught a taxi and traveled the several blocks to where I actually did live, Charles was waiting for me, to disconnect the Nagra and hear what had happened. We had a good laugh over Renzullo's comments about my limp.

WHEN I ARRIVED the next evening, the Sheraton Centre Hotel was a blaze of lights. I was feeling a little more comfortable on this occasion because my dinner jacket was somewhat looser than my suits, so there was more room for the Nagra.

Renzullo was waiting for me in the lobby, prompt as ever. There was a piano bar on the left, with an attractive girl playing some sad songs, and Renzullo suggested a drink. Under normal circumstances I would have loved to listen to her, but that night I pointed to my black tie and said I didn't have time. We took the elevator and ascended to the sixth floor, room 619. That was the first thing I had to remember to tell Ben, when I called him later that night to report in.

Garuti was there, of course, but so surprisingly, was Del Peschio, looking a little suspicious at first, though he cheered up after a while. The paintings were on the bed. Now it had all come this far, I was tempted to give them a cursory look but, for the last time I hoped, I told myself I had to act like a real dealer. I got out my magnifying glass.

"Take your coat off, Mr. Blake."

"Sorry, but I can't stay that long," I said, waving the suggestion aside with my glass and kneeling down. Even under magnification they looked fine to me though I could just make out the specs of a light-colored paint on the Bronzino. I presumed this was from the overpainting. The crack on the Del Sarto, which Garuti had fussed about, was fairly short and not very wide and was not bad enough, I felt, to affect its value (though even after all this time I didn't really know about these things).

After the inspection, I got to my feet, grunting with satisfaction. I smiled at each of them in turn. "Going to offer me a drink to celebrate?" I pointed to some beers near the television set. "One of those will do."

Another of my mistakes. It was an awful German concoction, sweet and sour at the same time. I couldn't stand more than one swig so I gently put it down next to my magnifying glass on the television set and raised the question of money. As before, in the car on the way in from Kennedy, it was an excellent distraction.

"So, $58,000 in cash at 1:30 P.M. tomorrow. I take it that's in order?"

"No, Mr. Blake, $60,000."

What was *this?* We had agreed: $28,000 for the Del Sarto and $30,000 for the Bronzino, $2,000 less than what Renzullo was now asking. It was a sneaky trick of Renzullo's; how greedy people became when it came down to it. Presumably he thought that, with the deal about to go through, he could squeeze me up to the round figure.

He was right, for once. Although a real dealer would no doubt have quibbled, this time I took the easy way out and didn't rock the boat.

"Yes," I said. "All right, in hundred-dollar bills."

"Till tomorrow then," said Del Peschio.

"*Ciao*, Mr. Blake."

Renzullo came down in the elevator. "One thing, Mr. Blake," he said when we were safely out of earshot of the others. "You will also have $6,000 for me—my commission?"

"Yes."

"You pay me here, beforehand, in the lobby."

"As you wish."

"And for Zorza, $8,000. You give me that also."

"No," I said firmly. I had been expecting this, and for legal reasons we wanted Zorza to take possession of the cash. "No. We are dealing in cash, Renzullo. If Zorza is to work for us again I have to be sure he gets his money. That means giving it to him in person."

"He will not come."

"That's his problem—and yours. I'm not giving you his $8,000. That's final."

In the lobby the girl was still singing her sad songs. Renzullo looked sad now—or perhaps just cunning.

"Okay, Mr. Blake. Okay. Also, you promised me a bonus. Is that still good?"

"Yes—yes," I lied. "I will give that to you when I give Zorza his money."

Renzullo's face creased into a smug grin. Maybe the cunning beggar had been angling for that all along. "Good. I will get Zorza, Mr. Blake, I will tell him. We—Garuti, Vincenzo, you and I—we meet at one-thirty. The meeting will take half an hour—yes? Maybe twenty minutes. Then we will meet Zorza, you and me later on, for the other payments—yes?"

"Fine."

"Where shall we meet, and when?"

"How about that bar on Third Avenue, in the Sixties, where you called from the other night? What's it called?"

"The Sign of the Dove. Okay. When?"

"Three o'clock. You will tell Zorza? If he doesn't turn up, no money."

"I will tell him, Mr. Blake, do not worry." We shook hands. "So, we make good business after all, eh? After this there will be many good things . . . till tomorrow then. Enjoy your dinner and sleep well, Mr. Blake, sleep well."

17

The Swindle

I DIDN'T SLEEP AT ALL, of course. By the time Charles called at 8:30 A.M. the next day I was up, dressed and shaved, and raring to go. The big holdup, so I understood at that stage, was the money. Ben van Inwegen thought it would be safer if he gave me real money and there were certain formalities he had to go through that wouldn't have applied if counterfeit notes had been used. In one of the customs vaults at the Investigations branch they had half a million dollars, the result of a heroin seizure, just sitting there; the notes themselves would be used as evidence in the trial, which was why they could not be put in a bank to earn interest. So Ben was trying to get permission to use $74,000 of this money and he had told me it should take an hour or two that morning to get the necessary clearance. Then every note had to be photocopied—both sides—again for legal reasons. With 740 hundred-dollar bills this meant 1,480 photocopies, which would take time even though they had a special machine to do it.

Ben called around 9:30 that morning and introduced three new aspects to the operation he was planning to mount. First, he said they now had moved two of the customs agents into the suite adjoining Garuti's; they had bugged the room and were already listening to the conversation in room 619 (the conversation was in Italian, of course). Second, Ben said they had rigged up a number of video cameras in the lobby of the Sheraton Centre. Since Renzullo had asked for his $6,000 commission to be handed over in the lobby, customs wanted that transaction on film. Ben instructed me to hand over this commission in as public a space as possible, where it could be caught on camera and witnessed by the agents he would have stationed in the lobby. Third, he said that today he wanted me to wear a radio transmitter as well as being wired for sound. I would at all times, he said, be surrounded by nine armed customs agents, each of whom could listen in to my conversations with the Italians. If there was the slightest bother they would know what to do—and be on hand to do it.

Ben said I was to be brought to a rendezvous point on the West Side so that all his officers who did not know me could take a look before the operation proper began.

I had nothing to do that morning except hang around. Yet I couldn't sit still. I tried reading—couldn't concentrate. Made a cup of coffee; then a second; then a third.

Renzullo was scheduled to call at 10:30 A.M. just to confirm that everything was going according to plan. The phone rang at 10:20: it was Charles, asking if I was okay. Yes, I said, thanks, and he rang off. Immediately the phone rang again, but this time I heard nothing at the other end.

"Hello? . . . Hello? . . . I can't hear you, can you hear me?" I shouted into the receiver. Nothing. I was so strung up that I now began to worry about the phone. Were they on to me after all? Was today an elaborate trap on their part as well as ours? Was my phone tapped by them as well as by customs? Even if the Italians did not know I was not Blake, maybe they were planning to double-cross me anyway, take the money, shoot or mug me, and keep the paintings. I would have some protection from Charles, Ben and the others, but things could happen very quickly, before the customs agents could intervene. I was not behaving at all as I imagined I should be: and in no way as they do in the movies. Now we were so close I was just plain frightened.

I rang Charles and thankfully he was very calm, gentle and rational. He told me quietly not to panic, that the mysterious phone call was probably nothing of the kind, that it was just a hiccup in the phone network, and that it happened all the time (it doesn't—in England maybe, but not in New York).

No sooner had I put down the phone on Charles than it rang again. It was still not quite 10:30, but there was no mistaking the voice.

"Mr. Blake." It was Renzullo—calling early. Did that mean he was going to cancel? Or did he want to change the arrangements? I was back in a terrible state.

"Renzullo?"

"So, Mr. Blake. Everything is good—yes? We make the deal?"

"Of course, of course." My spirits lifted—momentarily.

"At what hour, Mr. Blake?"

"As arranged, Renzullo. One-thirty is good."

"Half-past one, in the hotel lobby."

"And afterward at three, at the Sign of the Dove."

"Okay, Mr. Blake. Till one-thirty."

He seemed calmer than I did. While talking with him I realized that I had overlooked something. The paintings, especially the Del Sarto, were quite large, and as yet I had nothing to carry them in. I needed a large—a very large—portfolio. It would look unconvincing if I didn't have something: a man like A. John Blake would have several expensive portfolios for transporting his canvases around the world. And, with my cane and limp, it would have to be a case that I could carry with just one hand. Where to find such a thing within the hour of free time remaining to me?

In the Yellow Pages under "Artists' Materials" there were about half a dozen shops roughly within my part of New York. The first three I tried had nothing. The next two had portfolios, but nothing nearly large enough. Then I found a shop that had something large enough, but didn't take American Express—and there wasn't time for me to get to my bank first and pick up some cash. What with having all the shop assistants search their basements for large portfolios, it was by now nearly eleven o'clock and I was no further forward.

The seventh shop I tried said, yes, they did have a large portfolio and, yes, they took American Express. "Where are you?" I asked and, to my surprise, the girl gave an address less than five blocks from my apartment. Trust New York to have exactly what you want right on your doorstep. The girl said the portfolio was rather dusty, but that they would hold it for me.

Some idea of my level of prudence during this time can be had from the fact that whenever I walked about in New York as myself I always walked against the flow of the traffic. In other words, I only ever walked uptown on Second Avenue or downtown on Third. And I only ever went west on even-numbered streets and east on odd ones. My reasoning for this was, ridiculously, that if by chance Renzullo or the others should see Peter Watson in the street, and notice the resemblance to Blake, then by the time they did so their car or taxi or bus would have passed me by and they would be unable to catch up with me except by going around the block, by which time I might have disappeared. So my walk of five blocks actually involved a couple of detours and meant it was nearly 11:30 by the time I got to the shop.

The portfolio cost $42. Was it, I wondered as I signed the credit form, destined to be the last exotic expense on a budget that had started so long ago? Or was everything still going to fall apart at the last minute?

I got back to my apartment just in time to wet my hair and flatten it down, tie my bow tie and retrieve my new black cane from the closet. Would this be the last time?

Eddie Choo and Ben's technical men were on time. They were very thorough. The right side of my body was literally covered with tape as they carefully fixed the Nagra and its microphone: it was going to hurt when the time came to pull it all off. The radio transmitter they fixed to my left side, with the microphone stuck to the shoulder blade near the small of my back. Every time I breathed I felt about thirty strips of tape creak. I still *felt* lopsided when I looked at myself in the mirror, but Renzullo and the others hadn't noticed anything odd on the previous three occasions so I was a little more confident that morning. Eddie told me the transmitter would get hot about twenty minutes after it had been turned on but that "it should be no more than uncomfortable."

In passing he told me not to stand near any television sets.

"Why not?" I asked.

"Oh, these things sometimes throw up interference."

What was that about feeling more confident?

By now the doorman in my apartment building was beginning to give me some very odd looks. I was, after all, behaving a little like Superman: one minute I would arrive home with curly hair and an ordinary tie; the next minute strange men would arrive and I would leave with them, with smarmed-down hair, a bow tie, a cane and a limp.

We left the apartment at about twenty to one. I could tell the doorman was dying to ask what the hell was going on, but I stared him down. The Sheraton Centre Hotel, where Garuti was staying and where the transaction was to take place, is on Fifty-second Street and Seventh Avenue. But first, Ben wanted a rendezvous with his team over on Fifty-fourth Street between Eighth and Ninth. This is a curious kind of block, very industrial with warehouses and workshops lining the busy cross-town street. It would have been an unusually wide street but for the fact that, between Eighth and Ninth, the traffic parked not along the curb but end-on to it, leaving the roadway narrower than usual. Despite this, when we arrived just after one, Ben and Charlie had double-parked and were causing quite a jam.

I was asked to remain in Eddie's car until all the other customs men were assembled. I was praying that we weren't being followed because by now our group of men, many with walkie-talkies and standing about in full view of the traffic jam that Ben's car was causing, were beginning to attract comment. It was obvious we were plainclothes law enforcement officers, and one or two people started to hang around waiting for action.

They were unlucky. Eventually all Ben's men were present, and I emerged from Eddie's car wearing a double-breasted camel-colored overcoat and feeling more like the Godfather than Superman. Ben's agents all took a good look at me and, to a man, seemed unimpressed. Given my getup, I can't say I blamed them.

Ben then took the opportunity to ask, quite casually it seemed, whether I thought Renzullo and the others would be armed. My instincts told me they weren't the gun-toting types and I said as much to Ben. But I added that they should not be underestimated, Garuti especially. Ben nodded enigmatically and said, "If you can do it naturally, ask Renzullo in the lobby if anyone is armed."

"Sure," I said, feeling a little dizzy. That's New York for you.

What would I do if Renzullo admitted he was armed? And if he was, would he admit it?

One of the other agents, a huge bear of a man, ambled over and handed me a brown cardboard folder.

"$60,000," he said. "For Garuti."

I took it and placed it at the bottom of the empty portfolio, where no one would think of looking for cash.

Next he gave me an envelope with a small figure "6" penciled in the top left-hand corner. "Six thousand for Renzullo." And an envelope with an "8" in the corner. "Eight thou for the priest."

I was rich. I stuffed the envelopes in my overcoat pocket and got back into the car with Eddie. There was some hilarity on the pavement, and when I asked why he told me that the bear, as I will call him, had at first put Renzullo's commission in a white envelope which, on the flap at the back, said, "Property of U.S. Customs; personal use prohibited." Just the kind of touch I needed.

At 1:25 P.M., Eddie dropped me off at the corner of Fifty-fifth and Eighth, three or four blocks from the Sheraton Centre and out of view of the hotel's lobby. I could see Charlie across the street and I knew that two or three officers would follow me discreetly as I made my way to the hotel. Why did I need an escort? They were concerned that a prosperous-looking man with a limp might get mugged during that three- or four-block walk. It would certainly have been an ironic end to the project.

For my part, I wondered how wise it was to have Charlie tail me that day. After all, he had been present at the airport just two days before. I was afraid that Renzullo would recognize him and smell a rat. No one else thought it a real problem but I thought it a risk we didn't need to take.

It was sunny that Monday but very windy. The portfolio, measuring forty-two inches by thirty, was like a large black sail under my arm.

After all those months of trying, of disappointments, of earthquakes and of fakes, here I was embarked on what was possibly my last five hundred yards of limping. I felt strangely solitary, even though I knew I was surrounded by special agents. And even now I still felt slightly silly with my bow tie and cane. . . .

As I emerged into Seventh Avenue from Fifty-third Street, I straightaway spotted Charlie lurking on the far side of the street, and beyond him, hovering in the lobby of the Sheraton

Centre, Renzullo himself. I kept moving but a fresh worry struck me. Renzullo didn't know exactly where I lived but he did know it was somewhere on the Upper East Side. At the moment, I was coming from the wrong direction. Even worse, when I thought about it, I was walking. Would a wealthy dealer, with a limp, arrive for such a transaction, carrying an unwieldy portfolio, on foot? I doubted it, and as I crossed the road my mind raced to find an excuse. A gust of wind swept down the avenue and blew the portfolio around. I had to swivel to accommodate the eddy, stop and wait for it to die down. That bought me time. I decided that if Renzullo did ask any suspicious questions about the manner of my arrival I would say I had been visiting my picture framer, who had his workshop on Fifty-sixth and Ninth.

I could now see Renzullo through the glass panels of the hotel, smiling that self-satisfied grin of his and moving toward the revolving doors to welcome me. The comic interludes weren't over yet. With my cane and enormous portfolio, I got stuck in the revolving doors. To anyone watching, like the customs agents, I must have seemed a real Inspector Clouseau, clumsy and exasperating. For me—well, I was beginning to sweat again.

Renzullo began by trying to push the doors back so that the portfolio would be freed, but it was too firmly wedged for him. He went off in search of help from the hotel management. Fortunately by this time one of the hotel doormen, standing on the pavement outside the building, had seen my dilemma. He was built like a rhinoceros and he gave the doors a short, sharp charge with his shoulder. The doors jerked into movement and he threw his weight behind them and pushed steadily, slowly, forward. The crumpled portfolio followed me around, making a loud scraping sound.

I watched nervously in case the imitation leather should disintegrate and throw out some of the hundred-dollar bills I had hidden inside. No, I made it safely into the hotel; the black sail was badly mangled at one corner, but otherwise intact. I turned and waved my thanks to the doorman. Not one of the customs agents had moved a finger to help me.

I looked up to find Renzullo watching me. I pointed to the portfolio and whispered confidentially, "The money's in there, that's why I was so worried." He nodded and moved closer. Beyond him I saw a couple of the customs agents I had been shown to about half an hour before. They were casually talking near the hotel reception desk, as if they were about to check in.

"So, Mr. Blake, you have the commission?"

I tapped the pocket of my overcoat. "In here." There was something curious about the way Renzullo was dressed that day, something unusual for him. I couldn't make out what but it lodged in the back of my mind.

The problem now was that we weren't in the middle of the lobby so I couldn't be sure the video cameras would pick up any transaction carried out where we were standing. I therefore tried to edge nearer the center of the lobby even though Renzullo obviously wanted to get his hands on the cash straightaway. I managed to do what I wanted by whispering again, "Come over here, away from these people; there is one question I want to ask you first." I limped across to the center of the reception area which, thankfully, was fairly clear. I rested the portfolio against my leg and took out the envelope with the small "6" penciled on it. I held it out to Renzullo, though when he grasped it I didn't let go.

"I take it, Renzullo, that no one is silly enough to be armed today?" And I pulled the envelope back toward me.

Was there a slight lowering of his eyes as I asked this? A small but definite hesitation? "Mr. Blake, please. You know us—what?— eighteen months; do you think we would do such a thing as to carry guns? Please, we do not have guns. Do not worry."

Was that a too-fulsome denial? Or had I lost nearly all grasp of reality that day, when everything he did seemed suspicious?

Anyway, after this Renzullo pulled the envelope back again. Still I held on.

"I take it the three o'clock meeting is on?" I pulled the envelope back.

"Yes, yes, of course. I talked to Zorza." He pulled and I let go.

However, just as he was about to pocket the envelope, I said, "Aren't you going to count it?"

He felt the thickness of the notes, yet wouldn't open the envelope in public. "No, Mr. Blake, I trust you."

"Then you are a fool."

At this he smiled and prised apart the envelope with the thumb and forefinger of one hand. He was satisfied with what he saw and I was now satisfied that we had spent enough time on this transaction for Ben to have a convincing film. Renzullo slid the envelope into an inside pocket and said, "Let's go upstairs. Shall I carry your portfolio?"

"No, thank you. The money is in it."

We walked to the elevators, and I must say that the customs officers around us were very smooth. Just as Renzullo pressed the elevator button, two men—Eddie Choo and another young agent —materialized from nowhere. When the elevator arrived they got in with us, apparently deep in a convincing conversation about theater tickets. I was still sweating like the walls of a Turkish bath but also dying to burst out laughing at the same time.

As the elevator rose, I made a weak joke about hoping the beer in Garuti's room would be better today than it had been the night before. I was still perturbed by whatever it was that was wrong with Renzullo's appearance, though I couldn't put my finger on it. The elevator jerked to a stop and the doors began to open. At this, Eddie and his pal started arguing about which floor their room was on. As Renzullo and I left the elevator, they "found" their "key," which told them they, too, were on the sixth floor and they followed us out. However, they turned right out of the elevator alcove, whereas we turned left.

Room 619 was, I suppose, about twenty-five yards down the corridor, on the right. I had told Renzullo that, to prevent my being "jumped" by them, since they were three and I was alone, I wanted the paintings in such a position so as to be visible from the corridor when the room door was opened. I had also specified that I was to be the person closest to the door at all times during our meeting.

When we reached the room I stood across the corridor while Renzullo knocked and called softly, "*Siamo noi* [It's us]." Down the corridor, fifty to sixty yards away, Eddie and his pal were "struggling" with their key.

A short pause, a rattle in the lock and the door to 619 was swung back by Garuti. Sunlight flooded the room, which faced south, and silhouetted the portly profile of Del Peschio against the window. He stood at the far side of the bed, behind the paintings, which were propped against it so that I could see them from where I was standing in the corridor. Everything looked in order so I signaled Renzullo to lead the way into the room. I followed and closed the door behind me. I checked that there was no one in the bathroom, which was just inside the door on the left, or in the large closet opposite the bathroom. There was a lot of wrapping paper on the floor of this closet, presumably what had been around the paintings when the priest had smuggled them in.

After the usual greetings, I was invited to check the paintings again. I did so cursorily. For one thing, I was nervous and didn't want to waste time and risk making a gaffe. For another thing, the radio transmitter was now getting very hot and burning into my flesh just below my rib cage on the left. Too much bending would make it worse. And, in any case, I seemed to have mislaid my magnifying glass. So I just checked that the crack in the Del Sarto was still in the same place, that the marks were there on the back of the Bronzino—and pronounced everything ship-shape.

Unzipping the portfolio, I reached inside and took out the brown cardboard folder the bear had given me. I untied the tape laces, opened it out and brandished the contents.

"$60,000, in hundred-dollar bills. Who wants to count it?"

Del Peschio was elected and stood by the television removing the elastic bands which were around each bundle of notes. I turned to Renzullo and said, "Why don't you wrap the paintings for me, while Vincenzo is counting? I saw some paper in the closet there."

He translated for Garuti and the two of them set to it.

I moved to sit on a chair against the wall when I suddenly noticed the television, half concealed by Del Peschio's body. It was turned on, with the sound turned down, and *showing signs of interference*. I quickly got to my feet and disappeared into the bathroom under the guise of a call of nature.

When I came out Del Peschio had finished and pronounced the money "all there." (I was relieved by this since, after all, I had not actually counted the notes myself.) Garuti and Renzullo were just finishing the packing of the paintings with plastic padding, brown paper and masking tape.

Suddenly, I knew what was wrong with Renzullo's appearance —and froze, if it is possible to freeze and sweat at the same time. It wasn't a big difference, but it might be significant. Renzullo was normally a casual dresser; when he wore suits they tended to be scruffy and he rarely buttoned either his jacket or the neck of his shirt, even when he was wearing a tie. Today, however, his shirt was buttoned all the way up, his tie was pushed close up to his collar and his jacket was buttoned. To me, in my state, that could mean only one thing: he was concealing a gun beneath the jacket. I tried to locate it as he bent to help Garuti with the packaging. Now that I had worked out what was wrong with Renzullo, he started behaving very suspiciously to my eye. Were he and Garuti making a thorough job of packing the paintings? Or were they just going through the motions, intending to swindle me at the last minute and at the point of a gun? Was that a bulge under Renzullo's right armpit? Or was he lopsided around the hips, like me? I couldn't be sure.

The portfolio accommodated the paintings perfectly—it even zipped up. Renzullo lifted it and carried it toward the door. In doing so he was breaking our rule about me always being closest to the corridor . . . and escape.

"I can manage, Renzullo."

"No, no, Mr. Blake. There's no problem." He opened the door and disappeared down the corridor, in the direction of the elevators. Garuti followed him. Behind me Del Peschio had a firm grip on the money. Behind *him* was the television, again showing silent interference. The transmitter in my side was very hot.

There was nothing for it but to follow Renzullo and Garuti. If they had disappeared with the paintings they would regret it, since they couldn't get away and I could block Del Peschio's escape with the cash. What I was worried about was: if they were prepared to double-cross me they must be prepared for me to make trouble for them. And what form would those preparations take? I shuddered to think.

"*Arrivederci*, Del Peschio," I said over my shoulder as I left the room.

"*Ciao*, Mr. Blake." He didn't move and kept his hold on the money.

Out in the corridor it was darker than in the room. I could not see the paintings or Garuti but I could see Renzullo. He was standing half in and half out of the elevator alcove. Was Garuti there too? Or had he disappeared to another room with the paintings? We hadn't thought of that. Renzullo was beckoning with that sickly grin of his, and there was no sign of Eddie, Charles, Ben or any customs agents. That grin suddenly became menacing. I tried to talk to Ben indirectly through the radio transmitter.

"Are you alone, Renzullo?" I shouted as I limped slowly to-

ward him. "Where is Garuti and the paintings?" Surely Ben
would pick this up as a cry for help and storm out of the room
next to Garuti's. Nothing happened.

As I covered the twenty-five yards or so toward Renzullo I
remember noticing that the hotel carpet was a dirty shade of red-
brown check—and that the walls were a nondescript gray-yellow.
And I will never forget noticing that Renzullo's right hand was
resting on his hip.

As I approached Renzullo he didn't move, just stood, smiling at
me, his hand still on his hip. With ten feet to go I reached the
edge of the elevator alcove and my field of vision suddenly
broadened. There was Garuti: he was standing with his back to
the elevators, the portfolio behind him, leaning against a long
mirror. Was he intending to bar my way to both the elevators
and the paintings? A trickle of sweat scored down my cheek.

Two more steps and three things happened at once. The elevator arrived; Renzullo held his right hand out toward me—a black,
metallic object which glinted was in it; and two customs agents
stepped out of the elevator.

Would Renzullo shoot? He didn't know, of course, what he was
getting into, which only made circumstances more dangerous. He
might have meant only to frighten and intimidate me. The customs agents would not take that chance, however, and would
shoot; Renzullo would shoot in retaliation and out of fear. His
gun was pointing at me. "Death takes us piecemeal," wrote one
of the Greeks, Seneca, I think, ". . . not at a gulp." Wrong.

The black, shiny object in Renzullo's hand wasn't a gun. He
had had my magnifying glass in his back pocket and had just
remembered it. I had left it on the television set in Garuti's room
the night before. Renzullo looked astonished when I gave a huge
flinch and a muffled yell when he brought it out. I was so keyed
up that I was capable of anything.

I took the magnifying glass and then grasped the portfolio
which Garuti proffered.

"*Ciao,* Mr. Blake," said Garuti.

"*Ciao,*" I replied weakly, shaking hands.

"Mr. Blake, till next time," said Renzullo, grinning his grin as I
backed into the elevator.

"Good luck, Renzullo," I cried. "Don't spend it all at once."

As the elevator doors closed, the last view I had of Renzullo was as he headed back to room 619 with Garuti to divide up the proceeds. They didn't know it, but they were followed by Eddie Choo and another agent. And then another and another.

I rode the elevator to the lobby level, where I was met by Charles. We shook hands, and I gave him the paintings. They would be needed as evidence.

I also gave him my black cane. A souvenir.

Epilogue

THE ARRESTS WENT SMOOTHLY, thank god. Renzullo, Garuti and Del Peschio were dividing up the money when, in one sudden rush, no fewer than eight customs officers burst into room 619. Six forced the door from the corridor and two others slipped in from the adjoining room through the connecting door, which had been surreptitiously unlocked. Renzullo was the only one who said anything. He was so surprised his plan had backfired that, for once, he lapsed into Italian and began swearing.

Zorza never kept the appointment set for later at the Sign of the Dove on Third Avenue. Presumably, he waited for a call from Renzullo to confirm the meeting. That call never came.

Eventually, Charlie went around to Zorza's mission, the St. Agnes Rectory at 143 East Forty-third Street, and arrested him there. As Charlie read the charges the priest fainted.

All four were taken first to customs headquarters, downtown in the World Trade Center, where they were interviewed and photographed. Then they were moved across to the offices of the U.S. attorney, in St. Andrew's Square—i.e., from Charles's office to

Minna's. In St. Andrew's Square they were interviewed again before appearing in court later on in front of U.S. Magistrate Leon-
ard Bernikow and a grand jury.

Blake, too, was "arrested," "handcuffed" and taken downtown.
Leaving the elevator at the offices of the U.S. attorney, Blake
bumped into Del Peschio, who was also handcuffed and yet who,
incredibly, smiled at him. Farther down the corridor sat Zorza,
looking pale and very definitely not smiling. At that stage Renzullo, Del Peschio and Garuti may not have been certain who the
"traitor" among them was—was it Blake or was it Zorza? But
Zorza, of course, had no such doubts.

The plan at that point was to have Blake arrested and indicted
along with the others. That way the Italians would be kept in
doubt for some time as to who was really to blame for the way
the whole plan had gone sour. They might even think some outside agent had got on to "us" without a tip-off. I was worried
about reprisals and this plan at least meant that some time would
elapse before the others found out the truth about Blake—when
he didn't appear in court for the trial, the charges against him
having been quietly dropped by the government. Tempers might
have cooled by then, and revenge be seen as only compounding
their problems.

It soon emerged that no such plan would be followed. Minna
and her boss, Shirah Neiman, argued—probably quite correctly—
that the U.S. Government should not tell deliberate lies when is-
suing indictments. So Blake's name was left off the charge sheet
and he didn't appear in court that day. It made me very nervous,
but there was nothing I could do.

The court proceedings took about three hours and didn't end
until evening. After much haggling and translating for Garuti's
benefit, three indictments were finally handed down against all
four defendants. They were charged with:

• Conspiring to smuggle stolen paintings into the U.S.
• Conspiring to sell stolen paintings
• Receiving and concealing stolen goods

Renzullo and Zorza were further charged with making a false
declaration on customs importation documents. If found guilty
on all the charges, the defendants faced a maximum of ten years
in jail and/or a $10,000 fine. That night, however, they were all

released on bail of between $25,000 and $30,000, Zorza's bond being provided by the Consolata Order, of which he was a member.

They straggled off into the night just before eleven o'clock, and I followed some time later at a safe distance.

I HADN'T BARGAINED on the press coverage the arrests would spark. The customs publicity department had worked through the night, and next morning's *Daily News* splashed the case all over its front page: "Nab Priest, 3 Others, in Art Scam." The *Post* and the New York *Times* also carried extensive reports, naturally leading with the fact that a priest, and one attached to the staff of the Holy See's Observer to the United Nations, was involved. Later that day the television and radio news networks followed up after a special news conference laid on by customs. At that meeting Mr. Wilbur Nichols, one of Charles's bosses who had played absolutely no part in the arrests, proudly displayed the recovered paintings.

By this time Zorza had been suspended from his duties at the UN Mission and it had been made clear by the staff of the Holy See's Permanent Observer that Zorza was "only" a voluntary worker. These developments, together with the discovery that Zorza belonged to the Consolata Society, whose members take a vow of poverty, made for some ironic headlines as the papers ran with the story for a second day.

By this time, too, the news had flashed around the world, making headlines as far apart as Britain (the *Times*, of course, and the *Sun*), and Australia (the Melbourne *Age* and the Sidney *Morning Herald*). In Italy, naturally, most of the main papers, like *Il Messaggero*, *Il Tempo* and *Corriera della Serra*, carried the story, leading on the priest's involvement. Fortunately, none of the reporters pressed U.S. Customs on the identity of their informant.

THE LEGAL PROCEEDINGS were to last until the following September, by which time all four defendants had decided to do a deal with the government. They would plead guilty to some of the charges, thus saving the court time and money, and preserving for the time being my own anonymity—since I wouldn't have to give evidence. In return the government would drop what remained of the indictment. A classic piece of plea bargaining.

Two events of interest occurred while this plea bargaining was being worked out during the summer months. The first concerned Zorza and the second, Garuti.

The day Zorza had been arrested he had let slip two things which, to my way of thinking, reflected his guilt. He told Minna's boss, Shirah, who interrogated him, that, if challenged at the airport about the paintings he was not declaring, he would have said that the pictures were part of his father's estate. This amounted to an admission that he was prepared to lie about the paintings. Second, when his interview at customs had finished, he turned to Charles and said, "Okay. We go to prison now." In other words, Zorza knew he had done wrong and what the consequences were.

Later, however, he was to change his story. He told the court that, although he had falsely filled in his customs declaration form, describing the paintings as books, he did not know that the pictures were stolen. Now he lied to the court. He also said that he had been offered $8,000 by Renzullo to act as courier but had turned down the money, adding, however, that if Renzullo wanted to use the cash to make a contribution to his Brazilian project that was fine. This was all in flat contradiction to what I knew, of course, but it was instructive for me to witness at firsthand the way defendants, even supposedly honest priests, "modify" their stories for the benefit of the court.

But this wasn't the main point of interest concerning Zorza. When Renzullo had been searched on the day of arrest, a notebook-cum-diary was found in one of his pockets. Besides having some dates and calculations in it, figures which confirmed my own account of various events in the story, this notebook also contained some fresh names.

The two most intriguing names were a Miss Turkham and a Mr. Bove. Charlie recognized the first one—it belonged to a woman who worked on the staff of Sotheby's in Manhattan. When Minna contacted her, Miss Turkham stated that she had never heard of Renzullo but she did know a Mr. Bove.

It appeared that some months earlier Mr. Bove had taken into Sotheby's a number of beautiful pieces of ancient pottery, ap-

parently Sicilian and with some wonderful paintings on them.
The Sotheby's staff had been enchanted by the pottery and eager
to have them auctioned. Just to be on the safe side, however,
they had sent them across to the Metropolitan Museum to be au-
thenticated.

Which was just as well. Miss Turkham was told by the staff at
the Metropolitan that, although the pottery was indeed beautiful,
certain of the warriors depicted were holding their spears "in the
wrong way" and that some of the trees in the background did not
grow in Sicily. In short, Mr. Bove's pottery was fake.

The antiquities were returned to him—but that was not the
end of the story. About six months later Miss Turkham was
offered the same pottery again. It was so distinctive there could
be no mistake. This time, she told Minna, it was brought in by
someone quite different. And she proceeded to describe a fairly
tall man, an Italian who had become a naturalized American,
who wore a small moustache and the collar of a Roman Catholic
priest. Zorza.

Once again, of course, Zorza claimed that he was never told
that the Sicilian pottery was fake.

The incident concerning Garuti was not so very different. It
emerged during the plea bargaining that he had received stolen
paintings before. Garuti's story was that he had bought them in
good faith, of course, and only later on had found out that they
were stolen. He told the court that he had reported his discovery
to the local police in Cremona. All well and good, except that the
Italian police could not have been entirely convinced of Garuti's
probity because a civil action followed, and Garuti was made to
pay some sort of tax or assessment on the paintings. Garuti, it
turned out, also had his own contacts in the Cremona police who
had ensured that he was treated more leniently on that occasion
than he might have expected.

So far as I was concerned, Garuti and Zorza had "form." They
had known very well what they were doing.

Their lawyers must have drawn very similar conclusions, and
this possibly had something to do with the deal that was struck.
Rather than risk ten years in jail, they all pleaded guilty to a
lesser charge on condition that more serious ones be dropped. All
except Renzullo, that is.

Not surprisingly, Renzullo felt he had been the one most

duped by Blake. In retaliation, he wanted his day in court. He wanted to see who Blake really was and to test the Englishman's credibility against his own. Besides the threat of prison that was now hanging over him, Renzullo had been humiliated by Blake in front of his colleagues and friends, people like Battiato and Viappiani. As the others began to plead guilty, however, Renzullo's stance began to look increasingly misguided.

Del Peschio went first. In fact he collaborated right from the arrests. This was one of the reasons why the U.S. Government formed the view that Del Peschio was the least culpable of the four. I am not so sure. Maybe he was just cleverer.

He was, after all, president of Italcraft, whereas Renzullo was secretary. And Del Peschio had always managed to be around when money was discussed or changed hands. When Battiato had smuggled the *St. John* I bought from Baratti I had actually given the second portion of money to Del Peschio; until his father died suddenly he was to have been the man who introduced me to Garuti; and he had, of course, turned up mysteriously at the Sheraton Centre Hotel and been the one who actually took possession of the money and who did the counting.

We shall never know whether Del Peschio was a fringe figure or the *éminence grise* of this band. Or whether it was weakness which made him collaborate with the government, or cleverness, a proper appreciation that this particular game was up. Either way he was to receive the lightest sentence.

Garuti fell next; then, after a delay, the priest. Finally, reluctantly, Renzullo was persuaded that, with the other three admitting so much and pleading guilty, they could be used as witnesses against him. And since in reality he was by far the most culpable, with all his negotiations with Blake on tape, it was simply silly for him to stick it out. He capitulated.

The final court appearances of these four taught me my last cynical lesson about the law and projects like this one.

Del Peschio, Garuti and Renzullo each pleaded guilty to the transportation of stolen paintings into the United States. "The charge," according to the Honorable Robert J. Ward, district judge, "was a serious one."

Del Peschio, because he collaborated with the government and corroborated much of John Blake's evidence, was given one year's probation.

Garuti, because he promised to hand over *another* stolen painting in his possession (in other words, he admitted to being even
more guilty than the charges against him reflected), was given
five years' probation.

Renzullo was given three years in jail, all but three months of it
suspended.

Zorza pleaded guilty to bringing in the paintings and to filing a
false customs declaration—smuggling, in everyday language. This
charge carried a maximum of two years in prison and/or a $5,000
fine. The judge made it plain in sentencing that the court "had
evidence of awareness" on Zorza's part—that he knew exactly
what he was doing.

Yet the priest put on quite a performance for the judge, weeping openly and saying he "was terribly sorry." The judge gave
him three years' probation.

The sentences were a disgrace. Immediately he got outside the
court, Zorza's performance changed. The weeping suddenly
stopped and he laughed and joked with his lawyer about the way
they had "beaten the system."

As soon as he got back to Italy, Garuti's cooperative attitude
changed also. He didn't turn in the other stolen painting as he
had promised. About three weeks after his return, the U.S. Customs representative in Rome had to travel to Cremona—more
than three hundred miles away—and reclaim the picture. Garuti
had had no intention of turning it in unless forced.

To my way of thinking, the U.S. Government was beaten three
to one. Del Peschio, Garuti and Zorza were, effectively, free men.
Only Renzullo actually went to jail.

Throughout the court hearings, everyone had been considered
sympathetically—everyone, that is, except Renzullo. Yet he was
the one I felt a bit sorry for. I wasn't weeping crocodile tears—he
was culpable, of course, nothing could change that. But I had
got to know him best—and had begun to sort of like him. And,
given that the others, each in his own way, had so misled the
court, I felt Renzullo had been unfairly treated.

REFLECTING on these light sentences back in London, I decided
to do one final piece of research: I examined the sentences which
the courts had handed down to convicted art thieves. The sample

wasn't very large—since so few actual thieves seem ever to have been caught—so too much should not be read into the following examples. Nonetheless they are, I think, worth some attention.

The courts seem to have awakened to art theft at about the time I did, late 1978/early 1979. At any rate, at that point the sentences meted out started to get heavier.

For example, John Crenshaw, who pleaded guilty to two thefts at the St. Louis Art Museum in January and February 1978, was sentenced to four years imprisonment later that year despite the fact that two men believed to be his accomplices on the thefts were found murdered in the months following his arrest. At more or less the same time, Ronald Monsouris, former Chief of Security at the Santa Barbara Museum, received only one year in jail for the theft of three Monets from the museum.

Perhaps the tide began to turn—albeit temporarily—with the conviction of Paul Petrides, the Paris dealer I have already referred to, and the man who is the author of the three-volume *catalogue raisonné* on Utrillo. He was sentenced to three years in jail but was also saddled with a fine of more than $500,000 for dealing in stolen paintings, the court clearly deciding to hit him where it hurt most, in his pocket.

Then, for a while, the courts became quite fierce. In September 1979 the New York court of appeals upheld the conviction and fifteen-year sentence of George LiVecchi, involved in the theft of Picasso's *Flowers in a Blue Vase* from the Rochester Memorial Art Gallery. In April 1980 David Thomas, a twenty-five-year-old philosophy student at Suffolk University, was given thirteen years in jail for stealing old masters from a Cohasset, Massachusetts, private collection including a Rembrandt, a Brueghel, an El Greco and a Van Goyen. In the same month Laud Spencer Pace, twenty-nine, was given ten years for the theft of four Cézannes from the Art Institute of Chicago.

But by 1981, the signs were that sentences were again falling off. Charles Richmond, despite having at least four previous convictions for art theft, and a record that went back to 1976, received only five years for three separate thefts from different galleries, including that of a Utrillo from Wally Findlay. And Dr. Kurt Wagner, a Hollywood plastic surgeon, got away with three years (plus 300 hours of community service) for receiving valuable antiques stolen from the Beverly Hills mansion of Sheik Mohammed Al-Fassi.

It may be, then, that for some reason or another the courts' sense of outrage over art theft has peaked and, as a result, deterrent sentences are no longer being handed down. This would certainly help explain the exceptionally light sentences awarded to Renzullo and the others.

And what made it doubly frustrating was the fact that, in my case and unlike any of the other cases I was able to trace, the entire chain—fence, courier, resale men—had been caught. Usually, it was just the thief who confessed under pressure or the fence alone who was lured into a "sting." My case, with the whole chain captured, including the main organizer who had been duped into entering onto U.S. soil, was the perfect instance when exemplary justice should have been done.

The more I thought about the light sentences, the more I began to see just what a mess the art trade has got itself into with regard to stolen works. Sentencing is only one aspect of it. On top of that you have woefully inadequate art squads and hopelessly incomplete records which, together, mean that we now have the worst of all possible worlds. In London at Scotland Yard the art squad has rarely been more than three people; in Italy there is just Siviero and, at most, four Carabinieri officers; in Paris, M. Gill Raguideau works largely alone; in New York the Police Department just has Bob Volpé, the FBI has Tom McShane, and U.S. Customs relies on Charles who also covers other fields like pornography. Small wonder then that when I checked the records for recoveries they showed that, on average, in Italy only 10 percent of *recorded* thefts are ever seen again and in the United States 13 percent.

The incomplete records possibly do the most insidious damage of all. After all, what could better suit the purposes of the dishonest dealer? The records are so bad that, if a Madison Avenue or Fifty-seventh Street gallery owner is offered something vaguely suspicious he can check the records, safe in the knowledge that, nine times out of ten, the theft of the work will not be recorded. Then, if at some later date it is proved that what he has bought *was* stolen, he can always put his hand on his heart and swear that he did all he could to check it out before he bought it. Since the records are so incomplete he can't be held responsible . . .

The records of stolen art are so bad that, in some ways, they probably do more harm than good. A bleak conclusion.

SIVIERO, when I visited him to make my final report on the project, was as phlegmatic as ever. We met in the room in his Florence home where the whole conspiracy had started so long ago. Out came the same brand of malt whiskey and the same sugared nuts. The De Chirico portraits were still there, as was the beautiful terra-cotta bust by Nanni di Banco. Siviero said he understood my frustration at the light sentences handed down. Even in Italy, he said, the courts were lenient—did I not remember the case of the Ephebus, which had involved a statue worth $1 million and a shoot-out? After appeal some of the thieves got off with eighteen months. And he knew that in America the situation was even worse.

He shrugged but added that the light sentences were particularly disheartening in this case because it was a classic example of the way the international traffic in stolen art operates.

"In general the thieves, as in this case, are not terribly knowledgeable about art. They steal what is available, without too much risk to themselves and often operating with inside knowledge that the person who owns the art in question is going to be away on a certain date.

"The thieves pass the pictures—or the sculpture or the furniture—on to a receiver and get what they can. The receiver is the man who counts. He is usually in the art world—a dealer or a restorer, as in this case. He will know quite a bit about art, enough to tell the good stuff from the rubbish; and he will have a gallery or a workshop where he can store the stolen merchandise without it seeming too obviously out of place.

"On top of that he will have a network of contacts in the art world and will be well-enough established to be able to afford to hang on to the paintings, or whatever, for some time, while the heat dies down. Dealers hang on to quite legitimate paintings for months, until either the right opportunity for a sale crops up, or time enough has elapsed for others to have forgotten the circumstances of the acquisition, where the pictures came from and how much they cost.

"A restorer is especially fortunate since he travels from gallery to gallery, from museum to church, collecting and dropping off works he is repairing. He hears the gossip about what is stolen, who is buying, which galleries are making money, which alliances are forming, who the trade is suspicious of and so on.

"Sooner or later he finds an outlet. Some of those stories about mysterious American millionaires, who 'commission' thefts of particular paintings, may have a grain of truth in them occasionally. But this is a much more typical case. Italy has so much art, in so many accessible locations, that nearly all thefts take place because some petty crook knows a receiver in the art world.

"Once a buyer has been found, the actual smuggling is never very difficult. We have had several instances of diplomats smuggling art in their pouches; and almost as many when men of the cloth have been involved. Zorza was both, so this case is, if you like, doubly typical."

Siviero offered me another sugared nut. Night was drawing in across the Arno. "You are worried about retribution—yes?"

"A little bit," I said. "U.S. Customs advised me to change my telephone numbers and to go unlisted. And to move house if I could. And I was followed once in New York. I saw Garuti on Forty-second Street but I managed to get into a cab and lose him. We checked out their lawyers, and they are not Mafia lawyers, so far as we know. But I do wonder, from time to time, whether they will try anything."

Siviero lifted the malt bottle and refilled my glass. "I wish I could offer you some comfort, or protection, but after every recovery, after every trick we have to play in this game to get something back, I always remember what the lawyers used to tell their gangster bosses in Chicago back in the 1920s."

"What was that?"

"That there's one thing to be said for inviting trouble. It generally accepts."

HOWEVER, so far as my recovery was concerned, I was cheered, a little later, by a visit to the home of Marchese Roi, at his villa in Montegalda, between Vicenza and Venice. It was a wonderful house—small, as villas go, but beautifully appointed. Inside, there were marble floors, Bassano drawings in the sitting room, carved bookcases. Outside, the house was surrounded by geometrically laid-out lemon and lime groves, deep green flame-shaped cypress trees and the family's own fourteenth-century chapel with a gorgeous brown-red, terra-cotta roof. The marchese himself was an elegant, civilized man who showed me around as we drank his own brand of champagne. It was fitting that the Del Sarto should come back to such a home.

Index

Baratti negotiations of, 123–29, 152, 154–61
blackening name of, 57–67
fake clippings on, 120–21, 141, 239
"London flat" of, 166–75, 179, 188–89
"Manzu" negotiations of, 165, 173–89, 193–94, 199–207, 212–13, 222
nickname of, 68
Renzullo negotiations of, 116–23, 126, 130–37, 140–53, 158–59, 162–63, 192–93, 222, 224–25, 239–70, 279–89, 291–92, 294–302
smuggling by, 144, 158, 162–64, 308
tapped telephone of, 267–70, 279–81
wired for sound, 282–87, 291, 293
Blunt, Anthony, 6–7
Boccachio, Tony, 85–88
Bollandists, 73
Bologna railway station, bombing of, 161
"Bolognese, Franco," 95
Bonham's (gallery), 4, 74–75
Bonnard, Pierre, 81
Bordone, Paris, 138
Bosch, Hieronymus, 95
Boston Museum of Fine Arts, smuggling by, 12
Botticelli, Sandro, 9, 16, 74, 169
Boudin, Eugene, 31
Bourdon, Sebastien, 96
Bouts, Dieric, 53–55
Bove, Mr., 306–7
Braque, Georges, 143, 149, 150
British passports
false name in obtaining, 22–25
stolen, cost of, 22
Brod (gallery), 43, 48, 50
Bronzino, Il, 8, 16, 52, 53, 104, 168, 169, 180
background of, 247
stolen portrait by, 240, 246–49, 253–54, 258, 262, 268, 277, 281, 287, 299
Brooklyn Museum, 81
Browning, Robert, 244
Brueghel, Pieter, 16, 256
Brueghel family, 43, 45, 52, 71, 90, 114, 130, 222, 234, 310
Buenos Aires Museum of Fine Arts, 221
Burton, Robert, 215
Buscetto, Tommaso (Zuccheto), 87–88, 113
Byron, Lord, 158

Byzantine icon, stolen, 82

Calvaert, Denys, 95
Campi, Giulio, 145
Canaletto, Antonio, 45, 52, 69, 70, 81, 222
disguised painting of, 9–10
Canonico, Flavio, 106
Cappelle, Jan van de, 52
Caprioli, Domenico, 71, 76, 80, 139
Caravaggio, Michelangelo Merisi da, 100, 283, 286
background of, 13, 102–11, 135
"Blake's" copying of, 168
lost picture of, 169
Nativity (Adoration of the Child with St. Francis and St. Lawrence)
author sees photos of, 204–5
author's negotiations for, 183–89, 193–94, 199–207, 212–13, 222
Baratti and, 160–61
Caravaggio's painting of, 110
list of suspects in theft of, 16–17
price of, 28, 160
Siviero's help in pursuit of, 13–14, 16–17, 22, 35, 60, 77, 79, 82, 86, 113, 115, 123–24, 184–85, 189, 194–95, 199, 203, 206–7
theft of, 13, 111–12
still lifes supposedly of, 121–23, 125–29, 155–56
Carracci, Annibale, 96
Catania, Giuseppe, 84–88, 113, 154
Cavallino, Bernardo, 92
Cézanne, Paul, 16, 100, 221, 310
Chagall, Marc, 100, 162, 183, 191
Charles I (King of England), 223
Chase, Alexander, 132
Choo, Eddie, 272, 273, 276–79, 282, 293–95, 298, 302–3
Christie's (gallery), 4, 98
author observed by "Manzu" at, 178–79
cooperation in investigation by, 29, 32–33, 38–41, 49–55
London gallery of, 49
Park Avenue gallery of, 38
Sotheby's compared to, 50
Churchill, Sir Winston, 8
Ciechanowiecki, Andrew, 35, 36, 52, 68, 167
Cirile, Marie, 81

PETER WATSON was born in 1943 and educated at the universities of Durham, London and Rome. After postgraduate work in psychology at the Tavistock Clinic in London, he became assistant editor of *New Society* magazine. Since then he has been a member of the "Insight" team of the London *Sunday Times*, written the daily "Diary" column on the London *Times* and been that paper's New York correspondent.

Mr. Watson's previous books include *Twins*, an account of the curious coincidences in the lives of identical twins who have been separated at birth, and *War on the Mind*, an investigation into the uses and abuses of military psychology. His books have been translated into several languages. He is married and lives in London.